D1715880

EUROPEAN ARMIES OF THE FRENCH REVOLUTION, 1789–1802

C&C

CAMPAIGNS & COMMANDERS

GREGORY J. W. URWIN, SERIES EDITOR

European Armies of the French Revolution 1789–1802

Edited by Frederick C. Schneid

University of Oklahoma Press | Norman

Also by Frederick C. Schneid
Napoleon's Italian Campaigns, 1805–1815 (Santa Barbara, Calif., 2002)
Napoleon's Conquest of Europe: The War of the Third Coalition, 1805
   (Santa Barbara, Calif., 2005)
Napoleonic Wars (Washington, D.C., 2012)
The Second War of Italian Unification, 1859–1861 (London, 2012)
The French-Piedmontese Campaign of 1859 (Rome, 2014)

Library of Congress Cataloging-in-Publication Data

European armies of the French Revolution, 1789–1802 / edited by Frederick
C. Schneid.
     pages cm. — (Campaigns and commanders)
   Includes index.
   ISBN 978-0-8061-4039-1 (hardcover : alk. paper)
   1. First Coalition, War of the, 1792–1797. 2. Second Coalition, War of
the, 1798–1801. 3. Europe—History, Military—1789–1815. 4.
Armies—Europe—History—19th century. I. Schneid, Frederick C., editor, author.
   DC220.1.E97 2015
   944.04—dc23

                              2015011414

European Armies of the French Revolutions, 1789–1802 is Volume 50 in the
Campaigns & Commanders series.

1 2 3 4 5 6 7 8 9 10

Interior layout and composition: Alcorn Publication Design

Contents

Preface and Acknowledgments

This book is about the armies of Europe during the French Revolution. While much has been written about the French army and its transformation during the Revolution, a yawning gap exists in the literature on the European armies that fought against France. The genesis of this book derived from my years of research and teaching when it became clear that a single volume examining the composition, organization, and operation of the armies that waged war against revolutionary France was long overdue. Nothing in English provided a survey of the Austrian, Prussian, British, Russian, Spanish, German, Italian, and Turkish participants in the French Revolutionary Wars (1792–1802). This absence is even more striking when compared to the vast number of sources on the armies that fought the Napoleonic Wars (1803–1815). Thus, this book is intended as a starting point.

Historical generalizations that developed, beginning in the nineteenth century, in the French-focused narratives about the Revolutionary Wars established the false premise that the changes in the French army and its subsequent victories compelled the other European states to reform their military systems. The contributors to this volume, all experts in their fields, have published widely on military affairs related to their respective armies. Though their conclusions vary, they generally agree that the changing face of warfare during this period did not result in a "revolution in military affairs," which came later during the Napoleonic Wars. Nevertheless, Europe's other military establishments during the French Revolutionary Wars were compelled to address the threats posed by French arms.

I wish to thank the contributors for participating in this important project, and for their patience as it progressed from idea to publication. Chuck Rankin at the University of Oklahoma Press encouraged me to pursue the book, and kept at it over the years. I wish to thank the anonymous readers for their invaluable comments, which served to improve the manuscript. I hope those who read this book find it to be an important preliminary conversation on European armies during the French Revolution and explore the subject further.

EUROPEAN ARMIES OF THE
FRENCH REVOLUTION, 1789–1802

INTRODUCTION

FREDERICK C. SCHNEID

On a damp fall day in 1792, Johann Wolfgang Gottleib von Goethe, the German author, poet, and playwright, stood on the battlefield of Valmy with his prince Karl August of Saxe-Weimar. Formerly, Goethe served as Karl August's war minister. It was an unlikely post for such a scholar. He found the office too distracting and was excused from his duties, but he remained an ex officio member of the prince's cabinet. Goethe had little inclination for martial affairs but nonetheless was required on occasion to observe military maneuvers. Such had been the case in 1791, when Karl August called for Goethe to join him in Prussia, "where instead of stones and flowers, he would see the field sown with troops."[1] The following summer Goethe accompanied his prince to France as part of the German contingent serving with the Duke of Brunswick's invasion of the country.

On 20 September, a cloud-covered, rainy day, Goethe experienced war for the first time. He witnessed the serried ranks of Prussian troops advance against the French, who had only recently failed to stem the Prussian tide sweeping Paris. The Prussian cannonade was horrendous, but the French would not budge. In the midst of the advance, the Duke of Brunswick called his men back—"We shall not strike here."[2] The artillery duel continued, but as the afternoon wore on, the French remained and the Prusso-German army withdrew. Later that evening, Goethe sat with Karl August and a number of officers who were perplexed at the renewed determination of their enemy and their own general's loss of nerve. Pressed by his company to comment, Goethe presciently responded, "From this place and from this day forth commences a new era in the world's history, and you can all say that you were present at its birth."[3]

Being a writer, Goethe tended toward the dramatic, but nonetheless, the French victory at Valmy secured Paris, and gave the revolutionary government time to breathe and plan and pursue a war it inaugurated in the spring. Although those who had instigated the conflict in April 1792 were no longer in power by September, their political opponents, who had initially rejected the war, had become the war's greatest proponents. To the republicans in the National Convention, war provided an opportunity to mobilize the nation, "La Patrie," and export the Revolution.

The desperate French summer followed a tremendously successful autumn. The Kingdom of Piedmont-Sardinia became the victim of chance when revolutionary irredentism led to the French occupation of Nice and Savoy. In October, a French army invaded the Holy Roman Empire west of the Rhine and "liberated" Speyer, Worms, and Mainz. An audacious crossing of the great river and seizure of Frankfurt followed. Two weeks later, a second French army invaded the Austrian Netherlands and defeated an Austrian army at Jemappes. Victory, however, was short-lived as an Austrian counteroffensive in the spring of 1793 forced the French from Belgium and Holland.

The seesaw of victory and defeat was a hallmark of the first years of the wars of the Revolution. The French initially desired to limit the scope of the conflict, but it eventually became a continental affair. During the War of the First Coalition, 1792–97, virtually all of Europe, excluding Russia and the Ottoman Empire, was drawn into the war. Peace lasted less than a year before the Second Coalition was formed, inaugurating a second round of hostilities against France from 1798 to 1802. Although France emerged victorious from the first war, it found itself hard-pressed by the Second Coalition, and it nearly lost much of what it had gained earlier. By 1800, however, disagreements among the coalition partners and military victories at the hands of the French led to the end of the conflict. The combined resources of Europe were substantial, but political disagreements and lack of coordination among coalition leaders did not bring them the victory they anticipated.

The war was not initially viewed from Vienna or Berlin as one of ideology. Instead, their political and military responses retained their historical character, which included a profound distrust between the two German courts when concerning matters of strategy. Even the lesser German princes of the Holy Roman Empire were reluctant to support Emperor Francis II's call to arms. The true nature of the conflict, or what it had become, became apparent in January 1793, when Louis XVI, the former king of France, took his last steps to the guillotine. The audacity of the revolutionary tribunal's decision to execute the Bourbon ruler had the consequence of sending an ominous message to the royal houses of Europe. Two weeks later, the National Convention expanded the conflict by declaring war on Great Britain and Holland. Then six weeks later, the French added Spain to the list of the Revolution's enemies. It was fortunate for Catherine II (the Great) of Russia that her empire was far to the east; otherwise, she might not have had the luxury of avoiding the now general European war.

The hubris of revolutionary leadership soon gave way to fear of counterrevolution when French armies began to crumble in Belgium, on the Rhine, and along the Pyrenees. Fear fed extremism, and triumphant republicanism became revolutionary dictatorship. The Committee of Public Safety, empowered by the National Convention to save the Revolution and dominated by Maximilien Robespierre, determined to mobilize the nation's resources to preserve that which was now in danger. In August 1793, the Convention decreed a levée en masse. It was the first national draft—that could properly be defined as such—in European history. Volunteers had more than adequately fed the French army in the hundreds of thousands before the summer 1793, but the revolutionary leadership concluded that compulsory service had to be absolute if the Revolution was to be rescued from their enemies.

The creation of National Guard battalions and their subsequent federalization established an army comprised of professionals and revolutionary volunteers. The numbers of men who joined their local guard far exceeded the expectations of the revolutionary government. This polyglot army fled the field in Belgium in April 1792 but stood at Valmy the following September. The expansion of the conflict, concomitant with the execution of the king, the counterrevolution in western and southern France, and the creation of a revolutionary dictatorship, necessitated the mobilization of national resources on both ideological and military grounds. The volunteers of earlier years, however, clashed with the conscripts of '93 and '94. The political orientation of the conscripts, watched and fostered by the equivalent of political commissars, ensured their loyalty to the Revolution and the "proper attitude" while on campaign. Curiously, by the time the men of the levée arrived at the front, the situation had changed dramatically.

The tide turned once more in 1794. The counterrevolution was brutally suppressed, and French armies crossed the Pyrenees and plundered Catalonia. The Austrians suffered a decisive defeat at Fleurus, which secured Belgium and opened Holland to invasion. Frederick William II, the king of Prussia, desired to extricate himself from the war. Elsewhere, Russia eyed the remaining rump of Poland, and Austria's overwhelming commitments against revolutionary France offered Prussia the opportunity to wrest northern Germany completely from Habsburg influence. With these events as background, negotiations between the Prussian kingdom and the French Republic began in earnest. This first coalition against France was anything but unanimous with respect to its ultimate political objectives, and Prussia's secret negotiations with the revolutionary government were merely the first manifestation of the dysfunctional European alliance.

Austrian commitment to the coalition remained firm considering that Habsburg lands became plunder to French armies. Beyond Belgium, the French violated the Reich—the Holy Roman Empire—by occupying the west bank of the Rhine. Indeed, in Italy, the Habsburg duchy of Lombardy was only safe from the French threat as long as Piedmont-Sardinia remained intact. The dilemma in which Habsburg emperors Leopold II (d. 1792) and Francis II found themselves was that they were not merely dealing with this war in the west, but with Russian and Prussian designs on Poland.

In Britain, Edmund Burke, the esteemed Anglo-Irish member of Parliament, cautioned his compatriots of the danger of radical revolution. This warning occurred well before the monarchy was overthrown and the French Republic emerged. Despite some popular enthusiasm for the Revolution, Britain's general attitude toward France after 1789 remained cautious. More important than the ideological danger to Britain's political and social structure were the geopolitical implications posed by the French war in 1792. Historically wary of French expansion into the Low Countries and Italy, by 1793, London perceived France not as a new constitutional state, but as a threat to British interests in western Europe. Paris took note of this change in attitude, and a French declaration of war against Great Britain accompanied an invasion of Holland in 1793.

Britain had limited military options. Its ability to place a sizeable army on the European continent had always been problematic, but more significantly the French declaration of war came at a time when Britain was engaged in India. The conclusion of the Second Anglo-Mysore War reduced Britain's immediate focus on India, but limited operations continued throughout the subcontinent. Furthermore, substantial financial and physical resources were required to secure recent conquests. Scant forces could be spared for operations in Holland and Belgium, despite the proximity of the Low Countries to England. Throughout the seventeenth and eighteenth centuries, Britain's continental might derived from hiring foreign—notably German—regiments. The actual outlay of English manpower was minimal compared to those employed for British service. When France declared war on Great Britain in 1793, London anticipated raising substantial German forces to fight for its cause. Prior agreements with the Prussians and long-established relations with the Hessian princes were expected to provide Britain with sufficient manpower on the European continent. All of this, however, was an extremely expensive affair.

Britain's true military power remained in its navy and finances. Its treasury underwrote both coalitions while the Royal Navy wreaked havoc upon the French colonial empire and blockaded its ports. Only after 1796 did the British fleet and the home islands face an immediate threat when Spain entered into a French alliance. Nonetheless, British naval supremacy ravaged French commerce and provided vital support to French rebels in Toulon in 1793, and to the Turks facing General Bonaparte at Acre in 1799. The destruction of the Spanish fleet at Cape Saint Vincent in 1797, the French fleet at Aboukir Bay in 1798, and the Dutch at Texel that same year secured Britain from invasion. Even so, the French were still able to dispatch an expeditionary force to Ireland in 1798. While the Royal Navy provided valuable piece of mind, Britain had to commit land forces to move the French on the continent.

Perhaps more than any other European monarch, Carlos IV, king of Spain, dreaded war with France. The Revolution ideologically threatened the relationship between the two Bourbon houses. As long as Louis XVI sat on the throne, the Revolution could be ignored and overtures by the French government for a Franco-Spanish alliance rejected. After the overthrow of the French monarchy and the radicalization of the Revolution in 1792, Spain's refusal to make common cause led to a French declaration of war in 1793. Spain's military power had long since faded at the conclusion of the eighteenth century. Overseas empire necessitated the maintenance of an immense fleet to protect its transatlantic interests. Spain's armies were formerly the scourge of Europe during the seventeenth century;

this was no longer the case by 1792. The elevation of the Bourbons to the Spanish throne in 1700 removed France as the immediate and traditional enemy of Habsburg Spain. Subsequently, in the eighteenth century France and Spain allied against Britain and Austria. After the War of Spanish Succession, Spain's continental interests were limited to Italy. Madrid held the Kingdom of the Two Sicilies, but had lost Milan to the Austrians. Franco-Spanish attempts to seize Lombardy during the War of Austrian Succession likewise failed. The subsequent Bourbon-Habsburg alliance of 1754 removed any chance of Spain regaining Milan. To this end "Family Compacts," produced in 1733, 1743, and 1761, cemented the relationship between the Spanish and French Bourbon houses. Moreover, the lack of a continental enemy, and the neutralization of Italy during the reign of Carlos III (d. 1788), allowed the Spanish monarch to focus on a massive naval-building program with the intention of securing his overseas empire from British threats. This strategy meant severely reducing expenditures for the army. As Britain was Spain's primary rival throughout the second half of the eighteenth century, the ability to best Albion would be determined at sea and not on the European continent.

The Franco-Spanish familial alliance succeeded in forcing the British from the Mediterranean after 1768. This development resulted in Britain's temporary loss of the English Channel in 1781 and threats to British possessions in the Caribbean. In every case, however, victory over England meant victory at sea. The Spanish army was poorly maintained as the years after 1754 eliminated any continental interests. Hence, when France declared war on Spain in 1793, the Spanish army was is disrepair. The fact that French armies were initially worse off than those of the Spanish provided the Iberian kingdom with only a limited advantage. A Spanish invasion across the Pyrenees was short-lived, and by autumn, as the Spanish tide receded, it was rapidly exploited by a French invasion of Catalonia.

A confluence of Spanish and Austrian interests occurred in the Italian peninsula before the Revolution. The extended families of Spanish Bourbons and Austrian Habsburgs divided much of the peninsula. Although the Kingdom of Piedmont-Sardinia, the Venetian and Genoese Republics, and the Papal States remained independent of the two dynasties, Italy was a battlefield between French, Austrian, and Spanish royal houses for centuries. Yet, the fifty years preceding the Revolution comprised a rare period of Italian peace. The axis of Italian alliances altered dramatically when, after 1700, the French Bourbons ascended the Spanish throne. In 1754, the diplomatic revolution ended all hostilities in the peninsula as French Bourbons and Austrian Habsburgs joined forces to counter the threat from Prussia. The Bourbon-Habsburg alliance neutralized the Italian peninsula and made friends of former enemies. Even those kingdoms and republics that were not ruled by these houses found the general peace quite beneficial. Italian states reduced their expenditures significantly by scaling back their armed forces. Grand Duke Leopold, the ruler of Tuscany and the future Emperor Leopold II after 1790, virtually eliminated his army except for a palace guard.

The Kingdom of Piedmont-Sardinia remained the foremost indigenous military power in the peninsula. More than a decade before the Revolution, King Louis XVI of France married off his sister as well as his two brothers to a son and two daughters of King Victor Amadeus III, thus assuring familial bonds between the two kingdoms. This half century of tranquility was shattered by the French invasion of Nice and Savoy in 1792. The Italian kingdom was ill prepared for war, yet revolutionary France could not benefit from the poor state of defenses with its focus on Germany, Belgium, and Holland. Italy only became a center of attention after General Napoleon Bonaparte's lightning campaign against Piedmont in April 1796.

The princes of the Holy Roman Empire felt the benefits of the Franco-Austrian rapprochement at midcentury too. After 1763, war within the Holy Roman Empire occurred only once prior the French Revolution during the War of Bavarian Succession in 1778. The nature and duration of the conflict was limited, and a further war scare between Austria and Prussia in 1790 failed to develop into anything significant. The princes of the empire therefore took advantage of the general calm in central Europe to reduce their military expenditures. When war ultimately came to the empire in 1792, Austrian and Prussian pressure compelled the princes to marshal their small armies and contribute to their cause.

The Reicharmee, or Imperial Army, never manifested itself as a separate entity. Thus, it was that Goethe accompanied Karl August of Saxe-Weimar and his regiments, which were attached to the Prussian army under the Duke of Brunswick at Valmy in 1792. The empire's middling territories, most notably Saxony, Bavaria, Hanover, and Württemberg, found their armies incorporated into either the

Prussian or the Austrian-led forces on the Upper or Lower Rhine. There was little inclination on the princes' part to participate in the conflict, but political and military pressure dictated otherwise. When, in 1795 Prussia and France signed the Peace of Basel, a number of German princes took the opportunity to extricate their realms from the war. Bavaria and Württemberg, too, signed neutrality agreements with France in 1797, only to be disarmed by the Austrians and later compelled to fight against France during the War of the Second Coalition (1798–1802).

In Russia, Catherine II avoided the general European conflict for much of the 1790s. She played upon Austro-Prussian rivalries and took advantage of the war in the west to advance her territorial interests in the Ukraine and Poland. Pressed by William Pitt the Younger, prime minister of Great Britain, to join the First Coalition, Catherine demanded enormous sums as military subsidy, purposely putting her collaboration beyond the financial reach of England. Upon devouring Poland, she settled her affairs with the Turks in 1795 and accepted Pitt's proposals. Alas, she died shortly thereafter, before her army took the field. Her son and heir, Paul I, reneged on his mother's agreements for the moment.

The Russian army that Pitt sought to enlist into the war effort was formidable, its size considerable. Over the past century, Russian military power had grown. Peter I (the Great) Europeanized the Russian army during the early eighteenth century in order to compete successfully with the Swedes and Saxons in the Baltic and Poland. Russia's participation in the Seven Years' War consequently proved decisive in almost bringing Frederick the Great to his knees. The death of the Tsarina Elizabeth, euphemistically known in Prussia as "the miracle of the House of Brandenburg," saved the German kingdom from a most certain fate. Elizabeth's successor, Peter III, was a great admirer of the Prussian king, and he changed alliances. These issues were part of the rationale for military support for the palace coup that removed Peter from the throne and secured his wife, Catherine's, position to the Romanov throne.

Russian arms had been generally successful during the course of the eighteenth century when facing the Ottoman Empire. The Russian army's performance against Prussia was respectable, as was Russia's ability to absorb heavy losses yet soon return to the field in substantial numbers. There remained, however, an argument within the Russian army over the advisability of accepting a Prussian-style reform or, instead, of pursuing more of a Russian course. This was more than an academic discussion, and led not only to the overthrow of Peter III (d. 1762) but also to the assassination of Paul I, son of Catherine the Great, forty years later.

Paul too was dissatisfied with the army's performance in Poland despite its ultimate success in 1794–96. Ever an admirer of the Prussian military system, the tsar also sought to reform the Russian army along German lines. For these reasons, he was not inclined to join Russia to the coalition against France in 1796, despite his mother's promises to the British. Nonetheless, he could not ignore the dramatic French victory over Austria in 1797 as it altered the power equation in central Europe and Italy. He negotiated with Britain and Austria to bring his empire into a new coalition and provided much-needed strength to the continental resistance against the ever-expanding French Republic. Russia's military commitment to the Second Coalition proved decisive. A Russian army joined with the Austrians in 1799 to overthrow the French control in Italy, and menaced their position in Switzerland. An Anglo-Russian expedition to Holland further threatened French hegemony in the Low Countries.

The coalition, however, became a victim of its own success. At the moment of victory, political squabbling led to a critical rift between Russia and its allies. Tsar Paul withdrew his armies from western Europe and Russia from the coalition. When, in November 1799, a coup brought General Napoleon Bonaparte to power in France, he found France in a poor strategic situation. Yet, the Corsican upstart benefited from the fractured European alliances. He faced a continental coalition of one, Austria. Far from an inevitable victory, there is little question that Russia's absence was as decisive in the outcome as it had been at the war's inception.

In retrospect, European monarchs perceived the victories of the European coalition in 1792–93 as a product of French weakness as well as their own military superiority. When the tide turned during 1794–97, the question arose whether this setback was a product of the superiority of French arms, or failings in their own military systems. The generally accepted historical perception is that European monarchies and their military leaders shunned change. The conservatism of these institutions supposedly prevented any direct and immediate reforms. It is clear that there is some truth to this interpretation, as an institutional ossification clearly existed before to the Revolution—even in France. Yet, the problem with these general notions is that they assume that European military institutions were squarely focused on the French, that upon meeting defeat in 1792 and 1793, there was a dramatic concern for growing French military supremacy on the battlefield. These assumptions do not consider factors outside the French war that may have influenced European military thought and the response to the French Revolution. In a number of cases, military reforms were already under consideration when Europe went to war in 1792. In other cases, reform reflected strategic interests beyond the purview of the French war.

For three decades, European military institutions emulated the Prussian military system. Frederick the Great's ability to fend off, and on occasion decisively defeat, the armies of France, Russia, and Austria, led the rest of Europe to examine and, in many instances, copy the Prussian system. Furthermore, military reform and organizational change in the period preceding the French Revolution reflected lessons learned on the battlefield and military experience beyond western and central Europe. A century of wars with the Ottoman Turks profoundly influenced the development of Austrian and Russian armies. The British experience in America and continued colonial expansion in India affected the British way of war. French defeat during the Seven Years' War necessitated substantial organizational and tactical reforms accomplished by royal decree. In short, changes in the use of artillery, infantry tactics, and military organization were already in progress when war came in 1792. Nonetheless, reforms occurred, but armed forces were reduced considerably since the conflicts of midcentury. The extent to which these reforms had any practical impact on the battlefield would only be determined over the course of the wars of the French Revolution.

Notes

1. George Henry Lewes, *The Life of Goethe* (1874; repr., New York: Ungar, 1965), 370.
2. T. C. W. Blanning, *The French Revolutionary War* (New York: Arnold, 1996), 78.
3. Johann von Goethe, "The Campaign in France," in *Miscellaneous Travels of J. W. Goethe*, ed. L. Dora Schmitz (London: Bell, 1910), 118.

CHAPTER I

THE FRENCH ARMY

FREDERICK C. SCHNEID

No state set pace by the French army after 1763. It numbered merely 180,000 men, half its total compliment in the general wars of the eighteenth century. In terms of comparative strength, the French Royal Army stood behind Russia, Austria, and Prussia and only narrowly claimed more men than Spain. The severe reduction in size was the direct and immediate product of economic crisis and of the fact that France's bête noir on the continent had ceased to be such after the Habsburg-Bourbon compact of 1754 and the conclusion of peace with Prussia in 1763. The reduction in manpower is often represented inaccurately as an illustration of the military decline of the ancien régime.

I

The French army in 1789 was a lean, mean, fighting machine. In the decades prior to the Revolution, the army was a highly professional force, with a capable military administration to manage it. The professionalization of the French Royal Army prior to 1789 emphasized training, esprit de corps, proper technical support for the line army—dramatic improvement in the artillery and engineering corps—and a lively internal debate on the operational and tactical art of war.

The general history of the French army prior to 1789 often begins with the debacle of the Seven Years' War, the nadir of French military power. By June 1789, the French army addressed many of the problems that had plagued it more than three decades earlier. Its leadership, training, doctrines, and theories created a forward-thinking army not mired in the past. This development was witnessed in the first successful French colonial war since the seventeenth century, the American Revolution. As much as the war for America—as seen through the eyes of colonists—was a war for independence, the French royal administration, specifically Louis XVI and the comte de Vergennes, his foreign minister, perceived this conflict as an opportunity. On the grand strategic stage, the war provided an occasion to regain former colonial territory such as Quebec, but it also served as the first testing ground for the army and navy since their failure almost two decades earlier. Twenty years elapsed between the outbreak of the Seven Years' War and the American Revolution. An entire generation of Frenchmen had passed, and the leadership and direction of the army had changed. The result was victory for French arms in 1781, culminating in the siege of Yorktown and the practical education of officers and men that would later form the backbone of the revolutionary and Napoleonic armies.[1] It was during this war that the French Ministry of War also authorized the establishment of military schools to prepare youth from the gentry and nobility for professional military careers.

The problems faced by the French army in the first months of war in 1792 were not structural, but involved both the social revolution that gutted the officer corps and the gradual politicization of the army after 1793. The poor showing of the army in Belgium during the first month of war in April 1792 and the panic in response to the Prussian invasion during the late summer presents a cursory view that the army, wracked by revolution, was falling apart. It was not. The army suffered from crises that emerged during the first years of revolution, but its performance on the whole, in the first year of war, indicated that despite difficulties, it remained a significant force.

Despite the political turmoil of August 1792 and the social revolution that followed, the army remained untouched through the fall campaign. Other than the marquis de Lafayette, none of the army commanders after the 10 August revolution fled, were removed, or resigned their commissions. This would only come the following year. The French victory at Valmy (20 September 1792) was followed by a string of triumphs on all three fronts: the Austrian Netherlands (Belgium), the Rhine, and Italy. Coincidentally, the day after the Battle of Valmy general Montesquieu, commanding the Army of the Alps, crossed into Savoy, the patrimonial province of the Kingdom of Piedmont-Sardinia, and occupied it, along with the county of Nice. Indeed, French achievements continued less than ten days after the Duke of Brunswick began his lugubrious march back to Germany. General Custine, commander of the Army of the Rhine, captured in rapid succession the fortified cities of Landau, Speyer, Philippsburg, and Worms, completing his triumph with the taking of Mainz on 21 October. Custine took advantage of his position and speed of movement, crossing the Rhine and occupying Frankfurt, at the heart of the Holy Roman Empire, by 23 October.

On that day, the Prussian-led army withdrew across the French frontiers, enabling General Kellerman, commanding the Army of the Center, to double back to support French operations in Belgium. Dumouriez, now in charge of the Army of the North, advanced once again into Austrian territory. While Kellerman kept a watchful eye on Brunswick at Koblenz, Dumouriez attacked the Austrians at Jemappes and defeated them on 6 November. The following day Dumouriez seized the city of Mons, and the Austrian army abandoned Belgium. The only setback to this string of French victories occurred on 9 November when a Prussian counteroffensive compelled Custine to abandon Frankfurt and withdraw to the security of Mainz. All in all, French arms had much to commend in the fall 1792. Not bad for an army that is often portrayed as suffering from internal crises.

The structure of the French army in 1789 was thoroughly eighteenth century in character. The military reforms preceding the Revolution involved neither a reorganization of the regiments nor any substantial alteration of the basic military configuration. The army was divided conventionally into two branches, the infantry and cavalry. Artillery and engineers were subordinated to the former branch as a subcategory. Only under Napoleon a full decade later did artillery become an independent branch on par with the other two.

The disaster of the Seven Years' War led to more than a decade of reforms, which established a solid foundation for the army of the future. The quality of the prerevolutionary army can be seen readily in the fact that the senior leadership that emerged after 1792 was largely made of those who had served in the army prior to 1789. This was no coincidence, but a reflection of the army's quality before the Revolution. At that time, the French army was a shadow of its past glory under Louis XIV, yet it can be argued that the performance of the French army in the War of Spanish Succession (1701–14) and the War of Austrian Succession (1740–48) was inconsistent.

The French infantry formed the core of the army. In 1789, it comprised 110 infantry regiments divided into 2 combat battalions and a depot battalion. Five regiments served in the colonies, and twenty-two were foreign regiments hired into French service: eleven Swiss, eight German, three Irish, and one Belgian. Twelve Chasseurs à pied battalions formed the light troops, to keep pace with the Jaegers or Grenzers of the Habsburg and Prussian armies and the light battalions of the British army. The line regiments were raised by province and supported by a patron who served as the regimental colonel. The monarchy and the extended royal family directly raised several regiments as well. These household troops included the Gardes Françaises (infantry) and the Maison du Roi (cavalry).[2]

The cavalry, the most aristocratic branch of the army, consisted of sixty-two regiments. Two regiments of carabiniers formed the corps d'elite of the mounted arm. The heavy cavalry formed twenty-four regiments, followed by eighteen dragoon regiments, and another eighteen of light cavalry—six hussar and twelve Chasseurs à cheval. Foreign regiments included several regiments of heavy cavalry and one of hussars. The employment of contracted foreign regiments was an old tradition followed by virtually all European armies. The French were no different. By 1792, however, with the dissolution of the French monarchy, the revolutionary government canceled contracts, and many foreign troops deserted either individually or en masse. This was particularly the case of the Royal Allemand (German) heavy cavalry regiment, and the Saxe (German) Hussars. The colonel and troopers of the former regiment were implicated in aiding the royal family in its failed escape attempt at Varennes in June 1791.[3]

Despite its subordinate role to the infantry and cavalry, artillery had always been an important part of the French army. Its status and condition fluctuated during the course of the eighteenth century, but by 1789 it regained its significant role in the army. The artillery corps consisted of seven regiments and one colonial regiment. In June 1789, artillery Régiment de la Fère included a young lieutenant Napoleon Bonaparte. Miners, sappers, and engineers were attached to the artillery corps.

The army was wholly professional and volunteer. The foreign and royal household regiments met with suspicion as the Revolution evolved. The intimate relationship between royal patronage and the foreign and household troops caused concern with the National, Constituent, and later Legislative, Assembly. Between 1789 and 1791, instances of mutiny became commonplace among foreign regiments, and all too often the Swiss were used by the monarchy to guard the palaces and confront mobs. The increasing reliance on Swiss troops also reflected the lack of loyalty among the Gardes Françaises. Quite a few had deserted their posts in July 1789 and joined the Parisian mobs in storming the Bastille. Louis XVI responded by disbanding the regiment.

The progress of the Revolution led to disorder in the ranks. Desertions, resignation of commissions, and open acts of mutiny made the army a politically unreliable institution. Indeed, it was perceived as weak and incapable of coping with external threats. Appeals to the National Assembly from Minster of War La Tour du Pin failed to prevent soldiers from expressing their political will, and the army continued to wither. More than 50,000 soldiers left their posts prior to 1791.[4] When the constitution was finally promulgated in 1791, the "Royal" designation was removed from the army.

The army organization changed little in practical terms, although the professional regiments lost their provincial ancien régime names. They were replaced with numerical designations; thus, the famed Régiment d'Auvergne was now simply the 17th Regiment of the Line.[5] The elimination of feudal vestiges became an essential part of the revolutionary regime, even during its moderate course. The Royal Army became a French army, with the purpose of defending the constitution or, more appropriately, the Revolution. Nevertheless, the professional soldiers were caught between loyalty to their regiment and comrades and their affinity for the Revolution. This issue became increasingly tenuous after the establishment of a National Guard.

National Guard units began to organize during the summer of 1789, first in Paris and then throughout France. In its initial conception, the National Guard was not to be a substitute for the army, but a counterweight to it. Discussion concerning the army's role occurred in the fall of 1789, when it was decided that a national army would be composed of volunteers, rather than raised through conscription. This declaration was significant, as it represented an initial triumph of professionals over more radical revolutionary sentiments. Yet the call for volunteers met with only marginal success through 1791, and as war loomed thereafter, the National Guard became the institution to which the government in Paris turned to fill the ranks. This decision was quite important because prior to the call for volunteers or the federalizing of National Guard battalions in 1791, soldiers in the line regiments and those in the National Guard often faced off in the departmental towns and cities over the question of loyalty to the Revolution.

As early as the summer 1789 the professional soldiers of the army were faced with the dilemma of either supporting the Revolution or remaining steadfast in their loyalty as soldiers of the king. The mass desertions around Paris in June and July 1789 culminating in the participation of French troops in the fall of the Bastille is evidence of internal crisis.[6] Throughout the summer of 1789, French troops were called to establish order in various parts of France where grain riots or civil unrest necessitated action. Regimental garrison towns became centers of discontent, potential mutiny, and locals often denounced officers as disparagers of the Revolution. Lieutenant Louis-Nicolas Davout, a cavalry officer in the Régiment Royale Champagne at Hesdin, supported the Revolution but was condemned for his refusal to obey the city council's demands. He traveled to Paris to make his case but was dismissed from duty for "abandoning his post."[7] Davout's case is not an isolated incident, but the fluid political situation made it quite difficult for anyone outside of Paris, and even those within, to clearly understand the relationship between the political developments and the behavior of officers and men in the French army.

II

Edmond Louis Alexis Dubois-Crancé is perhaps one of the three most important figures in the history of the French army during the Revolution. Along with Lazare Carnot and Napoleon, Dubois-Crancé was a permanent fixture in the various revolutionary governments from 1789 through the coup of 18 Brumaire in November 1799. While Lazare Carnot is often referred to as the organizer of victory, and Napoleon's achievements on campaign in Italy in 1796–97 brought an end to the War of the First Coalition, Dubois-Crancé was responsible for the creation of a viable military force through his advocacy in the National, Constituent, and Legislative Assemblies and in the National Convention. It was Dubois-Crancé who advocated for the establishment of a volunteer army rather than a conscripted army. Furthermore, he was responsible for the *amalgames* of 1794 and 1795–96, which unified the divergent battalions of professionals and National Guard. He is largely responsible for the creation of a national army that was employed by Carnot at the grand strategic level and by Bonaparte at the strategic and operational level to great success.

Debate ensued in 1790 over the question of national conscription. Although the appeal among revolutionaries to establish an army representative of the nation fit well with the concept of "Liberty, Equality and Fraternity," the very act of a compulsory draft seemed to contradict revolutionary principles. At the recommendation of former army officers, including Dubois-Crancé, the Constituent Assembly agreed to the call for volunteers drawn from the National Guard.[8]

The National Guard was established as a civic force with the purpose of defending the Revolution from internal enemies, yet the need to fill the depleted ranks of the line army from the National Guard became the commonplace until 1797. On 28 January 1791 the Constituent Assembly called for 100,000 volunteers to fill the ranks.[9] This declaration was a recommendation, and none heeded the call. The failure to raise volunteers led to a more strident decree on 21 June 1791, which placed the National Guard on a national footing. To use a term drawn from the American Civil War, the National Guard was "federalized." Later during the summer 1791, the assembly issued several decrees, which required the drawing of 101,000 volunteers from the National Guard to form 169 new battalions for the line army.[10]

As new battalions formed, it became clear that many of the men had willingly joined the National Guard but did not appreciate being called up for duty with the line army. Tension between the line troops and the volunteers was apparent and continued through the inclusion of volunteers and then levies in 1792 and 1793 respectively. The volunteers looked upon the line troops with suspicion. After all, those soldiers chose to remain in the ancien régime regiments, rather than join the National Guard. The Blancs—the line troops noted for their white uniforms—and the Bleus—the National Guard with blue uniforms—were not particularly fond of each other, making training and coordination of battalions rather difficult.

By the spring of 1792 war loomed ever closer, and the state of the army remained poor. Desertions and failure to appear left the army lacking 51,000 men. When war came, the army was still understrength and the assembly responded with two decrees, one calling for the levy or draft of 50,000 men, and the other calling 20,000 National Guardsmen to Paris for the Feast of the Federation prior to dispatching them to the armies on the frontiers. The levy was called on 11 July concomitant with the declaration of "*La Patrie en danger.*"[11] The men drawn into the ranks were assigned first to fill the line battalions, second to fill the federalized national guard battalions called in 1791, and third, to establish forty-two new battalions as a strategic reserve.[12]

Jean-Paul Bertaud, the eminent scholar of the armies of the French Revolution argued that the difference between the volunteers of 1791 and 1792 was in their social class. The volunteers of 1791 came from the "bourgeoisie," while those of 1792 were "sans-cullottes," or the urban workers.[13] This claim may be true in the broader sense, but the soldiers who served in the former ancien régime battalions were of the same social order as the new draftees. Thus, one could argue that the volunteers of 1791 had less in common with the professionals than the new men of 1792. Nevertheless, the integration of recruits into the regiments continued to cause problems, as a lack of officers and noncommissioned officers made training and control a continual problem.

After a seesaw of war in the first six months, the success of French arms encouraged the republican government to expand its objectives and make more enemies. Between January and March 1793, France declared war on Great Britain, the Netherlands, and Spain. The decision to expand the conflict was made at the highest levels without consideration of the continuing dilemma over force size and structure. On 24 February 1793, the National Convention called for the levy of 300,000 Frenchmen.[14] Although virtually all accounts state that this decree was in response to the difficulty of keeping the army at full strength, the levy of 300,000 far exceeded any deficits and essentially doubled the size of the army. It is clear that the purpose of the levy was to accommodate the growing scope of the conflict and to ensure that there would be sufficient forces available to carry out operations.

The army size vacillated still through the spring of 1793, as the outbreak of the War in the Vendée and the Federalist Revolt sapped strength and the ability of the French war ministry to properly administer the levy. The result of defeat on the frontiers and internal crisis led to the 23 August 1793 decree of *levée en masse*. In theory, this decree is considered by many to be the birth of national conscription. The declaration called all able-bodied men to the colors, while the old would preach the glories of the Revolution, and women and children would prepare bandages and provide moral and material support for the army.[15] Indeed, the intention of the levée en masse was to mobilize the nation. The increased demand for troops through combat, attrition, and desertion necessitated a means to rebuild the ranks. Although some estimates claim that the levy created an army of one million men, this is simply hyperbole. It is clear from documents that the French army by the fall of 1794 numbered no more than 750,000 men.[16] The levy provided 400,000 men, or more than 50 percent of army strength by the end of 1794.

The significance of the levée en masse is not that it provided much-needed manpower in the midst of national emergency, as the strategic crisis that plagued France in August 1793 had abated by the end of the year. On the contrary, when the French army reached its greatest strength, the armies of the republic were already on the offensive. Despite the bloating of the ranks from the levy, the size of the army declined. Attrition and desertion denuded the army. In 1795 there were no more than 550,000 men, and in 1796 the army declined to 380,000 men.[17]

French Army Strength, 1789–1798[18]

1789	189,000
1791	138,000
1792	220,000
1793	550,000
1794	750,000
1795	548,000
1796	380,000
1797	380,000
1798	350,000

Since the federalizing of national guard battalions in 1791, discussion and debate followed over the organization of the army. In 1793, the military commission, headed by Dubois-Crancé argued fervently and without success that it was necessary to integrate the old and new battalions, that the former National Guard should be merged with the line army. Opponents in the assembly argued the converse, that the line army should be integrated into the National Guard. This view reflected the pervasive notion that the line army remained tainted by its association with the French monarchy. In reality, any *monarchiens* in the army in 1789 had left well before 1793.

The performance of the recently dubbed "demi-brigades" was mixed in 1792. Certainly, the professionals formed the cadre by which the volunteers and conscripted men learned the art of soldiering. Resistance to the proposed merger weakened when Lazare Carnot, minister of war, and member of the Committee of Public Safety openly supported this incorporation.[19]

The *amalgame* or integration of old and new battalions, Blancs and Bleus, established a truly national army. One ancien régime battalion and two National Guard battalions formed a new three-battalion demi-brigade of 3,200 men.[20] The designation of "regiment" was removed, as radicals associated it with the Royal Army. The term "demi-brigade" remained in use until the Consulate in 1800. The scope of the integration required two amalgames, the first in 1793–94 and the second in 1795–96. Carrying out the merger in the course of campaigns complicated this process. Although much was done during winter quarters, not all demi-brigades were fully incorporated when campaigning season began. Thus, the continued introduction of conscripts into the ranks and the nature of war in a particular theater determined the duration and extent of the amalgame. Indeed, a number of demi-brigades were still in process of integration for the second amalgame in the Army of Italy when Napoleon took command in 1796.[21]

Through the first eight years of the Revolution the various assemblies pursued an ad hoc process of recruitment and conscription. Victory over the First Coalition in 1797 gave respite to the military demands and enabled the Directory—the current revolutionary regime—to entertain a permanent procedure for conscription. General Jean Baptiste Jourdan advocated a system of annual conscription by lottery required of all men aged twenty. The number of annual draftees would be set by the legislature. On 5 September 1798, the Jourdan Law was approved and became the fundamental conscription law for revolutionary and later Napoleonic France.[22] It is perhaps one of the most important military developments in revolutionary France, as it provided for the conscription and maintenance of a national army, which had been forged on the battlefields of the War of the First Coalition.

III

The modest size of the French army in 1789 permitted the maintenance of a relatively smaller military administration. If one looks
however, at French military power in the late seventeenth into the
eighteenth century, it is clear that its large armies necessitated a
bureaucracy capable of managing hundreds of thousands of men.
The French military administration during the French Revolution
benefitted from the bureaucracy established earlier in the century
and therefore required only modification, rather than invention,
to accommodate the increasingly large size of its army. Although
France never possessed an army of 750,000 men prior to 1794, the
armies of Louis XIV and Louis XV averaged 350,000 in wartime.

The political conflict between the revolutionary government,
the monarchical and executive branches, and the ministry of war
were separate from the mundane daily functioning of the military
bureaucracy. While the post of minister of war was highly politi-
cized until 1799, the infrastructure of the military administration
was modified, but not overhauled. The situation would be analo-
gous to the position of secretary of defense in the United States and
the military administration of the Pentagon.

During the course of the constitutional monarchy (1789–92), the
minister of war was appointed by Louis XVI and was often at odds
with the increasingly radical legislature. In 1792, with the overthrow of the monarchy and the creation of the republic, the minister of war reflected the government's increasing extremism. Thus,
Louis-Marie-Jacques Amalric, comte de Narbonne served as war
minister through 1792 but was replaced by the intensely Jacobin
Jean-Baptiste Bouchotte in January 1793.[23]

Bouchotte's administration introduced political radicalism in all
its revolutionary glory. Although a former soldier, his interests were
the political loyalty of the army and its generals.[24] His tenure was
extremely difficult, occurring at the onset and course of the civil
war and the expansion of the external conflict. Bouchotte had to
manage numerous military and administrative crises. Order came
only when Lazare Carnot, former captain of engineers, Jacobin, and
member of the Committee of Public Safety, assumed the responsibility for the war ministry.

Carnot is romantically referred to as the "organizer of victory."
During the years of his administration, Carnot brought order to the

revolutionary army. His direction was aided by the implementation of the amalgame and by the development and conduct of a coherent grand strategy. Carnot provided clear orders to the respective revolutionary armies in the field. Strategic directives from Paris were commonplace between 1794 and 1797. Under Carnot the military administration assumed greater efficiency in regard to logistics, weapons production, and strategic and operational planning.[25] The Bureau Topographique, often misunderstood by historians, provided detailed war plans for the armies.[26] Napoleon Bonaparte served in this office in August 1795, six months before his promotion as commander of the French Army of Italy.

Through Carnot, French military efforts gained cohesion in planning, logistics, strategy, and operations. The French minister benefitted as well from the conclusion of the civil war by the spring 1794 and the gradual victories against foreign enemies. During this period and previously under Bouchotte, members of the revolutionary government, either directly sent by Carnot or by the Committee of Public Safety, dispatched *representatives en mission* to relay orders to the army commanders or to oversee their actions. Carnot went personally to observe General Jourdan's Army of the North at Wattignies and to offer advice during the course of the battle. His dissolution with Jourdan led to the general's temporary removal, followed by his return to command a few months later for the offensive into Belgium in late 1794.[27]

The coordination and control of armies was complicated by the establishment of several armies in a single theater of war. Historically, most European states allocated one field army per campaign theater. The French followed suit through the eighteenth century, thus, allotting one army for Italy, one for Spain, one for Belgium and one for the Holy Roman Empire. During the first year of the Revolution four armies were established, the Army of the North, Army of the Center, Army of the Rhine, and the Army of the Midi (later Italy). By 1793–94 however, the increased manpower permitted the creation and allocation of several armies in a single theater, so that in Belgium in 1794 the French dedicated the Army of the North, the Army of the Ardennes, and the Army of the Rhine and Moselle. There were then two in Italy, Army of the Alps and Army of Italy; two for Spain; and two for Germany. The ability to coordinate the operations of multiple armies in a single region was complicated further by logistical requirements.[28] It was therefore imperative that operations be conducted with a conscious effort at coordination. Carnot brought increasing order, but was ultimately aided when Prussia and Spain withdrew from the war in 1795. This enabled Carnot to focus on merely three theaters of war—Holland, the Upper Rhine (Germany), and Italy.

The military administration and the army commanders were able to control their substantial forces due to prerevolutionary organizational and theoretical reforms. The battalion composed the basic military unit of European infantry for almost a century. The combination of two or more battalions comprised a regiment. When the French army was organized into field armies during the Seven Years' War, its large size and the need for more efficient command and control, as well as logistics, necessitated the creation of higher unit organization. Thus, the French army was the first to establish, in the postwar reform, the combat division. The division size varied initially yet by the later years of the Revolution included two or more brigades of two or more regiments—the later-termed demi-brigades. The division enabled army commanders to direct larger formations that were capable of independent movement and supply. The French armies of the Revolution retained the division as a standard organization, facilitating the operations of armies on the various frontiers. Division strength varied in the early years of the Revolution, but by 1800 it averaged 7,000 men. At times, specific operational plans called for the combination of two or more divisions into a larger formation subordinate to army command. The result was the *corps d'armée*. This formation remained ad hoc throughout the Revolutionary Wars and became a permanent fixture of the French army under Napoleon.[29]

The divisional system supported flexible operational plans and speed of movement. The ideas were drawn from Pierre de Bourcet, a French staff officer in the Royal Army who had served under French marshal Maillebois in Italy during the War of Austrian Succession. Bourcet believed that the coordination of divisions along parallel routes in a theater of war would speed movement and create strategic problems for an enemy. He elaborated on these ideas in his book *Principes de la guerre de montagnes* (1776). The concept of marching divided and fighting united derived from Bourcet's ideas.

Further theoretical reforms employed during the Revolution included those proposed by the comte de Guibert. A central figure of the military commission responsible for the overhaul of the French army prior to 1789, Guibert had written extensively on the French tactical system, publishing *Essai general de Tactique* (1772) and later *Défense du Système de Guerre Moderne* (1779). Guibert advocated the tactical flexibility of French battalions and their ability to change formation on the battlefield. The traditional formation employed in battle was *l'ordre mince*, or line, providing the battalion with a significant frontage for firepower. In the wake of the Seven Years' War, there had been an argument in favor of *l'ordre profond*, or attack column, to defeat the enemy with cold steel. Guibert believed both had their benefits dependent upon the tactical situation, but he also introduced a compromise, *l'ordre mixte*, a combination of column and line by a single battalion or employed by a regiment with columns on the flanks and line in the center. It offered firepower and mass.[30] While l'ordre mixte was an innovative idea, it was used rarely during the French Revolutionary Wars. Guibert advocated the training of a professional force capable of tactical maneuvers that included *mince, profond,* and *mixte.* During the course of the Revolutionary Wars, French infantry evolved from the masses of attack columns— easy enough to train the hundreds of thousands of volunteers and conscripts—to the more complicated and l'ordre mixte.[31]

Beyond the French army's need to address problems with the infantry, the artillery arm performed poorly and ineffectively during the Seven Years' War. The French army once possessed the most advanced artillery and engineering arm in Europe. In the early eighteenth century, French artillery became more mobile and standardized under the Vallière system. The Prussian and Austrian artillery arms had outperformed the French during the Seven Years' War, and shortly thereafter the French introduced a new system to standardize artillery. Advancement in metallurgy and casting permitted lighter guns and more efficient gun carriages. Artillery became more mobile. This new Gribeauval system carried the French artillery through the Revolution and into the age of Napoleon.[32]

As an artillery officer, Napoleon was highly familiar with the new system and new artillery theories. Virtually all European military institutions continued to see artillery as a subordinate or auxiliary arm of the infantry and cavalry. French artillery officer Baron Jean-Pierre du Teil advocated that artillery be established as a separate branch of the armed forces alongside the infantry and cavalry. Even Guibert disagreed, seeing artillery as supplementary. Du Teil argued that the increased mobility and firepower could be used independently by concentrating artillery batteries on the field of battle and by using massed fire at a single point to break the enemy line. Traditionally, heavy cannon were deployed as positional batteries at the beginning of a battle and were rarely moved due to their weight. Lighter field pieces were attached to infantry regiments to supplement infantry fire. Du Teil believed that cannon could now be used in larger concentrations and moved during the course of battle. He argued that regimental guns wasted the power and potential of artillery fire.[33]

Although Du Teil's concept of an independent artillery branch did not come to fruition until Napoleon became consul of France, his brother ran the Royal artillery school at Auxonne, which Napoleon attended in 1787. Indeed, Du Teil's theories of concentrated artillery fire and mobility on the field was taught to the artillery officers in the years prior to 1789, and the application of these theories on the battlefield could be found throughout the Revolutionary Wars.

IV

The decline of the French army's performance during the Seven Years' War was tied directly to severe problems in the officer corps. Traditionally the reserve of nobility, social status came to trump military hierarchy by midcentury. In the wake of the debacle, military commissions and investigatory committees examined the cause of defeat. It became quite clear that military professionalism had taken a backseat to privilege. The quality of French officers and their understanding of their business required further attention.

The transformation of the French officer corps prior to 1789 was critical to the success of French arms after 1789. Dubois-Crancé, Lazare Carnot, and Napoleon were already officers by 1789. Many—though not all—who became the senior officers of the Revolution and empire began their military careers as officers in the Royal Army. The emphasis placed upon military education and professionalism was fundamental to the establishment of a solid foundation for the Royal Army, which later became the national army.[34]

In the years before the Revolution, Louis XVI empowered a military reform commission to oversee the transformation of the Royal Army. Guibert was appointed a member of the committee. A merit-based system existed alongside the system of privilege, but performance and education played a central role.[35] The École militaire (Royal Military Academy in Paris) trained scions of the nobility since 1750. The reform commission advocated the establishment of military schools to prepare and inculcate sons of the lesser classes (generally the middle class) who exhibited intelligence and character and whose families desired that they enter the military profession. While general convention held that that nobles possessed an innate ability to lead, those of the other classes could be educated to lead. The notion that talent could be fostered and that education could be used as a tool to make leaders was directly drawn from basic Enlightenment principles.[36] The results of reform were seen as early as the American Revolution, when the French army in America, under the comte de Rochambeau, performed quite well, and the general—a professional officer—ensured that his subordinates conducted themselves as military professionals.[37]

After 1789, the life of an officer in the Royal Army became rather complex. As was seen with the experience of Davout at Hesdin, the loyalty of officers was questioned. Many officers, noble and non-noble, resigned their commissions in the first years of the Revolution. Many emigrated by 1792, and others joined the National Guard. Davout, among others of his contemporaries, spent restless time away from the army, yet in the call for volunteers in 1791, Davout joined the 8th Company, 3rd Volunteer Battalion de l'Yonne. His previous military education and command made him a natural choice for election to captain, followed shortly thereafter to his elevation as the lieutenant colonel of the entire battalion.[38] Davout's experience was typical of many with prior military experience and no doubt counted for the desertions and resignations from the Royal Army and the appearance of ci-devant noble officers in the National Guard. Additionally, the stagnancy of promotion in the Royal Army had led many veteran junior officers and noncommissioned officers to leave their ancien régime regiments and seek better opportunities in the National Guard. After the amalgames of 1794 and 1795–96, these men retained their ranks and became officers in the French army.

Davout's election as an officer reflected the radicalism of the Revolution and the reaction to the aristocratic nature of the former Royal Army. The creation of National Guard battalions necessitated the appointment of officers, and the democratic practice of election extended to these units. This was a wonderful reflection of revolutionary principles but resulted in disaster when popularity was initially prized over martial prowess. Within the first year of the French Revolutionary Wars, the error of the election process was made clear with horrible battlefield results. By 1793, the process changed with the restoration of promotion by merit and ability at the higher levels, and the retention of election of the junior officers. Nevertheless, the election of officers after 1793 eventually disappeared, as the necessities of war led to the elevation of experienced men.[39]

At the senior ranks, political appointment remained commonplace. Although much has been made of the appointment of favorites to military command in the Royal Army, the various revolutionary governments pursued similar practices. The appointment of an army commander was associated with politics. In 1792, as war loomed, the Constituent Assembly anointed Marshal Luckner, Rochambeau, and Lafayette as commanders of the three field armies. By August 1792, however, Lafayette had fled after an attempted coup against the revolutionaries who overthrew the monarchy, and Luckner resigned. These generals reflected the desire of Louis XVI and the moderate assembly to compromise on military leadership. Lafayette's failed coup and the 10 August Revolution led to the sacking of several senior generals, the eventual defection of General Dumouriez in 1793, and the prevalence of political promotions in the army during the years of the Terror (1793–94).[40]

The Jacobin regime had little tolerance for insubordination or for autonomy of its army commanders. Even victory could not necessarily save officers denounced for counterrevolutionary acts, such as defiance of orders from Paris, contempt for the revolutionary government, or failure in battle. The first dramatic example of the intolerance against these infractions was the denunciation, arrest, and execution of General Custine in August 1793, less than one year after his victories on the Rhine. General Houchard, another respected and capable general, followed him to the guillotine in November 1793. In part, this was a reaction to the defection of Dumouriez. One of the two heroes of the Battle of Valmy (September 1792), Dumouriez suffered defeat at Neerwinden in Belgium in March 1793. Afterward, he defected to the Austrians when representatives of the National Convention came to arrest him.[41]

After the Thermidorean Reaction in July 1794, the new revolutionary government, supposedly comprised of moderates, purged the army of political appointees in order to return to the policy of professionalizing the officer corps. More than one hundred generals were sacked in the process.[42] The result was a success. By 1795, the progress of the war had already favored France. A new military leadership emerged in the course of the campaigns, and while a number of skilled generals became victims of the Terror, the men who were now senior officers exhibited substantial sangfroid and possessed much experience. The result was a resilient and professional officer corps at all levels.

V

The Battle of Fleurus, fought on 26 June 1794, offers an interesting view of French revolutionary warfare in an atypical setting. The French Army of Sambre et Meuse, under the command of General Jean Baptiste Jourdan, stood on the defensive in the face of a Austrian attack to relieve the siege of Charleroi. The composition and conduct of the French army during this defensive battle illustrates the extent to which military reforms in the years since 1789 along with the professionalism of the officers who entered service prior to 1789 came together to achieve victory in difficult circumstances.[43]

The Sambre et Meuse army was formed by the amalgamation of the French armies of the Rhine et Moselle, Ardennes, and part of the North. It was commonplace for the ministry of war in Paris to create and later absorb or disband various armies on the frontiers dependent upon the strategic or operational needs. At the same time two armies operated on the Italian front, with an additional two in Spain, and two in Germany. Indeed, Belgium and the Rhine were the primary theaters of war and absorbed the vast majority of existing manpower drawn from the levée en masse. A seesaw of probes, feints, thrusts, and parries culminated in the French retaining part of Belgium but having lost the majority of its gains from the previous year. Carnot directed Jourdan—who had been removed from command by the war minister several months earlier for his "sluggish" generalship despite military victory—to take charge of the newly created army and advance into central Belgium, placing the fortified city of Charleroi under siege. To that end, with the siege affected, Jourdan moved his army northeast of the city to provide cover against an Austrian relief army. To achieve his objectives, the Army of the Sambre et Meuse boasted a strength of 72,000 men.

Jourdan's army did not operate alone, but General Charles Pichegru commanded the Army of the North. He was tasked with taking Tournai. This move occupied the Anglo-Allied Army under the Duke of York and General Clerfayt. Facing Jourdan stood the venerable Prince of Saxe-Coburg with the main Austrian army in Belgium. The prince divided his forces, dispatching General Beaulieu to Namur in order to distract Jourdan, and perhaps to convince him to divide his own army. The French general did not take the bait, and when Saxe-Coburg attacked at Fleurus, he was significantly outnumbered, having merely 46,000 men on the battlefield.

Jourdan deployed his eight divisions in a semicircular position three miles from Charleroi, while Hatry's division conducted the siege. The French opened their attack upon the fortifications on 18 June, and the sinister *terroriste* Louis de Saint-Just observed the conduct of operations as the representative from Paris. Fortunately for Jourdan, Saint-Just was more interested in taking Charleroi than in the general's direction of the battle. Saxe-Coburg thus gathered his forces, including the Prince of Orange's Dutch regiments and marched to the relief of Charleroi.

The French army used the available forests and towns to strengthen its position. General François Marceau's weak division was posted to the woods on the French right, along the Sambre River. Adjacent and to the north, Jourdan posted another division under General François Lefebvre (a future Napoleonic marshal) between Fleurus and Wagnée. The divisions of generals Championnet and Morlot held the center from Wagnée to Gossclies. The left was held by General Jean-Baptiste Kléber's ad hoc *corps d'armée* of two divisions (Generals Montaigu and Duhesme) held post in front of Courcelles. Jourdan held his cavalry in reserve, and was joined by Hatry after Charleroi surrendered on 17 June.

Saxe-Coburg surveyed the French position and determined that Jourdan had overextended his line, permitting the Austrian general to take advantage of the situation. Indeed, opportunity presented itself, yet Saxe-Coburg opted to attack Jourdan with five separate columns in front and flank. He therefore lost all advantage of Jourdan's faulty deployment. On the French left, Saxe-Coburg directed General Beaulieu with 10,300 men, having marched from Namur. The Archduke Charles, the younger brother of Emperor Francis II, commanded two columns totaling 15,500 men against Fleurus and Wagnée. General Quasdanovich, with 6,400, attacked the French center, while the Prince of Orange's columns of 13,000 assailed Kléber's divisions around Courcelles.

On 26 June the allied columns attacked. The Prince of Orange directed his forces against Montaigu's division on Kléber's far left. Although reinforced with an infantry brigade, Orange's artillery and cavalry forced the division beyond Courcelles, leaving Duhesme's division vulnerable. Fearing the collapse of his flank, Kléber dispatched Jean-Baptiste Bernadotte's brigade to secure Courcelles. Intense fighting for the next several hours resulted in the blunting of the allied advance. Orange had sufficient strength to force the French flank but insufficient numbers to occupy all of Kléber's divisions, and thus he exhausted his troops during the morning fight and then could not continue his advance in the face of determined resistance by Bernadotte's infantry. The prince withdrew his forces to their original position by late afternoon.

In the center, Morlot's division fell back toward Gosselies and held Quasdanovich, but a crisis emerged around Fleurus. Beaulieu's column pushed through Marceau's previously battered battalions. The French division gradually gave way with units routing. Marceau gathered what strength he could and delayed the Austrian advance through the woods as best as possible. Meanwhile, the Archduke Charles stormed through Fleurus, crashing against Lefebvre's division. The archduke's second column fell on Championnet's troops as well. This attack made moderate success until it ran into a redoubt supported by eighteen cannon, which Championnet had constructed to bolster his line. Nevertheless, Charles reorganized his battalions and threw them against Championnet, while keeping Lefebvre busy with his other Austrian column.

The French redoubt was taken roughly at the same time Marceau's division collapsed. Lefebvre found both his flanks compromised and the entire French right threatened. This was the critical moment of the battle. Lefebvre dispatched Colonel Nicholas Soult with three battalions and a cavalry detachment to stop Beaulieu's advance. Lefebvre's soldiers stood an offered fire against the Austrian attack, but the threat from Beaulieu's and Charles's columns increased the pressure. Jourdan responded to these events as he became aware of them. He directed Dubois's cavalry reserve against the Austrians facing Championnet. The attack supported by French infantry threw back the Austrian column. Jourdan then directed Hatry's division, the last reserve to the support of Lefebvre's battered division. Fresh troops succeeded in halting the Austrian attack. Part of Hatry's division further assisted Soult in holding the far right and eventually in compelling Beaulieu to withdraw.

Jourdan's victory was not guaranteed, and if Saxe-Coburg had had equal or greater numbers, the French may very well have lost. The organization of the French army into divisions made the command and control of the Sambre et Meuse much more efficient, especially in the midst of battle, when reacting to critical situations. Saxe-Coburg, however, followed eighteenth-century tradition of forming columns—the equivalent strength of divisions, but which lacked proper administration or staff and which were established for the immediate task. The performance of Lefebvre's, Bernadotte's, and Soult's battalions reflected a high quality of professionalism and skill. In fact, they were veterans of at least one previous campaign, and some of two. This experience enabled them to conduct themselves effectively under duress and with significant peril. Fleurus clearly illustrated the organizational advantages of the divisional system on the field of battle and the quality and professionalism of the new officer corps. The French army during the Revolution, therefore, merged the tradition of professionalism of the past with the revolutionary military policies to create a national army that succeeded in defeating its enemies on the frontiers and exporting the revolution under the bayonet into Belgium, Holland, western Germany, Spain, and Italy by 1797.

Notes

1. See Samuel F. Scott, *From Yorktown to Valmy* (Niwot: University Press of Colorado, 1998), for a detailed discussion of the French army from the American Revolution to the French Revolution.
2. Samuel F. Scott, *The Response of the Royal Army to the French Revolution* (Oxford: Clarendon Press, 1978), 217–24.
3. Ibid., 105.
4. Gunther E. Rothenberg, *The Art of Warfare in the Age of Napoleon* (Bloomington: Indiana University Press, 1978), 97–98; Andre Corvisier and Jean Delmas, eds., *Histoire militaire de la France: 2, De 1715 à 1871* (Paris: Presses Universitaires de France, 1992), 236. The numbers vary from 50,000 to 60,000 men. Strongly recommended is Samuel F. Scott, "The Regeneration of the Line Army during the French Revolution," in *Warfare in Europe, 1792–1815,* ed. Frederick C. Schneid (Aldershot, UK: Ashgate, 2007), 227–50.
5. Scott, *Response of the Royal Army,* 218.
6. Ibid. Chapter 2 is dedicated to the crisis of 1789.

7. A detailed discussion of the climate in the regular regiments is found in Pierre Charrier, *Le Maréchal Davout* (Paris: Nouveau Monde, 2005), 34–41; this incident is also mentioned in Jean-Paul Bertaud, *The Army of the French Revolution: From Citizen-Soldiers to Instruments of Power* (Princeton, N.J.: Princeton University Press, 1988), 29.
8. Bertaud, *Army of the French Revolution*, 44–45; John Lynn, *The Bayonets of the Republic: Motivation and Tactics in the Army of Revolutionary France, 1791–1794* (1984; repr., Boulder, Colo.: Westview Press, 1996), 49–50.
9. Camille Rousset, *Les Volontaires, 1791–1794*, 5th ed. (Paris: Perrin, 1892), 5. Rousset states that the numbers included 25,000 for the navy and 75,000 for the army.
10. Ibid., 9.
11. The *fédérés* were called to Paris on 8 June 1792; the levy of 50,000 was on 11 July. Bertaud, *Army of the French Revolution*, 78.
12. Rousset, *Les Volontaires*, 69.
13. Bertaud, *Army of the French Revolution*, 66–67; Lynn, *Bayonets of the Republic*, 48–49.
14. Rothenberg, *Art of Warfare*, 99–100; Bertaud, *Army of the French Revolution*, 90–96.
15. Bertaud, *Army of the French Revolution*, 104.
16. Corvisier and Delmas, *Histoire militaire*, 243.
17. Ibid., 243.
18. List from Schneid, *Warfare in Europe*, xv.
19. Rousset, *Les Volontaires*. Chapter 19 discusses the details of "embrigadement" or the *amalgame*. See also Bertaud, *Army of the French Revolution*, 150–52, and Lynn, *Bayonets of the Republic*, 57–60.
20. Rothenberg, *Art of Warfare*, 103.
21. Léonce Krebs and Henri Moris, *Les campagnes dans les Alpes pendant la Révolution*, vol. 2, *1794, 1795, 1796* (Paris: Plon, 1895), *pièces justificatives* [supporting documents], 371–74, provides a full reprint of the order of battle for the army, and pre-amalgame battalions are listed in the organization.
22. Rothenberg, *Art of Warfare*, 101–102.
23. Howard G. Brown, *War, Revolution, and the Bureaucratic State: Politics and Army Administration in France, 1791–1799* (Oxford: Clarendon Press, 1995), 66–67.
24. Alan Forrest, *Soldiers of the French Revolution* (Durham, N.C.: Duke University Press, 1990), 95.
25. Ken Alder, *Engineering the Revolution: Arms and Enlightenment in France, 1763–1815* (Princeton, N.J.: Princeton University Press, 1997), 264–65. Alder clearly establishes that Carnot, with the full support of the Committee of Public Safety and the assistance of his colleague Prieur de la Côte d'Or, directed military production.
26. Brown, *War, Revolution, and the Bureaucratic State*, 127–28.
27. Lynn, *Bayonets of the Republic*, 14.

28. A wonderfully valuable, but underutilized, history of logistics during the French Revolutionary Wars is Peter Wetzler, *War and Subsistence: The Sambre and Meuse Army in 1794* (New York: Peter Lang, 1985).
29. For the development and integration of the French division, see Steven T. Ross, "The Development of the Combat Division in Eighteenth-Century French Armies," *French Historical Studies* 4, no. 1 (Spring 1965): 84–94.
30. Rothenberg, *Art of Warfare*, 22–24.
31. Lynn, *Bayonets of the Republic.* Chapters 11 and 12 and the appendix present a detailed analysis of the application of tactics in the Armée du Nord.
32. Matti Lauerma, *L'artillerie de Campagne Française pendant les guerres de La Révolution: évolution de l'organisation et de la tactique* (Helsinki: Akateeminen Kirjakauppa, 1956), 12–22.
33. Ibid., 82–83, 85–90.
34. Two important articles on the reform of the officer corps prior to the Revolution are David Bien, "The Army in the French Enlightenment: Reform, Reaction and Revolution," in Schneid, *Warfare in Europe*, 143–74; and Harold T. Parker, "Napoleon and the Values of the French Army," in Schneid, *Warfare in Europe*, 217–26.
35. Rafe Blaufarb, *The French Army, 1750–1820: Careers, Talent, Merit* (Manchester, UK: Manchester University Press, 2002), particularly chaps. 1 and 2.
36. Bien, "Army in the French Enlightenment," 158–61.
37. See Scott, *From Yorktown to Valmy.*
38. John Gallaher, *The Iron Marshal: A Biography of Louis N. Davout* (Carbondale: Southern Illinois Press, 1976), 13–14.
39. Blaufarb, *The French Army*, chaps. 2–5.
40. Bertaud, *Army of the French Revolution*, 62–63, 143–45.
41. Lynn, *Bayonets of the Republic*, 78–79.
42. Howard G. Brown, "Politics, Professionalism, and the Fate of Army Generals after Thermidor," in Schneid, *Warfare in Europe.* Compare figures on page 182 with those on 188.
43. The sources for the narrative of the Battle of Fleurus are *Archives de la Guerre, Service Historique de l'Armée du Terre*, Château de Vincennes, B34 "Correspondance de Nord et de Sambre et Meuse," 16–30 June 1794, specifically the report by General Lefebvre to Jourdan, 26 June 1794. I must thank my former student Jordan Hayworth for providing me with a copy of this document. The battle narrative was also taken from V. Dupuis, *Les Opérations militaires sur la Sambre en 1794: Bataille de Fleurus* (Paris: R. Chapelot, 1907), and Robert Bruce et al., *Fighting Techniques of the Napoleonic Age, 1792–1815* (New York: St. Martin's Press, 2008). Most recently, Jordan Hayworth's work on the Sambre et Meuse army is published and must be consulted. See Jordan Hayworth, "Evolution or Revolution on the Battlefield? The Army of the Sambre et Meuse," *War in History* 21, 2 (April 2014): 170–92.

CHAPTER 2

THE PRUSSIAN ARMY

DENNIS SHOWALTER

To say that Prussia does not come out well in standard accounts of the French Revolutionary Wars is an understatement. Its policy is dismissed as shortsighted opportunism. Its army is described as a degraded simulacrum of its Frederician original. This essay offers an alternative perspective and, without inverting convention to depict wise statesmanship and effective war making, suggests that Prussia between 1788 and 1806 pursued a comprehensible and defensible foreign policy, based on a close and comprehensible synergy between diplomacy and force. In that context, the Prussian army was not a retrograde and arteriosclerotic foil to its revolutionary/Imperial French opponent.

I

Frederick II went to war in 1740 from the conviction that the European status quo was no longer viable. The accuracy, legality, and morality of that perception are less important than their consequences. A quarter century of conflict brought Prussia to the edge of destruction and left it devastated.[1] Frederick nevertheless remained determined to maintain Prussia's new position as one of its major powers. He regarded the Seven Years' War in particular as a product of Europe's miscalculation of Prussia's intentions and capacities and proposed to leave no room for doubt about either. After 1763 Prussia's peacetime army initially consisted of more than 150,000 men and grew steadily larger. Embodying the risks of trying conclusions with Old Fritz and his grenadiers, the army was the central element of a foreign policy assigning force the role of intimidation rather than implementation. For the rest of his reign, Frederick's state strategy was based on negotiation and deterrence.[2]

That policy culminated in the Potato War of 1778–79. Rather than being the fiasco described by misinterpreters of Clausewitz, this military/diplomatic confrontation resulted in Austria's backing down from its intention of acquiring Bavaria by purchasing it from its new elector. Of even greater significance, from being the disturber of Germany's and the continent's peace, Frederick until his death in 1786 became de facto defender of the sovereign rights established in 1648 by the Treaty of Westphalia and the international order confirmed at such cost during the Seven Years' War.[3]

Frederick's nephew and successor, Frederick William II, was willing enough to seek glory and territory where it was to be found. He earned a name for probing boundaries with more energy than finesse, launching diplomatic adventures without considering carefully their military or financial ramifications.[4] In practice, however, the new monarch never abandoned his uncle's hard-won position as rational actor, accepting the virtues of a policy of limited goals backed by credible force.

Credible force in Frederick William II's case was an army whose heart was its infantry: fifty-two regiments in 1787, sixty by 1806.[5] Each consisted of two musketeer battalions totaling around 1,600 men and a third, elite grenadier battalion (reduced to two grenadier companies in 1799), usually operating independently in the field. Numbered according to seniority, regiments were named after their "colonels in chief," aristocrats or distinguished generals, and usually identified by that name. The drill regulations, slightly modified in 1788, emphasized rapid fire in linear formation The infantryman's musket, although dismissed by one critic as "neither firearm, pike, nor club,"[6] was a weapon refined and developed along the lines of the modern assault rifle, with ease of usage and enhanced rates of fire favored over ballistic qualities. The complex drill movements usually associated with Frederick the Great were designed to facilitate quick deployment and disciplined execution of small arms drill under the worst, most confusing circumstances. The oblique order made famous by Frederick the Great was not an assault formation but a means of bringing overwhelming fire to bear on an enemy flank. The normal deployment of a battalion was in three ranks; the normal extension was over 150 yards; the usual allocation of reserves was zero. With its battalions side by side—also the norm—a regiment was fully committed. An exposed flank or a sudden breakthrough was a corresponding harbinger of disaster. The conventional counter was deployment in continuous and successive lines, regiments alongside and behind each other. A Prussian infantry line could advance to its front and maintain its alignment better than any of its counterparts. Any other maneuver was difficult—especially in the absence of any permanent command echelons above the regiment. Brigades were ad hoc creations; divisions were a foreign concept, under test in France but otherwise unproven.

Prussian cavalry was divided into three categories. The thirteen regiments of cuirassiers were big men on heavy horses, armed with straight swords and wearing breastplates, intended as a battlefield striking force. The twelve regiments of dragoons had minimized their original role as dismounted fighters and developed into medium cavalry, backing up the cuirassiers. There were ten regiments of hussars and one of lancers: light cavalry, frequently employed apart from the army's main body as scouts and raiders, with a reputation for devil-may-care boldness that ensured they never lacked for volunteers. Cuirassier and dragoon regiments had around 800 men at war strength; hussars, around 1,550. Regiments of the same type were usually brigaded together.

During this period, the Prussian artillery underwent repeated reshuffling in an effort to improve its firepower and mobility. While making no significant innovations in equipment and doctrine, the artillery did improve training and morale incrementally.[7] The elite horse artillery reached a strength of ten batteries by 1805. The models of guns and types of ammunition were reduced as well. By 1806, about a third of the sixty-odd batteries were armed with 12-pounders, the balance with 6-pounders. By general agreement the material was too heavy, especially given the poor quality of the gun teams. Once in position, however, the Prussian artillery was an effective tactical instrument—as the French discovered at Pirmasens and Kaiserslautern.

The Prussian army was built around a recruiting/conscription system prefiguring selective service as practiced in the United States during the 1950s and 1960s. Prussia's economy could not spare its most vigorous element for even a few of its most productive years. Nor could the state properly train every eligible man. A process of random selection seemed as irrational to Prussia's monarchs as to America's Congress. Instead, regiments were assigned a recruiting district, or canton, further broken down into company areas. All males in the district were entered in the company recruiting rolls

THE PRUSSIAN ARMY   39

at age sixteen. If the companies did not fill their ranks by voluntary enlistment, then eligible cantonists were conscripted.

The key word was "eligible." While every male was registered, only those who met the height requirement of 5'7" or taller, who were non-noble, who were not sons of officers, who did not directly own a farm, or whose families were worth less than 10,000 talers were eligible for induction. These criteria reduced the typical company pool to between 15 and 20 percent of the enrollees. As an example, in one company-sized recruiting area of 771 hearths (Amt Bochum), there were approximately 135 households that met the minimum requirements for conscription at any time during the cantonal era. This population filled a yearly cantonal requirement of about three soldiers—scarcely a high blood tax by any standards. Moreover, once the conscripted cantonist learned the basics of his new craft, he was eligible to be furloughed to civilian life and the civilian economy for an average of ten months a year, spending only two with the colors to refresh his memory and reflexes. All these factors combined to produce tractable, if not necessarily enthusiastic, soldiers—much like their American counterparts two centuries later.[8]

The army's numbers were made up by volunteers. Even in wartime, Frederick the Great had asserted, recruits should be raised in one's own country "only when sternest necessity compels."[9] By 1786, 110,000 of the 190,000 men under Prussian arms were outlanders. All authorities agree, however, that the foreigners in Prussian service were a far cry from what they had once been. The Enlightenment, with its rejection of war as violent and unnatural, had begun to penetrate village schoolrooms and pulpits. The general economic upturn in central Europe after 1763 absorbed many potential soldiers. Prussia's harsh discipline and deteriorating conditions of service encouraged desertion.[10]

Frederick William was as unlikely a warrior–king as could be imagined. His uncle had cashiered his father for incompetence during the Seven Years' War. Frederick William did not seek to compensate by mastering the soldier's trade. His victories were won in the boudoir; a string of mistresses and illegitimate children offered a direct contrast to Frederick's misogynistic Puritanism. Where Frederick was caustic, remote, and austere, Frederick William was courteous, gregarious, likeable—and willing to listen to advisers who sensed new directions in the craft of war and the treatment of soldiers.

The German Aufklärung (Enlightenment), which reached its full bloom in the 1770s, had a significant impact on military thought between the Rhine and the Vistula. Like its counterparts in literature, art, and philosophy, the new generation of military theorists was less concerned with establishing scientific systems than with broadening and disseminating practical knowledge.[11] Frederick's wars, moreover, had shaped images in Germany suggesting that war was a human endeavor as well as the province of reason. The Seven Years' War was the first conflict in history to be reported from the bottom up as well as from the top down. Significant proportions of the Prussian army's junior officers and enlisted cantonists were literate. As much to the point, these men usually had someone at home anxious to learn if all was going well. The large number of memoirs published by survivors and participants reinforced the argument that the genius of Frederick the Great depended significantly on the courage and goodwill of the common soldiers and junior officers.[12]

The process of rebuilding pride in service began with an institution particularly congenial to the late eighteenth century. Regimental schools emerged everywhere in Prussia during the 1770s and 1780s. Intended primarily to provide instruction in marketable skills, they had a stabilizing function as well. By providing soldiers' children with academic and practical instruction, they encouraged fathers to stay with their families and remain in the ranks. Potsdam provided the model. Beginning in the early 1780s, all children of the garrison from five to thirteen were required to attend a school whose facilities and curriculum were state-of-the-art, with salaried teachers expected to limit corporal punishment as they taught not only basics but more esoteric subjects like essay writing and high German.[13]

Nor did enlightened personnel policies stop at the classroom door. Frederick William had long criticized, albeit in a casual fashion, what he regarded as the excessive strictness of the army's discipline. A series of orders abolished, at least officially, the more extreme physical punishments. Cavalry NCOs, for example, were instructed to refrain from verbal abuse and could be punished, even cashiered, for getting physical with recalcitrants. Only squadron commanders could order flogging, and the maximum sentence allowed was thirty lashes. A new "Regulation on Recruitment" was introduced to curb the frauds and abuses that had hindered enlistment and retention of the foreigners who were still so important to

Prussia's military effectiveness. Frederick William proclaimed that anyone joining the army could count on lifelong security. Soldiers' homes were expanded in capacity and accessibility. Regiments organized invalid companies for those veterans still able to perform housekeeping duties. Family allowances were introduced for men with children under thirteen. Pensions were increased and in part made retroactive to veterans of the Seven Years' War and the Potato War campaign.[14]

Changes in personnel policies were accompanied by changes in organization. In 1787 each line infantry company received ten *Schützen.* These sharpshooters were selected for physical fitness and mental alertness and were given special instructions in marksmanship and skirmishing. There were too few of them, however, to make much difference to the way a battalion fought. Instead, the Schützen proved a valuable source of young, active noncommissioned officers. Those picked for the assignment were as a rule more interested in gaining promotion than improving their fieldcraft. Colonels and captains for their part welcomed these "chosen men," as they came to be known in the British service, more as assets to unit command structures than as a select group of specialists whose tactical skills were of limited use in peacetime.[15]

More visible, and more tactically significant, were the twenty fusilier battalions also created in 1787. At the beginning of his reign, Frederick the Great had organized a corps of riflemen, drawn as far as possible from foresters and hunters. The Jäger eventually developed into a regiment of around 2,000 men at war strength whose ten companies were used independently. Though they participated in set-piece battles, the Jäger are more accurately compared to the ranger battalions of the contemporary U.S. Army: an elite force for special operations. Otherwise, light infantry was never a high priority for Frederick the Great. To the extent he bothered, the king depended on formations formed ad hoc from the army's dregs.

The new fusilier battalions, by contrast, were built around existing grenadier and line battalions and were selected from some of the best companies from the army's garrison regiments. The fusiliers were intended not to work closely with the battalions of the line but to operate semi-independently in wooded or broken ground against enemies like the Croats and Grenzers of Austria or the combined arms legions used by France in the Seven Years' War. These were true irregular forces, not the as-yet nonexistent skirmishers of the

French Revolution. The best way of challenging them was to combine the virtues of discipline and initiative. The fusiliers wore green uniforms instead of the traditional blue. They carried a more accurate version of the regular musket, and they used hunting horns for signaling. They fought in two ranks rather than the regulation three. Fighting in open order, they were expected to maintain a common direction, never get too far from each other, and open and cease fire on command—or risk a flogging. The Prussian army was still the Prussian army.

Man management in the fusiliers was also innovative. Fusilier companies were expected to cultivate personal and small-unit initiative—to the point of living off the countryside. Discipline was based heavily on appeals to professionalism and comradeship: common commitment to a common enterprise. Physical punishment was expected to be a last resort. Being a Prussian fusilier, in short, was something special, and the battalions seldom lacked high-quality recruits.

Frederick William initially sought to distinguish the fusiliers from his uncle's misbegotten Free Battalions by insisting that their officers be of noble birth. In practice, Frederick William allowed exceptions, while the light infantry regulations of 1788 even permitted the commissioning of sergeants. Ambitious bourgeois sought and received commissions in the fusiliers: by the 1790s about a quarter of the fusilier officers were untitled. On the other hand, the official emphasis on preserving the aristocratic character of these new units' leadership kept the fusiliers from being regulated to the army's sidelines as something less than real soldiers.

Field training wore out uniforms and equipment at rates alarming to the army's bookkeepers. Practice ammunition was doled out in rounds. Nevertheless, as light troops Prussia's fusiliers were not to be despised—particularly for new creations. Officers like the future reformer Neithardt von Gneisenau took advantage of their own experience (in his particular case service in North America with the Ansbach-Bayreuth contingent) and utilized an increasing number of unofficial, plainly written handbooks to train their companies and battalions in open-order tactics.[16]

The new conditions of service offered prospects for professionalizing the army as a whole. Foreigners would have been easier to recruit and retain; more Prussian natives might have been encouraged to seek military careers despite legal and social pressures against such a decision. A possible consequence might have been a standing army built around committed long-service regulars, "thirty-year men" with good benefits and solid prospects for a pension. In wartime the mobilized cantonists could take their cue from the professionals. The tactics recommended for Prussia's fusiliers strongly resemble those employed by British light troops in the French and Indian War, adopted widely by line units in the American Revolution, and developed by the Light Division in the Peninsular War.[17] Speculation on the prospects for Prussia during the Revolutionary Wars invites those interested in might-have-beens.

II

The Prussian army nevertheless met and passed with flying colors the kind of operational test for which it was in good part configured in 1787. The stadtholder of the Dutch Republic, facing domestic crises that flared into a mini-revolt, turned to Prussia for assistance. In mid-September Frederick William dispatched 25,000 men under Ferdinand, Duke of Brunswick, who had won laurels in independent command in the Seven Years' War. The task force included several light units, among them two fusilier battalions and part of the Jäger regiment. They set the invasion's pace despite bad weather and bad roads. Brunswick, elderly but canny, understood political as well as military offensives. He announced that those who did not interfere with his troops would not be harmed. In a short time the Prussians occupied Utrecht and Amsterdam without significant resistance. The stadtholder's position was restored. His opponents kept silent, changed sides, or fled the country in the face of Prussian bayonets.[18]

This neatly executed counterinsurgency operation is usually either interpreted in a political context as one of the ancien régime's last triumphs before the Revolution or dismissed as inconsequential compared to the large-scale military operations just over the horizon. It was in fact a solid affirmation of the Prussian army's quality as a deterrent force, formidably capable of maintaining the state's interests in its designated zones of influence. To contemporary observers there seemed no question that the Prussian army was an effective instrument of Prussian policy under its new monarch, as it had been under the great Frederick. Prussia did not only gain an alliance with a grateful stadtholder in 1788. On 13 August, Frederick

William also signed a treaty with Great Britain. London's concerns about Prussian territorial ambitions regarding Poland—concerns fully justified by subsequent Prussian policies—were overcome in good part by the performance of Prussia's soldiers.[19]

The Prussian army exercised its deterrent role successfully in eastern Europe as well. In 1787 Austria and Russia once more went to war against the Ottoman Empire. As the price of its neutrality, Prussia suggested Poland's western territories. Frederick William backed his claim by deploying almost 150 battalions in Silesia and along the Saxon frontier in the fall and winter of 1789. Austrian emperor Leopold II, who succeeded his brother Joseph in February 1790, decided to switch sides rather than fight. The July 1790 Convention of Reichenbach established the diplomatic basis for Prussian territorial gains at Poland's expense. A year later, Prussia's rapid mobilization against Russia led Empress Catherine to reconsider her objections to Poland's dismemberment and convinced Austria to transform the Reichenbach agreements into a full-fledged alliance.[20]

These diplomatic successes were by no means the unmixed result of unilateral saber rattling. Yet events from 1787 to 1791 clearly showed that whatever might be the Prussian army's possible shortcomings compared to ideal military standards, no European power was willing in practice to call the Prussian king's bets. Prussia was still the least of the great powers, with a corresponding risk of overplaying its cards. Yet for all his inadequacies as a military monarch, Frederick William II was at pains to avoid the kind of overstretch epitomized in the brawler's axiom "Never let your mouth buy more than your hands can pick up."

The king's prudence showed most clearly in his attitude toward France. From the beginning, Prussian policy was based on limited commitment to the anti-French coalition. Indeed, the case can be made that the Prussian army of the early 1790s was too convincing for the Prussian state's good. Frederick William II faced a corresponding temptation to modify the passive deterrence of Frederick the Great's final twenty years into a riskier active policy of opportunistic intimidation. The Seven Years' War nevertheless cast a long shadow. Frederick William was determined to avoid his predecessor's fate of fighting a war for Prussia's existence without reliable allies. Instead, he proposed to take as much or as little of the war as he willed. That approach was facilitated by the relative geographic remoteness from the French threat, the revolutionaries' relatively widespread perception of Prussia as a natural ally—reflecting a sense of identity with the enlightened, secular state purportedly created by Frederick the Great—and the relatively limited appeal of revolutionary ideology in Prussian lands. Even in the western provinces, historically open to influences from across the Rhine, initial enthusiasm for the French new order rapidly diminished as the effects of French occupation became manifest.[21]

Poland offered far more promising opportunities for low-cost aggrandizement. When in October 1792 Prussia declared itself willing to continue the Austrian alliance only if compensated by Polish territory, Vienna saw no alternative to accepting Poland's final dismemberment. The Russo-Prussian partition treaty of January 1793 touched off a general insurrection that proved especially successful against overextended, badly led Russian forces. Catherine requested Prussian aid; and Frederick William could congratulate himself on having outdone his uncle. The new Polish lands, less rich than Silesia, but almost as large, had been acquired in cooperation with Prussia's eastern neighbors. From the beginning that cooperation had reflected the presence and the performance of Prussia's army. Austria wanted Prussian troops to fight the French. Russia needed them to suppress the Poles. The Prussian expeditionary force had its share of problems against an increasingly desperate enemy but played a central role in crushing the insurrection and in erasing Poland from Europe's map for over a century. The Poles refused to stand for a decisive battle, but the Prussians wore them down and wore them out. The fusilier battalions again showed to advantage in the "little war" against partisans. The hussars resurrected a light cavalry tradition eroded by barracks and parade grounds.[22]

Exact responsibility for the outbreak of war between revolutionary France and the central European powers in 1792 continues to be debated. If France declared war first, Prussia and Austria had begun moving troops toward the French frontier weeks earlier. If the Girondins sought to extend the blessings of liberty, equality, and fraternity across the Rhine, the king of Prussia and the Austrian emperor perceived the long-term advantages of crippling France by repeating on a joint and larger-scale Prussia's performance of 1787 in the Dutch Republic.[23]

The Prussian king's decision was substantially validated by an army that between 1792 and 1795 performed up to and beyond reasonable expectations. Prussia's senior officers were no worse than their British and Austrian counterparts or, on the whole, their French enemies. The Duke of Brunswick, frequently cited as an example of arteriosclerosis in high command for his performance in the Valmy campaign, entered France with an army half the projected size, faked the French out of their boots in a skillfully orchestrated advance through the Argonne Forest. He might well have continued a successful campaign of maneuver had it not been for Frederick William's impatient insistence on pushing toward Paris even at the price of a battle.

Brunswick's behavior at Valmy was at best lackluster. Early morning fog and heavy French artillery fire slowed the Prussian deployment. The decision to halt the main infantry attack almost as soon as it began nevertheless reflected a loss of nerve alien to the Frederician system in its heyday. At the same time, the general and often-cited sense of defeat and embarrassment so eloquently described by Goethe nevertheless merits taking with a goodly measure of salt. Valmy can legitimately be written off as a case of opening-night jitters. Inexperienced troops facing strong positions in bad weather seldom achieve glory. Brunswick himself showed to better advantage in the next campaigning season, whose primary result was the successful recapture of Mainz.[24]

Tactically and operationally, Prussia's performances improved exponentially in a short span of time. Prussian contingents in the Rhineland, their principal operational area, had no opportunity for the kind of pitched battles Frederick II had waged a generation earlier in Bohemia and Silesia. The region's wooded, broken terrain forced deployment in relatively small combined-arms task forces. While these did not become organic units like the French divisions, they were usually kept together long enough to develop some cohesion. For the most part, their commanders handled them capably. After some seasoning, the line battalions combined well-regulated volleys and well-controlled local counterattacks to match, if not always to master, the élan of their opponents. Prussian light infantry proved formidable opponents against French foragers and raiding parties. In large actions as well, the fusiliers taught some sharp lessons at high tuition in marksmanship and skirmishing.

The theater of operations offered no opportunity for the use of massed cavalry in the style of Seydlitz and Ziethen during the Seven Years' War. Prussian cuirassiers and dragoons nevertheless proved effective in brigade and squadron strength, despite uniform changes that favored the parade ground more than the battlefield. The hussars consistently outrode and outfought their French counterparts in the skirmishing and outpost fighting that dominated the campaign. Furthermore, for all the praise heaped on the French artillery reforms under Gribeauval, Prussian guns were seldom silenced or driven from the field by their opponents.

Another encouraging aspect of the army's performance was its morale. Prussian light units developed a strong identity as the army's elite, who performed their missions or went down fighting. In particular the Jäger, barely respectable when the war began, won a reputation as a fighting force second to none on either side. The line battalions were not far behind in self-image. Particularly in the Rhineland, supply systems consistently broke down. Living conditions were Spartan at best. Much of the fighting was cut-and-run operations against an elusive enemy who occasionally mounted the kind of fierce mass attacks western armies had not faced since the height of the Ottoman wars of the seventeenth century. Singly or in combination, such conditions had devastated European armies for over a century. Prussian desertion rates, however, remained acceptable, particularly in the context of French propaganda stressing the advantages of turning coat in the cause of freedom.

The Prussian army is the exception in this anthology. All the other armies, even the British, either fought a major battle, a Jemappes, Fleurus, or Tourcoing. Prussian troops, true to their role in Prussian strategy, managed to avoid serious combat. The only exceptions were two engagements during the Rhineland campaign of 1793. The broken, mountainous terrain and the dense network of small but strong fortifications combined to restrict the scale and the stakes of combat to stereotypical eighteenth-century parameters. In that environment, the Prussians played a leading role in two neat victories, Pirmasens and Kaiserslautern.

Prussia's withdrawal in 1795 from the anti-French coalition and its conclusion of the separate Peace of Basel has usually been interpreted as a consequence of economic crisis and diplomatic myopia. Standard general accounts describe the exhaustion of the war chest left by Frederick II, forcing Prussia to depend on foreign subsidies. Austria was unwilling and unable to underwrite her old enemy. Britain's offer of financial support was contingent on Prussia's troops operating for all practical purposes under British command and in

British interests. This reversion to Prussia's days as a subsidy state was regarded as intolerable, even at the price of abandoning Prussia's territory west of the Rhine to French rule. Frederick the Great had relied heavily on subsidies to keep the field for much of the Seven Years' War. Frederick William did not perceive a similar urgency. Nor was he about to mortgage Prussia's future by embarking on war to the knife against France because of a British hostility that seemed to be based as much in ideology as in self-interest.[25]

III

The policy of opportunistic neutrality Frederick William II bequeathed to his son in 1797 suited the latter's temperament. Saturnine and pessimistic at the age of twenty-seven, Frederick William III tended to assume the worst about most situations. He comes off poorly in most histories for failing to take counsel of Prussian hawks on the nature of the French threat. In fact, Frederick William's cautious outlook fitted Prussia's immediate realities.[26] His refusal to be drawn into the ramshackle Second Coalition of Russia, Austria, and Britain seemed the soundest of common sense as the new alliance blundered from one military disaster to another. France proposed an alliance as early as May 1798, but that prospect too had a cloven hoof. Lying as it did between contending powers, with no natural frontiers to speak of, Prussia faced the alternative risks of leading the forlorn hope for one adversary or of becoming everybody's battlefield.[27]

What saved the kingdom from having to choose sides for almost a decade was its army. From the French point of view, Prussia was better conciliated than fought. For anti-French coalitions, actual or potential, Prussian soldiers were increasingly regarded as necessary in a successful continental war. Prussia's military reputation was also enhanced by default. Austria's performances against the French grew worse instead of better as the century waned. Russian soldiers knew how to fight and die, but their commanders failed increasingly to cope with French tactical and strategic flexibility. Britain's military contributions in Europe between 1793 and 1802 are best described as inadequate, if not pathetic, despite marked subsequent improvement.[28]

Frederick William III was by no means blind to the risks of French aggrandizement. In June 1802, he met with Tsar Alexander of Russia and came away with a personal commitment to the allied cause. The king, however, had absorbed his great-uncle's commitment to the principle that Prussia was not a royal fief, to be taken to war at the will or whim of its monarch.[29] Nor was the first consul (soon to become emperor) of France backward in showing good will. In his effort to win Prussian support, Napoleon offered temptations even the great Frederick might have found difficult to resist.

In the reorganization of western Germany under French auspices in the aftermath of the 1801 Peace of Lunéville, Prussia's benevolent neutrality was rewarded by extensive territorial gains in Westphalia and to the north of Thuringia.[30] These acquisitions bore a certain risk. They shifted Prussia's center of gravity westward, making it more directly involved in the ongoing Anglo-Austro-French rivalry. The new lands, however, significantly improved the links between the monarchy's eastern and western halves. They seemed as well to prove the continued wisdom of Frederick William's foreign policy. Prussia's unprepossessing monarch appeared to have achieved the dream of every gambler: to win without betting.

Could Prussia continue to straddle the fence without splitting itself open? The answer by the turn of the century depended almost entirely on the actual and perceived effectiveness of an army facing a clear challenge to its half century's dominance of Europe's military scene. France, not Prussia, now set the standards of warfare. Adapting to second place is never easy in a milieu where a close run counts for nothing. The French army was likely to improve rather than decline. It was also backed by significantly greater human resources than anything Prussia could hope to match. For three quarters of a century, the state's ace in the hole had been a recruiting system that systematically tapped native manpower without exhausting it. That in turn allowed the maintenance of an army able to sustain Prussia as a first-rank power—as long as no other state copied or improved upon the method. The levée en masse did not permanently bring all classes of French society into uniform. By the mid-1790s, most of the bourgeoisie were keeping their sons safely at home, or in staff and noncombat assignments. The real difference between the armies involved numbers. Now France too had begun mobilizing its lower classes systematically and had several times as many of them to call into service.[31]

The manpower imbalance was exacerbated by the steady decline in foreign enlistments after 1795. By 1802, the Prussian army counted only 80,000 professionals to 140,000 cantonists. Increasing the army's domestic cadres was theoretically possible. Official figures gave just over 2 million eligible cantonists in 1799 and 2,300,000 in 1805. By the time all the legal exemptions were calculated, over 300,000 men could be conscripted in a given year.[32] Numbers, however, were by themselves a red herring. Prussia's position relative to France prefigured that of the United States or the Federal Republic of Germany relative to Russia during the Cold War. Matching France man for man was impossible, even without the accompanying risk of gridlocking a society arguably already too finely tuned for its own good.[33] Nor did even the most ardent Francophobes ever believe Prussia could defeat Napoleon's burgeoning empire singlehanded. Proposals like Karl Friedrich von dem Knesebeck's "Fatherland Reserve," with its advocacy of a popular levy based on the universal obligation to perform military service, were correspondingly widely criticized as more likely to weaken than improve both the army's effectiveness and the state's strategic position.[34]

Nor were the naysayers mere military mossbacks more frightened of disrupting their system than of attacking its shortcomings. They argued cogently that the French army of the new century, the force the reformers explicitly or implicitly proposed to counter, was not the half-disciplined "armed horde" of the early 1790s. Napoleon and his marshals instead led regiments strongly comparable to those that had marched to glory with Frederick: large cadres of experienced professionals supplemented by conscripts little different from Prussia's cantonists.[35] To match such an adversary, Prussia must develop a quality army able to counter mass and skill with even greater fighting power.[36] Conceptualizing such a force was no easy task in the context of rapid, continual changes in the craft of war, combined with a state strategy that when most successful in averting the risks of war kept Prussian troops and officers from updating their operational experience.

Beginning with Frederick the Great, the Prussian army had been influenced by the belief that successful war fighting required both knowledge and education. War, Frederick argued, was not a matter of improvisation but a subject that could be treated theoretically. Concepts derived from historical study and applied to specific cases could substitute for direct experience.[37] The man most responsible for applying Frederick's legacy to the Prussian army of the early 1800s was Gerhard von Scharnhorst. He had both a distinguished combat record and a reputation as one of Germany's best military theoreticians when Frederick William III convinced him to transfer from the Hanoverian army in 1801. Scharnhorst's first significant act in his new appointment was to found the Militärische Gesellschaft. This institution's ultimate purpose was to develop "an aristocracy of education"—not limited, technical instruction, but *Bildung*, the cultivation of individual character and understanding by the open, systematic exchange of ideas and information within an intellectual community.

Scharnhorst proposed not to challenge directly the Prussian army's traditional, and to date successful, way of doing things, but to introduce, a few at a time, a new generation of leaders with a common background who would advise and assist their nominal superiors in commanding the state in arms that Scharnhorst saw as necessary for Prussia's survival. These new men provided as well an unobtrusive infusion of fresh blood. Most Prussian senior officers were in their sixties—a sharp contrast to a French high command whose average age was well under forty. A decade of peace had offered, however, no opportunities to develop a corps of battle-tested counterparts to Napoleon's marshals. Making a clean sweep, replacing generals with men a decade or so younger, was no guarantee of improved efficiency. Attempting such a process was likely instead to have the negative result of polarizing an officer corps that needed above all to work together.[38]

Prussia's military reform movement nevertheless did not emerge from the ashes of the Peace of Tilsit in 1807. Before the beginning of the nineteenth century, overlapping and lively debates on specifics flourished. Chief among them was doctrine: how the army fought. Even committed supporters of traditional linear formations could not deny the impact of French assault columns covered by swarms of skirmishers. Nor could they ignore the evidence that open-order tactics were best countered only by open-order tactics. Images of musketeers in line being picked off one by one, until only isolated files were left to fire into the smoke at their invisible tormentors, had just enough basis in reality to give weight to the reformers' case.

Increasing the number of fusilier battalions and the percentage of Schützen in the line regiments could be no more than a palliative. Instead, the advocates of military reform cited both French and Prussian experience to stress the need for changing the army's patterns of recruitment, education, and training. Mercenaries and cantonists held in ranks by traditional discipline had limited prospects against what a steadily increasing body of professional literature described as a national army that incorporated in its ranks a cross section of France's population and infused formal instruction with patriotic enthusiasm.

By 1806, consensus was growing in the officer corps on replacing the canton system and its elaborate structure of exemptions by universal liability, with those conscripted serving a limited time unbroken by extensive furloughs. Accompanying this fundamental restructuring was support for treating common soldiers humanely, appealing to their goodwill and intelligence without moving too far in the direction of relying on enthusiasm and instinct at the expense of training and discipline. In that context, men like Gneisenau, Scharnhorst, and Carl von Clausewitz sought to synthesize the open-order tactics of the Revolution with the closed linear formations that had continued to prove their worth when properly handled.[39]

Logistics were also overhauled. Field requisitioning methods were simplified. Baggage, supply, and ammunition trains were reduced. Here, however, Prussia confronted a gap between myth and reality. Reformers, for example, cited as a precedent for increased requisitioning the alleged contemporary French practice of living off the land. Critics replied by calling up images of whole regiments collapsing into marauding bands of foragers. The doubters had clearer perceptions than the visionaries. Even the revolutionary armies had never really been self-sustaining. Napoleon's tendency to ignore logistical concerns brought his operational plans to the edge of disaster time and again. If case-hardened veterans of a dozen campaigns broke ranks because of hunger, could more be expected of relatively domesticated Prussian troops? The army's revamped logistic system's shortcomings were highlighted in 1806, when the wagon trains faced consistent difficulty in keeping pace with troop movements. The Prussian army that took the field for the Jena campaign was nevertheless a good deal leaner than it had been since the Seven Years' War.[40]

Organization was the third focus of the pre-Jena reformers. Almost from the beginning of the Revolutionary Wars, the French had employed permanent divisions combining infantry, cavalry, and artillery, with enough support and logistic services to sustain independent operations. Under Napoleon, the divisions were integrated into army corps, miniature armies of between 10,000 and 20,000 men whose combat power and sustainability were exponentially greater than the same numbers organized as divisions.[41] Scharnhorst's advocacy of a divisional system for in the Prussian army was, how- ever, was a minority position. One set of critics argued that the rap- idly changing conditions of war made it unwise to set any organization in cement. Others believed in the Frederician system's continued utility—particularly for an army that expected to fight a defensive war. A divisional system might be well-adapted for an army desiring to pose threats of invasion. Prussia's deterrent strat- egy, on the other hand, did not call for such a force structure.[42] Not until the 1806 campaign was actually under way was a divisional system introduced, and the divisions were badly balanced, lacking both fire power and shock power.

Contemporaries and scholars frequently blame the collapse of Prussia's state strategy in 1805–1806 on the culpable shortsighted- ness and irreconcilable factionalism of its administration: Frederick William III and his political advisers.[43] The position's flaw is its Prussocentricity: the assumption that Prussia from the beginning essentially miscalculated the intentions of imperial France. The key to Europe's situation lay not in Berlin but in Paris; it was the mushrooming in 1803–1804 of Napoleon's unfocused ambitions and what seemed the limitless capacity of the French army to enforce its emperor's pretensions. Diplomacy became for Napoleon no more than the conduct of war by other means.[44]

Prussia, with its Frederician heritage of wars waged for limited political objectives, was slow to recognize the paradigm shift in French behavior. Yet a solid body of evidence suggested that Prussia still held a trump card in its army. When Napoleon threatened to occupy the Electorate of Hanover in 1801, Frederick William pre- empted him. Instead of forcing the issue, Napoleon opened peace negotiations with Britain.[45] When war broke out once more between France and Britain in 1803, French troops overran the Electorate of Hanover, creating exactly the kind of direct geographic contact that Frederick William had sought to avoid. French diplomats, however, described the operation as temporary and suggested that continued Prussian neutrality would be amply rewarded. In the event, Prussian troops did occupy Hanover without resistance in October 1805, and the French garrison withdrew expeditiously.[46]

This success only reinforced the confidence that had led to Frederick William's refusal to join the Third Coalition, pitting

Russia and Austria against Napoleon on the Continent. The king's decision was facilitated by a belief, scarcely unreasonable given past experience, that the adversaries were evenly enough matched to wear each other down. The French might win, but at a cost, making the Prussian army an even greater factor in European affairs. Like Napoleon III sixty years later, Frederick William's political decision in the event left his state facing France alone. The acquisition of Hanover was followed in the aftermath of Austerlitz by a series of one-sided negotiations binding Prussia to supply troops for Napoleon's war with Russia and close its ports to British ships and goods. As a final indignity, rumor had it that Napoleon was willing to return Hanover to Britain in return for peace.

Rather than accept client-state status, reduction to the level of Bavaria or Württemberg, Frederick William declared war. He had the full support of a Gallophobic war party headed by Queen Marie Louise, who, according to some accounts, refused her husband sex until he consented to draw his sword. The king also hedged his bet. While negotiations were still incomplete in the summer of 1806, Russia was willing, indeed more than willing once Austria had withdrawn from the war, to support Prussia as part of a Fourth Coalition including Britain and Sweden. The only drawback was Prussia's credibility. With French envoys also discussing peace terms with Alexander, it seemed necessary for Prussia to take the lead and show goodwill.

That meant fighting—but not a fight to the finish. Prussia declared war in September. That left just time enough in the campaigning season for one major battle. All the Prussian army had to do there was to bloody Napoleon's nose, buying time for Russian bayonets and English guineas to bring their respective influences to bear. This was not an optimal strategic situation, but neither was it generally perceived as being outside the capacities of Prussia's military establishment. The war hawks of 1806 included many of the officers most active in the military-reform movement. While men like Clausewitz and Scharnhorst were unlikely to sharpen their swords on the steps of the French embassy, neither did they see themselves as engaging in a forlorn hope to salvage Prussian honor. Nor, based on over a decade's experience, were there any obvious reasons to expect disaster—at least before the campaign began.[47]

Prussia's deficiencies in the Jena/Auerstedt campaign reflected the state's failure to prepare for an inevitable, all-out war with

France. Prussia's state strategy for over a decade, however, had been designed to avoid exactly that contingency. Despite its limitations, the Prussian army of 1806 can reasonably be described as being well into the process of introducing the new ways of war developed over the previous decade. In comparative terms, the Prussians were about where the Austrians stood three years later at Wagram. Not until at least 1810 would Britain's principal field army in the Iberian Peninsula reach the tactical and administrative levels at which Prussia stood just prior to Jena. Russia as late as 1814 remained unregenerately unreformed and significantly successful. One might even suggest that Prussia's army had adapted too well to what a later generation would call mid-intensity war and counterinsurgency operations, while in the process taking for granted the continued ability to win the modern equivalent of a Leuthen or a Rossbach. A good horseman named Helmuth von Moltke observed a half century later that one does not drive even the boldest steed against an obstacle it cannot hurdle, and at Jena/Auerstedt Prussia engaged one of history's greatest armies at the peak of its effectiveness, commanded by one of history's greatest captains at the height of his powers. Defeat at such hands exposes weaknesses. It is by no means proof of dry rot.

IV

French troops opposing the Prussians were in general poorly trained and poorly disciplined even by revolutionary standards. Command was increasingly exercised de facto by delegates of the National Convention. It was at their urging, backed by the very real prospect of a haircut by the "national razor," that on September 13 General of Division René Moreaux set out on a night march toward Pirmasens with 12,000 men and fifty-two guns. The Duke of Brunswick, expecting the move, kept his men fully dressed and thereby gained time to assume positions taking full advantage of the complex terrain. Moreaux formed his infantry into three deep columns and sent them forward around 10 A.M. without much regard for the Prussian deployment. Prussian guns engaged the assault from both flanks, driving the French toward the center and throwing them into confusion. Those who kept coming were mowed down by the infantry's steady battalion volleys. The French bunched, then broke, and the Prussian cavalry went in. By 1 P.M. the French were a mob of fugitives. The 7,000 Prussians engaged suffered fewer than 200 casualties. They took nine times that many prisoners, buried 800 dead, and captured nineteen guns—thirteen of then falling to a single cavalry regiment.

The battle of Kaiserslautern between November 28 and 30 was on a larger scale but a similar pattern. Lazare Hoche took command of the demoralized Army of the Moselle in October and promptly marched it into the Vosges looking for a fight. Brunswick fell back, found a solid defensive position behind the low-lying Lauter River, and waited. He had time to build field entrenchments for his 23,000 men, including a small Saxon contingent, before Hoche and his 36,000 showed up.

The armies felt each other out on the 28th. On the following morning, Hoche crossed the Lauter in force, but the numerically superior French artillery consistently overshot its targets. One column ordered to envelop the Prussian left instead got hopelessly lost. Several infantry attacks were scattered by regimental-strength cavalry charges before the French right flank took advantage of the terrain to throw a mass of skirmishers against the Prussian left. This attack *en debandade* got almost to the ditch in front of the Prussian redoubt before going to ground in the face-off battalion volleys followed by "rolling fire"—an officer's euphemism for everyone firing as fast as he could reload—and then a bayonet charge that threw the French back into the woods along the Lauter.

On November 30, Hoche tried again. A four-battalion attack on the left was repulsed by a sharp counterattack, and when the French artillery reported that it was running low on ammunition, Hoche ordered a withdrawal. Brunswick responded by taking the offensive in the center. The Prussian infantry moved forward, covered by its own skirmishers, until it reached the Lauter, when Brunswick received alarming news form his left flank. A series of French attacks was pushing back relatively weak Prussian forces. The main fieldwork, the "Gallows Redoubt," and its fusilier battalion garrison, held out and anchored the position until one of Brunswick's regiments shifted from the center, bought time with the bayonet for the duke to bring across another infantry regiment, one of cuirassiers, and a battery of 6-pounders, and pushed the French back with Prussian hussars in pursuit.

At the cost of eight hundred casualties, the Prussians and Saxons inflicted over three thousand. The victory had no lasting results—but that reflected the subsequent collapse of the Austrian contingent. Forgotten by military historians, Pirmasens and Kaiserslautern nevertheless helped solidify the Prussian army's reputation as a force well able to deal with the military challenges of the French Revolution on its terms: a valuable ally, an undesirable enemy, and a worked-in tool of Prussian policy.[48]

Notes

1. See Frederick II, "Das politische Testament von 1752," in *Die Werke Friedrichs des Großen*, ed. G. B. Volz, 10 vols. (Berlin: Hobbing, 1912–14), 7:164ff.; "Das Militärische Testament von 1768," in Volz, *Die Werke Freiedrichs des Großen*, 6:246ff. Theodor Schieder, "Macht und Recht. Der Ursprung des Eroberung Schlesiens durch König Friedrich II von Preußen," *Hamburger Jahrbuch für Wirtschafts-und Gesellschaftspolitik* 24 (1979): 235–51. The most recent and comprehensive indictment of Frederick is Franz A. J. Szabo, *The Seven Years War in Europe, 1756–1763* (London: Pearson Longman, 2008).

2. Frederick II, "Das politische Testament von 1752," 164ff.; "Das Militärische Testament von 1768," 246ff. See Dennis E. Showalter, *The Wars of Frederick the Great* (London: Longman, 1996), 321ff.

3. Showalter, *Wars of Frederick the Great*, 345–50. Johannes Kunisch, *Friedrich der Grosse: Der Köing und seine Zeit* (Munich: Beck, 2004), 503–23, credits Frederick with less success in changing his image. Paul Bernard, *Joseph II and Bavaria* (The Hague: Nijhoff, 1965), remains the most detailed English-language analysis of the diplomatic issues.

4. Wilhelm Moritz Freiherr von Bissing, *Friedrich Wilhelm II, König von Preußen: Ein Lebensbild* (Berlin: Duncker and Humblot, 1967), is a popular work but Friedrich Wilhelm's only biography. Lothar Kittstein, *Politik im Zeitalter der Revolution: Untersuchungen zur preußischen Staatlichkeit* (Stuttgart: Steiner, 2003), covers the king's reign effectively.

5. Cited in Friedrich Meinecke, ed., "Aus den Akten der Militaerreorganisationskommission von 1808," *Forschungen zur brandenburgischen und preußischen Geschichte* 5 (1892): 139.

6. For details of the Prussian army after 1763, see Curt Jany, *Geschichte der Preußischen Armee vom 15. Jahrhundert bis 1914*, vol. 3, *1763–1807*, 2nd rev. ed. (Osnabrück: Biblio, 1967), 81ff., which remains the most detailed account. Peter Hofschröer's volumes in the Osprey Men-at-Arms Series, *Prussian Line Infantry, 1792–1815* (London: Osprey, 1984); and *Prussian Cavalry of the Napoleonic Wars*, vol. 1, *1792–1807* (London: Osprey, 1985), contribute overviews focused on drill and uniform regulations.

7. See the analyses of contemporary artillery innovation in France by Howard Rosen, "The Systeme Gribeauval: A Study of Technological Development and Institutional Change in Eighteenth-Century France" (PhD diss., University of Chicago, 1981); and Matti Lauerma's

classic *L'Artillerie de Campagne Française pendant les Guerres de la Révolution* (Helsinki: Finnish Academy of Science, 1956).

8. Hartmut Harnisch, "Preußische Kantonsystem und Ländliche Gesellschaft: Das Beispiel des mittleren Kammerdepartements," in *Krieg und Frieden: Militär and Gesellschaft in der frühen Neuzeit*, ed. B. Kroener and R. Pröve (Paderborn: Schöningh, 1996), 137–65; Jürgen Kloosterhuis, ed., *Bauern, Bürger und Soldaten: Quellen zur Sozialisation des Militärsystems im preußischen Westfalen 1713–1803*, 2 vols. (Münster, Selbstverlag des NW Staatsarchivs Münster 1992), 1:61; and "Zwischen Aufruhr und Akzeptanz: Zur Ausformung und Einbettung des Kantonsystem in die Wirtschafts- und Sozialstrukturen des preußischen Westfalen," in Kroener and Pröve, *Krieg und Frieden*, 167–90.

9. Frederick II, *Werke*, 6:226–27.

10. Christopher Duffy, *The Army of Frederick the Great* (New York: Hippocrene, 1974), 57ff., establishes the negative aspects of late-Frederician Prussian service. See Kurt Schützle, "Über das Rekrutierungssystem in Preußen vor und nach 1806/07 und seine Auswirkung auf die geistig-moralische Haltung der Soldaten," *Militärgeschichte* 17 (1977): 28–35; Jörg Muth, *Flucht aus dem militärischen Alltag. Urachen und individuelle Ausprägung der Desertion in der Armee Friedrichs des Großen* (Freiburg: Rombach, 2003); and Michael Sikora, *Disziplin und Desertion. Strukturprobleme in militärischer Organisation im 18. Jahrhundert* (Berlin: Duncker and Humblot, 1996).

11. Azar Gat, *The Origins of Military Thought from the Enlightenment to Clausewitz* (Oxford: Clarendon Press, 1989), 25ff., 86ff.

12. See J. W. Archenholz, *Geschichte des Siebenjaehrigen Krieges in Deutschland*, 6th ed., 2 vols. (Berlin: Haude and Spener, 1860); C. F. Barsewisch, *Meine Kriegs-Erlebnisse während des Siebenjährigen Krieges 1757–1763* (Berlin: Wansdorff, 1863); and, for enlisted perspectives, *Preussische Soldatenbriefe*, ed. H. Bleckwenn (Osnabrück: Biblio Verlag, 1982).

13. The best brief treatment of this subject is Peter Paret, *Clausewitz and the State* (Oxford: Clarendon Press, 1976), 46ff.

14. The most important royal orders have been published in E. von Frauenholz, *Das Heerwesen in der Zeit des Absolutismus*, vol. 4 of *Die Entwicklungsgeschichte des Deutschen Heerwesens*, ed. E. von Frauenholz, Walter Elze, and Paul Schmitthenner (Munich: Beck, 1940), 298ff.

15. *Instruction für sämtliche Infanterie-Regimenter und Füsilier-Bataillone. Exercieren der Schützen betreffend* (Berlin: Felix, 1789); Jany, *Geschichte der Preußischen Armee*, 160, 165–66.

16. E. F. von Fransecky, "Gneisenau," *Militär-Wochenblatt* 41 (1856): 412; Robert A. Selig, "Light Infantry: Lessons from America? Johann Ewald's Experiences in the American Revolutionary War as Depicted in His *Abhandlung über den Kleinen Krieg* (1785)," *Studies in Eighteenth Century Culture* 23 (1994): 111–29.

17. See Peter E. Russell, "Redcoats in the Wilderness: British Officers and Irregular Warfare in Europe and America, 1740 to 1760," *William and Mary Quarterly* 35, no. 4 (1978): 629–52; and David Gates, *The British Light Infantry Arm c. 1790–1815: Its Creation, Training, and Operational Role* (London: Batsford, 1987).

18. Operationally focused accounts include T. P. Pfau, *Geschichte des Preußischen Feldzuges in der Provinz Holland im Jahr 1787* (Berlin: Rottman 1790); P. de Witt, *Une Invasion prussienne en Hollande en 1787* (Paris: Plon, 1886); and R. Senckler, *Der Preussiche Feldzug in den Niederlanden im Jahre 1787* (Berlin, 1893). Simon Schama, *Patriots and Liberators: Revolution in the Netherlands, 1780–1813* (London: Vintage, 1977), 64ff., is a modern survey.

19. Still useful on this subject is Friedrich Karl Wittichen, *Preußen und England in der europäischen Politik, 1785–1788* (Heidelberg: Winter, 1902).

20. T. C. W. Blanning, *The Origins of the French Revolutionary Wars* (London: Longman, 1986), 54ff.; and Steven T. Ross, *European Diplomatic History, 1789–1815: France against Europe* (Garden City, N.Y.: Anchor, 1969), 37ff., are readily accessible general analyses.

21. T. C. W. Blanning, *The French Revolution in Germany: Occupation and Resistance in the Rhineland, 1792–1802* (Oxford: Clarendon Press, 1983).

22. William W. Hagen, "The Partitions of Poland and the Crisis of the Old Regime in Prussia," *Central European History* 9 (1976), 115–28, remains a solid overview. See Jerzy Lukowski, *The Partitions of Poland, 1772, 1793, 1795* (London: Longman, 1999). Jany, *Geschichte der Preußischen Armee*, 314ff., is detailed and positive on Prussia's military performance. Hermann von Boyen, writing from the perspective of the reform movement, is more critical, especially of the line formations and their senior commanders; see *Erinnerungen aus dem Leben des Generalfeldmarschalls Hermann von Boyen*, ed. F. Nippold (Leipzig: Hirzel, 1889), 1:40ff.

23. See Frank Attar, *La Révolution française déclare la guerre à l'Europe. L'embrasement de l'Europe à la fin du XVIIIe siècle: 1792* (Brussels: Editions Complexe, 1992); Steven T. Ross, *Quest for Victory: French Military Strategy, 1792–1798* (South Brunswick, N.J.: Barnes, 1978), 15ff.; and the excellent overview in Blanning, *French Revolution in Germany*, 69ff.

24. Brunswick's success at Mainz was facilitated by the unpopularity of the French, who came as liberators but remained as conquerors. See T. C. W. Blanning, *Reform and Revolution in Mainz, 1743–1803* (Cambridge: Cambridge University Press, 1974), 275ff. For Valmy's matrices and ramifications, see Emmanuel Hublot, *Valmy, ou la défense de la nation par les armes* (Paris: Fondation pour les Études de Défense Nationale, 1987). See also Samuel Scott, *From Yorktown to Valmy: The Transformation of the French Army in an Age of Revolution* (Niwat: University Press of Colorado, 1998), 165ff.

25. John M. Sherwig, *Guineas and Gunpowder: British Foreign Aid in the Wars with France, 1793–1815* (Cambridge, Mass.: Harvard University Press, 1969), 45–53, understates the role of state pride in Prussia's decision. For the increasingly antirevolutionary, anti-French tone of British social and political conservatism, see I. Christie, *Stress and Stability in Late Eighteenth-Century Britain: Reflection on the British Avoidance of Revolution* (New York: Oxford University Press, 1984).
26. Thomas Stamm-Kuhlmann, *König in Preußens großer Zeit. Friedrich Wilhelm III. Der Melancholiker auf dem Thron* (Berlin: Siedler, 1992), is an excellent analytical biography.
27. See John M. Sherwig, "Grenville's Plan for a Concert of Europe, 1797–99," *Journal of Modern History* 34 (1962): 284–93; and Paul Bailleu, ed., *Preußen und Frankreich von 1795 bis 1807. Diplomatische Correspondenzen*, 2 vols. (Leipzig: Königlich Preußischem Staatsarchivs, 1881–87), 1:193–94.
28. See Russell F. Weigley, *The Age of Battles: The Quest for Decisive Warfare from Breitenfeld to Waterloo* (Bloomington: Indiana University Press, 1991), 292ff.; Gunther E. Rothenberg, *Napoleon's Great Adversaries: The Archduke Charles and the Austrian Army, 1792–1814* (Bloomington: Indiana University Press, 1982); and Kurt Peball, "Zum Kriegsbild der Österreichischen Armee und seiner geschichtlichen Bedeutung, in den Kriegen gegen die Französische Revolution und Napoleon I," in *Napoleon I und das Militärwesen seiner Zeit*, ed. W. von Groote and K. J. Mueller (Freiburg: Verlag Rombach, 1968), 129–82. The British experience is presented in G. J. Evelyn, "'I learned what one ought not to do': The British Army in Flanders and Holland, 1793–95," in *The Road to Waterloo: The British Army and the Struggle against Revolutionary France, 1793–1815*, ed. A. J. Guy (London: Stroud, 1990), 16–22; and Piers Mackesy, "Abercromby in Egypt: The Regeneration of the Army," in Guy, *Road to Waterloo*, 101–10. Richard Glover, *Peninsular Preparation: The Reform of the British Army, 1795–1809* (Cambridge: Cambridge University Press, 1963), also remains useful.
29. Stamm-Kuhlmann, *König in Preußens großer Zeit*, 173ff.
30. See the note of 17 January 1802 to the French ambassador, in Bailleu, *Preußen und Frankreich*, 2:67ff.
31. The paradigm shift is developed admirably in Gunther E. Rothenberg, *The Art of Warfare in the Age of Napoleon* (Bloomington: Indiana University Press, 1970). See Peter Paret, "Conscription and the End of the Old Regime in France and Prussia," in *Understanding War: Essays on Clausewitz and the History of Military Power* (Princeton, N.J.: Princeton University Press, 1993), 53–74; Alan Forrest, *Conscripts and Deserters: The Army and French Society during the Revolution and Empire* (New York: Oxford University Press, 1989); and W. S. Moody, "The Introduction of Military Conscription in Napoleonic Europe, 1789–1812" (PhD diss., Duke University, 1971).
32. The canton system's revised regulations of 1792 are in Frauenholz, *Das Heerwesen in der Zeit des Absolutismus*, 309–36. See F. F. Wilke,

Handbuch zur Kenntnis des preussischen Cantonwesens (Stettin: Leich, 1802). Jany, *Geschichte der Preußischen Armee*, 435ff., is a good summary.

33. Martin Winter, *Untertanengeist durch Militärpflicht? Das preußische Kantonsystem in Brandenburgischen Städten im 18. Jahrhundert* (Bielefeld: Verlag für Regionalgeschichte, 2005), presents the limitations of social militarization through the canton system.

34. Johannes Ziekursch, "Die preußischen Landreservebataillone 1805/06. Eine Reform vor der Reform?," *Historische Zeitschrift* 103 (1909): 85–94.

35. See Michael J. Hughes, *Forging Napoleon's Grande Armée: Motivation, Military Culture, and Masculinity in the French Army, 1800–1808* (New York: New York University Press, 2012); Jean-Paul Bertaud, *The Army of the French Revolution: From Citizen-Soldiers to Instrument of Power* (Princeton, N.J.: Princeton University Press, 1988); and Alan Forrest, *Soldiers of the French Revolution* (Durham, N.C.: Duke University Press, 1990).

36. See for example Friedrich von der Decken, *Betrachtungen über das Verhältniß des Kriegsstandes zu dem Zwecke der Staaten* (Hanover: Helwing, 1800).

37. "Elements de castrametrie et de tactique," in Frederick II, *Ouevres*, ed. J. D. E. Preuss, vol. 29 (Berlin, 1856), 4.

38. Among the voluminous writings on Scharnhorst's early career, the most relevant on this subject include Guenther Wollstein, "Scharnhorst und die Franzoesische Revolution," *Historische Zeitschrift* 227 (1978): 325–52; Hermann Büschleb, *Scharnhorst in Westfalen: Politik, Administration, und Kommando im Schicksalsjahre 1795* (Herford: Mittler, 1979); and Charles White's excellent *The Enlightened Soldier: Scharnhorst and the Militärische Gesellschaft in Berlin, 1801–1805* (New York: Praeger, 1989). See Georg Hebbelmann, *Das preußische "Offizierskorps" im 18. Jahrhundert: Analyse der Sozialstruktur einer Funktionselite* (Münster: Lit, 1999).

39. The debates are summarized in White, *Enlightened Soldier*, 76ff., and Peter Paret, *Yorck and the Era of Prussian Reform* (Princeton: Princeton University Press, 1966), 73ff.

40. See Paul Heinsius, "Der Wandel der Logistik in den Napoleonischen Kriegen," in *Die Bedeutung der Logistik für die Militärische Führung von der Antike bis in die neueste Zeit*, ed. Horst Boog (Herford: Mittler, 1986), 87–108; and Martin van Creveld, *Supplying War: Logistics from Wallenstein to Patton* (New York: Cambridge University Press, 1977), 42ff. Peter Wetzler, *War and Subsistence: The Sambre and Meuse Army in 1794* (New York: Lang, 1988), is an excellent case study of revolutionary logistics at their grass roots.

41. Steven T. Ross, "The Development of the Combat Division in Eighteenth-Century French Armies," *French Historical Studies* 4 (1965): 84–94; Robert M. Epstein, "Patterns of Change and Continuity in Nineteenth-Century Warfare," *Journal of Military History* 56 (1992): 378–88.

42. See Ernst von Rüchel, "Über einige militärische Diversitäten," in *Denkwürdigkeiten der militärischen Gesellschaft in Berlin* (1803), 3:401–402; and Carl von Clausewitz, *Nachrichten über Preußen in seiner großen Katastrophe*, Kriegsgeschichtliche Einzelschriften 10 (Berlin: Mittler, 1888), 428.

43. See particularly Brendan Simms, *The Impact of Napoleon: Prussian High Politics, Foreign Policy, and the Crisis of the Executive, 1797–1806* (Cambridge: Cambridge University Press, 1997). His approach strengthens the interpretation of the army's position as "competent by definition," a court of last resort outside the internecine squabbling at high government levels.

44. Paul Schroeder's "Napoleon's Foreign Policy: A Criminal Enterprise," *Journal of Military History* 54 (1990): 147–62, presents an argument developed in detail in his *The Transformation of European Politics, 1763–1848* (New York: Oxford University Press, 1994). David A. Bell, *The First Total War: Napoleon's Europe and the Birth of Warfare as We Know It* (Boston: Houghton Mifflin, 2007), presents Napoleon as the central figure in a developing European mentality affirming war's apocalyptic and redemptive character.

45. Hanover was the patrimony of Britain's royal house, a key entrepôt for British trade with northern Europe, and a correspondingly vital British interest. See Philip G. Dwyer, "Prussia and the Armed Neutrality: The Invasion of Hanover in 1801," *International History Review* 15 (1993): 661–87.

46. Philip Dwyer, "Two Definitions of Neutrality: Prussia, the European State System, and the French Invasion of Hanover in 1803," *International History Review* 19 (1997): 522–40.

47. The diplomatic aspect of this account is derived from Frederick R. Kagan's magisterial *The End of The Old Order: Napoleon and Europe, 1801–1805* (Cambridge, Mass.: Da Capo, 2006), 177; and Frederick Schneid's streamlined *Napoleon's Conquest of Europe: The War of the Third Coalition* (Westport, Conn.: Praeger, 2005). For the military details, see the highly self-serving "Die Preussische Kriegsvorbereitungen und Operationspläne von 1805," in Großer Generalstab, Abteilund für Kriegsgeschichte, *Kriegsgeschichtliche Einzelschriften* (Berlin: Mittler, 1883), 1:1–101.

48. John E. Stine, "King Frederick William II and the Decline of the Prussian Army, 1786–1797," (PhD diss., University of South Carolina, 1980), 139ff., is a critical overview based on archival holdings from the then German Democratic Republic. Jany, *Geschichte der Preußischen Armee*, 235ff., provides details and is predictably affirming of the army's performance. Paret, *Yorck*, 70, highlights the Jäger regiment's enhanced standing. Günther Gieraths, *Kampfhandlungen der brandenburgisch-preussischen Armee, 1626–1807* (Berlin: De Gruyter, 1964), 170ff., is useful for its list of the small-scale detached operations characteristic of the fighting along the Rhine, where the light

troops showed to such advantage. Großer Generalstab, Abteilung für Kriegsgeschichte, *Pirmasens und Kaiserslautern: Eine Erinnerung an das Jahr 1793*, Kriegsgeschichtliche Einzelschriften 16 (Berlin: Mittler, 1893), is a detailed case study with all the strengths and weaknesses of the General Staff school of history.

CHAPTER 3

THE AUSTRIAN ARMY

LEE EYSTURLID

D uring the long, on-again-off-again wars generated by the events of the French Revolution, the Habsburg monarchy would contribute the largest single contingent of troops to the fight.[1] For the Austrians, the wars fought over this nine-year period were a long-term disaster. Entering the war with a small, professional army, the monarchy would constantly be at loose ends to find the financing and manpower to carry out the demands of a European-wide war. Worse yet, and critical to remember, was that the disparate Habsburg lands were incapable of the political revolution that had allowed a homogenous France to mobilize so many men and such vast resources. There could be no real appeal to nationalism, like in France, in a state that had over a dozen national and linguistic groups. Not only was Austria poor by French or English standards, but it was a thoroughly early modern state, incapable of internal, liberal political reform. The history of Austria's army and its leaders in these wars is, then, one of reaction and, when it occurred, temporary, superficial change. This said, and while the monarchy often saw defeat on the battlefield, its army's ability to outlast its opponent allowed for its survival and eventual recovery.

When the Revolution first broke out in France, there was only modest concern in Vienna. Of far greater concern at the time were relations with Prussia and Russia over the so-called Second Partition of Poland. The Habsburg emperor Leopold II warned France of its belligerence in threatening Louis XVI and Marie Antoinette in 1791, but showed little inclination to war. But the Austrians misjudged the French, or at least the Directory's, inclination for war, as events would show. The January 1792 demands for compliance with the old 1756 Franco-Austrian alliance simply pushed the monarchy cooperation treaty with its old nemesis, Prussia. Then, rather unexpectedly, Leopold II, a lover of peace and an enlightened monarch, died. He was replaced by his oldest son, Francis II (later Francis I, emperor of Austria). Young, inexperienced, and lacking his father's prudence, Francis would be unable to stem the slide to war.[2] Furious over the new, potential Prussian alliance and looking to discourage the other German states from participation, the Directory decided on war. On 21 April 1792, it declared war on the king of Hungary and Bohemia.

To gain an understanding of the Habsburg army, it is necessary to try and first come to grips with the rather diverse, if not confusing, nature of the monarchy itself. The empire sprawled across central Europe from what is today Belgium to southern Poland (Galicia) and from the Czech Republic (Bohemia) to the northern states of Italy. The pillar of the monarchy's holdings were the hereditary lands, the *Erblande*, which centered on what is now modern Austria.[3] Added to this, though indirectly, was the large, powerful, but organizationally medieval state of Hungary, whose nobles jealously guarded their privileges. The title of Holy Roman emperor also gave, at least in theory, the Habsburg ruler access to the resources and armies of the numerous German states. However, while often evoked during the wars, the imperial title proved of little real use, as states like Bavaria, Saxony, and Brunswick, to name only three, would prove more than willing to seek political accommodation with the French when threatened. The Habsburg ruler therefore had to try and tie together the loyalties of Germans, Magyars, Czechs, Flemings and Walloons, Poles, Croatians, Serbs, Romanians, and numerous other small groups including Roma.[4] Such a state existed due to the combination of some early modern reforms, combined with numerous concessions to medieval and noble preferences. This outdated system inherently undermined the monarchy's ability to raise troops and taxes. For this reason, despite its great physical size and relative wealth, Austria could never compete alone with its French opponent.

Government functioned during the period in question exactly as it had in the proceeding century, with only the most minor of changes. The only real reforms had occurred, as mentioned above, as a result of numerous setbacks suffered during the Seven Years' War. The Habsburg ruler for all but the very beginning of the wars of revolution, Francis II, was not just a conservative, but in the end a reactionary. The violence of French social change, when measured against the polyglot nature of his kingdom, made it clear to him that such reforms were impossible, and therefore none were attempted. Historians, often looking to find some level of real reform among the Habsburg government or army, too often are willing to mistake improvement for real change. During the period between 1792 and 1801, nothing of magnitude changed for the Habsburg army. So command of the state, and therefore the army, remained firmly in the hands of the monarch, who was absolute. In Vienna day-to-day affairs were run by a state council, the Staatsrat, while foreign affairs belonged to the Haus-Hof und Staatskanlei. Finance was handled indirectly by the council, under the direction of a chief financial officer. Finances were always tenuous, and the long wars required the running of a sizable debt combined with the need to get foreign loans (these coming mostly from Great Britain) and the issuance of paper money. With the renewal of fighting in 1792, Austria would face its reoccurring problem, as laid out by its then chief financier, Count Chotek. War brought inflation and rising prices, which made an increase in taxes problematic, but a burgeoning deficit made internal or external loans difficult to acquire. In reaction, Chotek appealed for greater voluntary contributions from the great families and the provinces in combination with another effort to secure foreign, read English, loans or grants.[5]

The leadership of the Habsburg military, the kaiserlich-königliche Armee (the imperial and royal army title for the armed forces as a concession to the Hungarians, as the Habsburg emperor was actually their king) of course rested with the monarch, but in the field, and Francis only once visited the army, command was held by the generals. Francis was not ignorant of military affairs and had seen some exposure to campaigning during a visit to the field in the Austro-Turkish War in 1788. He was not a military man, and was intelligent enough to realize that he would never be one, and he meddled only with overall strategy. This said, he often did not appoint the best men but rather seems to have shown a preference for mediocrities to command. Likely, this came out of the fear that all Habsburg rulers since the Thirty Year's War suffered—the fear of being overshadowed by a charismatic and successful field commander. Such had been the case with Wallenstein, whose success so frightened the Habsburg ruler of the time, Ferdinand II, that he had him assassinated.[6] Francis also had a clear preference for the advice of his civilian advisors, chancellors like Johann Franz Baron Thugut, Johann Ludwig Count Cobenzl, and Franz Count Colloredo. While generally competent, these advisors were willing to get directly involved in questioning military strategy and even operations. Their authority was increased in 1792 and would overlap with the uniquely Austrian organization known as the Hofkriegsrat. Dating to 1566 and made of a mixed body of military and civilian officials, the Hofkriegsrat acted as a planning staff and controlled the routine administration of the army, directing ordinance, engineering, and logistics, while issuing day-to-day orders. The organization was inherently bureaucratic and became notorious for its Byzantine abuses, where requests seemed to disappear into it, never to return. With a relatively small staff, some thirty officers and perhaps one hundred clerks, the Hofkriegsrat still looked to maintain control through streams of required reports that served to bog down the administration of the army at all levels.[7] It was only in the initial reform efforts of the Archduke Charles in 1801 that any real streamlining of the agencies was attempted, and then only without resulting in any real change.[8]

Habsburg generals' ranks are numerous and often confusing, but should be seen as secondary in relation to the individual commanders' aristocratic titles and actual appointments as commanders of field forces or administrative organizations. This reality meant that the Habsburg military establishment carried a ridiculous number of senior generals on its rolls, far more than could be of use, although they went without pay during peacetime. Since there was no permanent military organizational structure above the level of the regiment, all commands were created on an as-needed basis. Subdivisions like brigade, division, or corps, which the French would bring into being, would only first really appear in 1809. An army was assembled as a force, given a commander, and then divided, as needed, into wings, or *abteilungen*, each again then assigned a respective commander. Field forces were often, in following the strategic practice of the time, divided between several armies, the commanders of which answered not to each other but to the emperor. This potential problem of having an unknown commander running a force of unknown regiments was solved, ideally, by the presence of a professional staff corps. Once war had been decided on and the regiments called together, the quartermaster general staff, whose director held the rank of lieutenant field marshal, would assign officers to each army. While the staff officers were intended to assist in making decisions, their primary responsibility often devolved into securing topographical intelligence.[9] Since good maps were scarce, if nonexistent, it became a vital task for these officers to gain some notion of the lay of the land.

Another issue of concern for the Habsburg army was its logistical system. Along with the notion of the Hofkriegsrat as a bureaucratic nightmare, the General-Kriegs-Commissariat also moved imperceptibly slowly, if at all. This agency was also a mix of civilian-military personnel, although in time of war command was given to an active-duty officer. The agency's primary task during a conflict was to secure both food for the men and fodder for the horses and draft animals. This project was done through civilian commissioners, who then maintained offices in each of the provinces to act as go-betweens with the local governors. The system for collection and distribution of these supplies and resources was organized around the existence of several large-scale supply depots or magazines, *Hauptmagazine.* Supply from there was moved to depots with immediate contact with the army, or *Fassungsmagazine.* From here, the army maintained substantial supply trains, wagons, and draft animals that then filled the roads between the main force and these intermediate depots. While a permanent, and therefore ideally professional, field service existed for logistics, it remained picayune for the needs of the army at war and required an increase of nearly tenfold in personnel to even begin to meet needs.[10] Added to this was the need to contract civilian drivers and teams to move the heavy artillery, field bakeries, staff facilities, and bridging equipment. As can be imagined, Austria's army became notorious for its long and ponderous supply lines, which choked the roads behind an army and kept troop movement, on average, well below ten miles a day.

The manpower that filled the ranks of the Habsburg army came from a combination of voluntary enlistment and conscription. Only the Military Border districts, which will be mentioned below, saw universal service. Conscription was based on a systematic census that had been ordered in 1771 to list all inhabitants of Crown lands. From this list of men available for military service, numerous exemptions were permitted, by individuals, towns, and even entire provinces. Direct application of conscription was seen in the hereditary states, although the Tyrol remained exempt with its unique form of universal militia service. Critical in raising troops, Hungary and Austria's Italian holdings also remained outside the system. Further, individual nobles, government officers, and artisans or well-to-do farmers were exempted.

While desperate for manpower, the state realized as well the necessity not to undermine the tax- and wealth-producing elements among the town artisans and productive peasants. Therefore, the bulk of any conscription call fell upon the humblest classes, so that the army's rank and file was largely made up of the poorest peasants and day laborers. Accustomed to hardship and back-breaking labor, the average recruit was physically tough and resolute, but lacking of any personal initiative. Once conscripted, these men were to serve for life, although that was shortened during the war to twenty years, or until they could no longer serve due to sickness or wounds. Despite the long term of service, it was generally assumed that during any lengthy time of peace many of the men under arms would be discharged or given a long-term furlough. Due to the lengthy nature of the wars of the Revolution, the notion of being discharged for anything but incapacity was rare. As a result, conscription was unpopular throughout the empire, and recruiters made use of compulsion and tricks to fill their quotas. For the other branches, rules were often different, but numbers were smaller. The cavalry was supposed to only accept trained men from the infantry but often disregarded this for men with actual riding abilities. The artillery and engineers remained the most selective, and smallest, and would only take men who were Habsburg subjects, unmarried, and literate in German.[11]

The officer corps, about which historians are always better informed, was one of the great pillars of the monarchy's stability. Its multinational makeup, and the fact that it possessed members of unclear social origin, reflected the state itself. Most often higher ranks were given to noblemen coming from the Habsburg heartlands, with some representation from the great families (e.g., Esterházy, Colloredo, Kinsky, and Liechtenstein). However, the great nobility, who saw military life as arduous and lacking substantial reward, generally did not pursue the profession. Once having entered the service, most of the officers received their training by being assigned as a cadet. They were taught the ropes, in general, by one of the regiment's senior sergeants and, if all went well, received the official rank of sublieutenant in a year. Rapidity of acceptance as a cadet and the rate of promotion varied of course with the level of noble rank the applicant brought with him. Princes of the blood, like the Archduke Charles, would expect near immediate promotion into the general ranks, while minor nobles would linger for years in lesser ranks. For the minor nobles, war was the only avenue for potential, speedy promotion. While relatively rare, it was certainly possible under the demands of wartime for commoners to be commissioned. Up to the equivalent rank of major, promotion was handled by the regimental commander-proprietor, while the rank of colonel and above required a nod from the emperor. While not recognized as ideal, ranks below major could be "purchased," albeit with approval from the regiment's colonel. Widely condemned in the nineteenth century, purchasing was intended as a means to create a form of pension system for older officers, and a means to get them out of the army.[12]

During the mid-eighteenth century, efforts by Maria Theresa had made the societal position, and therefore the attractiveness, of being an officer much greater. In order to secure their loyalty, always a Habsburg anxiety, uniformed officers had been allowed access to the imperial court. Further, and predating the Revolution's use of awards, she had created the Order of Maria Theresa, given for service and bravery and open to officers of all social ranks and religions. These and other innovations, which would create families that became generational servants in the monarchy's army and administration, did little to raise the level of military education or innovation. Rather, the Habsburg officer corps was well-known for its lack of interest in intellectual development, and remained poorly educated.[13] Instead, the average Austrian officer, although there were occasional exceptions, went through the revolutionary wars wed to the methods used during the Seven Year's War, and the wars against the Turks. Rarely, if ever, were the monarchy's officers encouraged to think for themselves, and it was even rarer that they should take risks.[14]

The army's infantry regiments were famously separated by being considered either "German" or "Hungarian." These were nominal misnomers, as they related primarily to the place and style of recruitment and to the fact that the Hungarians insisted that the language of drill and command in "their" regiments remain Magyar. In fact, the German regiments included Italians, Czechs, Poles, Belgians, and other non-Germans while their Hungarian counterparts also included Romanians and Ruthenians. The actual language of command was driven more by the language of the troops than by official designation. As mentioned above, the Military Borders of Croatia, Hungary, Slavonia, and Transylvania had a distinct status. Created as a buffer zone against the Ottomans, the regions were populated with military colonists, known as Grenzers (Border troops).

The notion had been to create a permanent garrison line and to cut costs. During the Seven Years' War, Maria Theresa had ordered these excellent light troops reorganized as line infantry in order to increase the size of the field armies. Understandably, their overall abilities were decreased, and the seventeen regiments fielded would not fare very well during the revolutionary wars.[15]

The overall kaiserlich-königliche Armee was composed of some fifty-seven regiments of line—or regular—infantry, seventeen of Grenzers, thirty-five of cavalry, and three of field artillery. Attached to this list were fortress artillery districts, a central logistical office, and various engineers and technical troops. The infantry made up three-quarters of the troops available, the cavalry a quarter, with the artillery numbering a few thousand. Due to cutbacks and lack of funds, the army had only 230,000 men ready when the wars started in 1792. There was no uniformity to the composition of troops as concerned unit size or equipment types. As an example, the average German regiment, when at full-strength, possessed two service battalions of six fusilier companies each and a stationary garrison battalion with only four companies. Each deployed battalion had three 6-pounder cannon, including artillerists and assisting troops. A regiment, whether German or Hungarian, possessed a so-called grenadier division of two companies. These men were considered the elite of the regiment and wore a traditional grenadier bearskin. During field service, these companies were taken to make ad hoc grenadier battalions, which usually served as part of formal reserve or third line. In sum, a regiment would have nearly 4,500 men under arms. More likely, as in 1792, the average fusilier company, instead of having 4 officers and 230 men, reported 3 officers and only 120 men. Because many regiments carried more men, especially the invalided or sick, on their roles than were present, it is often very difficult to determine actual army strengths at a given time by simply counting regiments.[16]

As the wars began in 1792, the average foot soldier, or fusilier, was armed with either the Model 1774 or Model 1784 smoothbore musket. Although considered reliable, these were heavy weapons, even for the time. As was standard, both musket types allowed for the addition of a socket-mounted, triangular bayonet, measuring over a foot in length. In reaction to the setbacks of the War of the First Coalition, a reform commission would introduce a new musket, the Model 1798, which was much superior to its predecessors.

The caliber was reduced to 17.6 mm (.69), and lighter brass fittings as well as an improved firing lock were added. These changes reduced the weapon's weight by over a pound, a considerable sum. Because soldiers were able to use captured enemy ammunition, and the French fired .69 rounds as well, the weapon was seen, even by foreigners, as a real step forward.[17] Along with the musket and bayonet, each man carried a short saber for close-in fighting. Every soldier also carried some sixty rounds of prepared ammunition on his person, with another thirty-six rounds allocated to the battalions' pack animals. Although each enlisted man was allowed few personal effects, there was a copper kettle and a tent assigned for every five men. This equipment remained with the approximately thirty packhorses and four wagons that each battalion was supposed to possess.

The army's cavalry, which numbered on paper some 40,000 strong, was often considered some of the best—horse for horse—in Europe. Unlike the infantry, whose units were often reduced to cadre strength during peace, the cavalry's need for trained men required that regiments be kept at full strength all the time. In 1792, there were thirty-five regiments, broken down roughly between one-third heavy (carabiniers and cuirassiers), one third medium (dragoons and *chevaulegers*), and one third light (hussars and uhlans). Near standard organization for all types of cavalry was the basic unit of the squadron, about 150 troopers, then organized into divisions, usually three, although heavy units often had four. Habsburg cavalry was standard for the time, mixing the use of lighter firearms with the sword or lance. The heavy cavalry, especially the cuirassiers, where generally held in reserve during a battle as the intended "shock arm." For this purpose, they possessed heavier horse mounts and wore a front breastplate and metal helmet (unlike their French counterparts under Napoleon who wore armor on front and back). Although cuirassiers possessed pistols for sundry duties, their main weapon was a heavy, single-edged sword to be used in the charge. Light cavalry, the hussars, on the other hand, possessed a distinctive curved sword and carried a short-barreled musket.[18]

The third key branch, the artillery, had undergone a series of impressive and long-term reforms under the civic-minded Prince Lichtenstein in the middle of the eighteenth century but had failed to keep pace with French reforms in the 1780s. During peacetime, the monarchy's artillery possessed no real tactical formations as such and did not have permanent unit assignments as there were no permanent units above the regiments. Three so-called field regiments were mostly administrative organizations, keeping track of the branches' nearly 10,000 officers and men. When the army moved to a war footing, these men and guns were then assigned to serve the battalion fieldpieces as well as the line batteries. Further personnel were drawn together from the Bombardeur corps and fortress artillery to make up the reserve batteries assigned on the newly organized army level. These reserve guns were generally employed as so-called position batteries with a given place in the battle line.

All the guns and equipment relied for transportation in the field on the Fuhrwesencorps, which at its best often proved unreliable and slow. While the Austrians possessed guns in weight from 3- to even 24-pounders (this giving the weight of the shot), the most commonly deployed during the revolutionary wars were the 3-, 6-, and 12-pounders. The 3-pounders were generally assigned to individual battalions, meant to bolster immediate firepower, with the 6-pounders and 12-pounders held in reserve or position batteries. Actual range of the guns varied by size, with the heavy guns roughly reaching about 3,000 feet and smaller guns maxing at 2,400 feet with solid shot.[19]

Acting in adjunct to the three main branches were the staffs, the engineers, and the medical services. Once put on a war footing, the army immediately began looking for men to make up the great general staff, and the several, field-army level smaller staffs. Since there were always more officers than billets, finding men was not a problem, but finding competent men often was. Contrary to these logistical and planning staffs, there always existed a standing engineering staff with corresponding units. The kaiserlich-königliche Ingenieurs Corps, under the command of a general field marshal and comprising nearly two hundred officers of various ranks, included two battalion-sized technical-engineering units. There were the sappers, who specialized in building fortifications while the Minuer Corps covered both the attack and defense of fortified positions. A third group, the pioneers, served as labor for the first two organizations, and were only activated in times of war.

Medical services were inadequate at best, and in 1792 the outdated techniques and lack of personnel would be unable to keep up with the new level of losses that the French wars would create. During a battle, dressing stations were established behind the wings of the army, each with two staff surgeons and their immediate assistants. Often done in haste, operations necessarily revolved around the amputation of limbs. Regulations required that officers be treated first, with the rank and file to follow. Battalion and company surgeons, as they were titled, were not actual doctors. Most possessed a degree of some form, while assistant surgeons, normally enlisted men, got their training on the job. Complicating matters further was the fact that medical personnel were often not given officer rank and were held at the absolute bottom of the pay scale.[20] As a result, the average Austrian soldier had little hope of decent care if he was wounded on the field or fell sick on campaign.

During the wars of the Revolution, the Habsburg monarchy's "way of war" would remain in the tradition of the previous century. In strategy the dominant notion was to minimize the risks taken by the individual army commanders while protecting a baseline of supply. Maneuver, especially against an enemy's line of supply, was emphasized. The extreme importance placed on the maintenance of supply lines and access to depots explains much of the apparent timidity shown by Austrian forces throughout the Wars of the First and Second Coalition. In creating any strategy, Habsburg leaders, both civilian and military, were at pains to reconcile the potential for success with the willingness to risk the army in a battle. The ultimate achievement for any army commander would have been to maneuver one's opponents off their line of supply, forcing them to retreat (or surrender!). Such success would allow for detached corps to blockade and reduce enemy fortresses, which could then be converted to friendly depots and would open a new, secure, baseline.[21] In the field then, the Austrians would employ, on what was essentially an operational level, the cordon system. The intention was for the army, or armies, to cover an entire region, with a series of detachments strung between fortress strongpoints. Such a line would force the enemy to move against the fortresses, to blockade or besiege them, allowing the Austrians time to gather forces for a countermove. While this system had a clear mathematical appeal, and seemed to minimize the ability of incompetent commanders to err, it was brittle and outdated. Worse for the monarchy, the French quickly bested the system with hard-marching troops, limited logistical needs, and dynamic leadership.[22]

In tactics there was mirroring of the strategic and operational. Throughout the wars, the Austrian army would retain the essential battlefield that had been standard in the Seven Years' War. Basically, doctrine called for the deployment of the infantry into two lines, preferably anchored on a physical barrier such as a river or woods, with a third, smaller line behind that in reserve. The line was then separated into a center with left and right flanks. Senior regiments and the senior subordinate general commanded on the right. Along the line was then placed the artillery, the position batteries being essentially immobile, which together with the infantry was intended to create a wall of fire. On the wings, the army's cavalry played out the role of blunting any moves by enemy cavalry or any attempt to turn the flank. Since this formation assumed a long, rigid front (this meant up to eight infantry regiments and three cavalry regiments per flank), it was best suited to the defense. Deployment in rough or hilly terrain, or anything more than a modest advance through the lines into disorder, made the force impossible for a single commander to control. Specific infantry regulations called for firing within the battalions by platoon, which was intended to give a near-constant effect. It also meant that no battalion was without a reserve of shot if it came under an unexpected cavalry charge. While all the infantry went into battle with their bayonets fixed, the real emphasis was, and remained, a controlled fire. Because of their experience in the Turkish wars, where they had been badly outnumbered in cavalry, the Austrians still made use of condensed battalion-sized formations called "close-columns." The formation was generally applied in the presence of French cavalry, or when moving to the pursuit, but it required time to form and reduced fire and speed substantially. The formation made clear that many Habsburg commanders had little faith in their troops' ability to maneuver, as the closed column gave the commander much greater tactical control.[23]

The monarchy's cavalry also suffered from outdated notions of training and deployment. Operating during the wars under the regulations of 1784, which assigned complicated procedures for fire, the cavalry continued to prefer, both heavy and light, the shock of the charge. For the charge, squadrons were formed up three ranks deep, the men boot to boot. The squadrons would advance at a controlled trot to maintain order, and then at a few hundred feet from the enemy receive the order to charge, which was done at a gallop. Despite the quality of many of its regiments, both heavy and light cavalry were poorly used by the Austrians. Rather than massing the heavy cavalry, it was often used in limited numbers and with poor coordination. The army's hussars were also not used effectively for scouting, their ideal task, but rather were given out by squadron to screen or accompany smaller forces of detached infantry. Finally, the artillery had no specific rules for tactical engagement other than to add their fire to the line. Sometimes the heavier guns were combined into line of fire, rather than just the 3-pounders, often to great effect, but this was not a set tactic. Since the Austrian guns and projectile weights were inferior to their French counterparts, and since they were deployed in small groupings, their impact was always limited or inconsistent.

The Austrian armies that took the field, with their numerous allies, against the French in the War of the First (1792–97) and Second (1798–1802) Coalitions were, as has been made apparent above, a solid if somewhat obsolescent force. In the examination of the army through these long years of conflict, it is never clear that an overall grand strategy emerges. What, in the end, was the enunciated state policy of the monarchy concerning revolutionary France? With only the most minimal exceptions, the Austrians under first Leopold, and then Francis, never seem to have called for a full-scale war to remove the republic and restore the Bourbons to the throne. Perhaps the monumental nature of the task of restoration, especially after 1794, and the backing of questionable allies like Russia and Prussia, made this a non-reality. Instead, it appears, by way of the plans and cordon system employed, as a series of wars meant to restore the status quo prior to 1792. If that is the case, then the overall management of these two wars by the monarchy can be seen as an effective implementation of statecraft through a necessarily limited military tool. For it is impossible to suppose, as has been stated already, that Austrian leaders such as Francis or his reform-minded brother the Archduke Charles, had any notion that French style change was anything but impossible and also undesirable.[24] Therefore, by the end of 1801 the monarchy, although at the cost of men, money, and some territories had maintained itself intact in the face of revolutionary fervor.

The War of the First Coalition was in a sense a defensive war for the monarchy. Clearly uncertain how to react in the face of the radical changes then under way in France, the Austrian emperor would sign a defensively oriented convention with Prussia at the Declaration of Pillnitz on 27 August 1791. An incensed Directory, reacting for self-serving reasons, would then declare war in April of the next year on Leopold, not Austria the state, in an effort to reflect France's new calls to liberty.[25] The first year of the war, which pitted the novice and disorganized armies of the French against the combined forces of Austria and Prussia saw little real fighting. Rather, neither Austria nor Prussia trusted each other, nor did it appear that either was willing to chance the loss of Polish territory in order to "save" France. It is also clear that the Austrian army was ill-prepared for war. It lacked all the needed resources, the victim of tightfisted policies and severe spending reductions under Leopold II. Further, the promised forces of the Holy Roman Empire, which were called into service by Emperor Francis, failed to materialize.

By late 1792, the French, recovering from the withdrawal of the Austro-Prussian force, went over to the offensive, attacking Austrian Belgium. In an attempt to recover their position, the allies also moved to the offensive in early 1793, forming a wide cordon line running through Belgium and Rhenish Germany under the Prince of Coburg. Again, Austrian plans were upset by a grinding lack of supplies, the slow movement of the troops, and the indecisive nature of its leadership. Despite some hard-fought victories and the failure of the French commander Charles Dumouriez, Coburg achieved little. This success was about to be shattered, however, as the French, under the leadership of Lazare Carnot, would produce larger and now veteran armies. By the end of 1793, the French had stabilized their situation in Holland and Belgium. Further complicating matters for Austria would be reduction and soon the withdrawal of the Prussians from the anti-French alliance. French offensives planned for 1794 would therefore strike against an Austrian army that was increasingly suffering from overuse, undersupply, and defeatism. Concentric attacks by French armies in the spring served to drive most of Austria's remaining allies out of the picture while also driving Coburg from Belgium itself. By October, Holland had fallen.[26]

The start of 1795 saw Austria's Prussian, Russian, and Portuguese allies gone and the British field forces evacuated from the Continent. Still, confident of possible success, mostly the result of internal French political upheavals, Austria allied again with Russia. This hope ignored the fact that the army was exhausted and incapable of major field operations. Happily for the Habsburgs, this was also the case for the French. By September, the Austrians resumed their cordon strategy, deploying two armies of nearly 200,000 men along a four-hundred-mile front. Modest French efforts at an offensive failed, and by the start of 1796 the monarchy's prospects looked somewhat renewed.

The campaigns of 1796–97, which ended the War of the First Coalition, saw Austria's greatest victories of the entire period dashed by the rising Napoleon. Treating Germany as the main area of operations, the Austrians found a successful commander in the Archduke Charles. Having retreated in the face of the advance of two independent French armies for several weeks, the archduke then turned and gained the position between them through a pair of battles at Amberg and Würzburg in August and September. He then pressed his advance, driving the French all the way back over the Rhine, and was preparing to move farther when disaster in Italy called him away.[27] While successful in Germany, the old Austrian tactic of holding lines played into the hands of the energetic and recklessly bold General Bonaparte. He quickly destroyed the Austrians' Piedmontese ally and then defeated a series of Hapsburg armies, capturing the last nearly intact. When Charles arrived in early 1797 to fix things, he quickly found that the army was in a shambles and pressed for peace. Furious, but with little choice, Francis accepted an armistice and then a peace treaty dictated by Napoleon. The 1796 campaign in Germany had shown that, with proper leadership and some good luck, the monarchy's army could still be successful. It was, however, to be the last real success until 1809.

The War of the Second Coalition was an even greater disappointment than the first, and did little but further damage the army. It was, unfortunately for Austria, unavoidable in the face of further French offensives taken by the Directory. Trying to stem the French tide, Austria looked for allies in Russia and Great Britain, but would provide the bulk of the troops itself. Some military reforms had been attempted in the brief respite of 1798–99.[28] As Archduke Charles had correctly asserted, it would be impossible to achieve reform without a sustained period of peace. Changes that did occur were essentially superficial, dealing more with organization and increase in the number of regiments, a new musket, and some uniform simplifications. The argument between emphasizing skirmish warfare and maintaining unit discipline and ranks remained, but the traditionalists carried the day.[29]

The initial campaigns of 1799 saw an effort by the Austrians and the Russians to coordinate military efforts against the French in what is today modern Switzerland. Due to mutual distrust, these efforts came to naught. Neither the Archduke Charles, commanding in Southern Germany, nor Marshal Alexander Suvorov in Switzerland, could clearly defeat the French. Instead, the two men came to despise each other, both blaming the other for their failures. Of importance was the fact that the Russian army was so lacking in logistical support that the entire force had to be maintained by Austrian officers. By December of 1799, the coalition had disintegrated, and the Russians withdrew.[30] Further, the archduke was relieved for reasons of health. The campaign season of 1800 opened with a critical change: France was now under the singular direction of Napoleon, now dictator. He intended to focus his effort in Germany with General Jean Moreau's army of 100,000 while a reserve force of 60,000 assembled to support it. In Italy, he left a covering force under General André Masséna.[31] The Austrian plans were ambitious, with a main army, some 90,000 under Baron Michael Melas, advancing from the Maritime Alps on Lyon in France. Successful at first, Melas was forced to turn and fight a separate French army under Napoleon that was threatening his line of supply. Napoleon defeated Melas in the close-run battle at Marengo and forced the Austrian to sign an armistice. The dispersed Austrian forces in Germany, faced with a reinforced Moreau, and deployed in a cordon line, also accepted an armistice that ran to 13 November 1800.

Emperor Francis, with the advice of Baron Thugut and the promises of British funding, decided to renew the war.[32] New recruits were found, but the army remained demoralized. When the Archduke Charles turned down command of the army, Francis decided in favor of his amiable—albeit only eighteen-year-old—brother, the Archduke John, to take command. When the armistice came to an official end on 27 November 1800, both sides took the offensive. Moreau's plan was simple; he would advance his army to the Inn River and then attack whatever Austrians he could find. It is not clear what broader plans he may have made, except to press east along the left bank of the Danube in the general direction of Vienna. Moreau probably assumed that such a move would force the Austrians to battle, and they obliged him. The Austrian plan, the product of the ambitious and optimistic Colonel Franz Weyrother, was complicated and called for maneuvering against the French line of communications. Having concentrated the army on the Inn River, John's forces would move west and reach the Isar River in just three days. They would then cross the river at the town of Landshut, wheel south, crushing Moreau's left flank and thereby cutting his line of communications. The French then would be forced to yield their hold on the left bank of the Danube, potentially allowing the Austrians to regain their losses of the summer. Weyrother's plan, unrealistic in the face of the French plan, made less sense considering the cold, rainy weather and the forest roads the troops would be forced to cross.[33]

The battle occurred in the area surrounding the small Bavarian village of Hohenlinden, which sits fifty miles west of Munich and just north of the Inn River valley. The battle is memorable for the fact that this decisive Austrian defeat ended the War of the Second Coalition and was the last real victory for an army of the French Republic. Despite its importance, Hohenlinden was overshadowed by Napoleon's somewhat less spectacular, but soon enshrined, victory at Marengo, Italy, in June of that same year.

The town of Hohenlinden would figure prominently in both armies' plans. It was the hub for the roads that ran through the area and was therefore a key to operations. The town was all the more critical as the area between the Isar and Inn Rivers was heavily wooded and hilly, meaning that armies could only move effectively by road, especially with their artillery and baggage. It also meant that the Austrians and her German allies, trained to fight in traditional, eighteenth-century fashion, were ill suited for the terrain. However, the revolutionary French troops were now famous for their abilities to fight dispersed in any and all terrains, and to act independently at all levels.

Despite all these factors, the initial Austrian advance caught the French by surprise. Moreau, who was notoriously slow in initiating operations, now found himself temporarily on the defensive. Unfortunately, the Austrians had little idea of the actual French position. Worse still, the poor weather and the troops' inability to perform hard marches immediately slowed the Austrian advance to a crawl. It rained incessantly each day, and the dirt roads quickly turned into a quagmire, with regiments suffering from excessive straggling. As a result, both Weyrother and Franz Baron Lauer now advised the archduke to abandon his sweep around the French left for a more economic and direct move against Munich. This made sense in that Munich had a number of good roads running to it, which would shorten the marching needed. It also meant that the Austrian army would pass through Hohenlinden, some eighteen miles from its present position, which is also where the French were now headed. It was, for the Austrians, the worst possible battlefield in the worst possible weather.[34]

The armies made first contact on 1 December, at the village of Ampfing, which sits immediately to the east of Hohenlinden. Under the command of General Michel Ney, the French advance guard fought a pitched battle against superior Austrian numbers but was compelled to retire after six hours. In a precursor of what was to come, the French troops inflicted heavy losses on the Austrians, showing markedly superior abilities to maneuver. John was buoyed by this initial success, despite the losses, and believed that the French were retreating. To capitalize on this, he ordered a general advance in columns to make the best use of the available roads. In doing so, he hoped to advance his 64,000 men across a broad front and on roads that traveled mostly east–west, which very much limited the ability for the independent columns to support each other. In his race to catch the supposedly retreating French, John further exhausted his worn and wet troops, who did not share his elation at a potential victory.

Moreau was again caught off guard by the Austrian attack but now rose to the occasion. Looking at the map, he quickly realized that, with some planning and hard marching, the chance to catch and crush the Austrian army was at hand. Seeing that the Austrians were advancing in belief of a French retreat, Moreau ordered his units to abandon the higher, wooded ground immediately before Hohenlinden, playing on John's hopes and creating a trap. The divisions that Moreau deployed, despite being on lower ground, sat at the points where the forest roads first came into the open before the town. This meant that the Austrians would be forced to try and deploy under fire from already drawn-up French troops. It also meant that the Austrian artillery would be strung out along the road and would never come into play. If the planned worked, the French divisions under Generals Claude Juste Alexandre Legrand, Emmanuel de Grouchy, Jean d'Hautpoul, and Ney, with 32,000 men, would hold the Austrian main advance in place on the anvil while the hammer swept in from the right. Marching as quickly as possible, considering the wet conditions, 20,000 troops under Generals Antoine Richepanse and Charles Decaen were moving alongside roads to get behind and into the Austrian left.[35]

Both armies spent 2 December on the move, the Austrians slugging along the roads toward Hohenlinden and the French either drawing up behind the town or marching east, parallel to the enemy. Both armies suffered from a combination of rain, sleet, and snow, and were now cold and wet. The French were aware that a battle was in the offing; the Austrian and German troops were simply trying to keep their formations. The day of 3 December began with the front Austrian columns making contact with the French near Hohenlinden, which they assumed was a rear guard. The battle evolved slowly with the piecemeal commitment of battalions and squadrons in localized actions. Within a few hours, however, the tide of battle around the town was turning and the Austrians were wavering.

As the situation grew worse for the Austrians along their front, the struggling troops of Richepanse and Decaen struck the left, with Richepanse nearly hitting into the enemy rear. Again, the fighting was piecemeal and confused, with units moving to the "sound of the guns" and being committed as they became available. Although the Austrians showed the will to resist briefly, the entire left flank soon collapsed, followed by the front line. Retreat almost immediately devolved into route, and much of the artillery and baggage abandoned as troops fled or surrendered. The real fighting was over by the early afternoon, and the Austrian army was in full flight.[36]

The Battle of Hohenlinden was a clear tactical and strategic success for the French. The disaster ended the Austrian army's ability to further resist a French advance, and Moreau seized several key fortresses and depots, allowing him to threaten Vienna. The situation left the monarchy with no option but to sue for peace, ending the war. The costs of the battle, fought primarily on 3 December, had been crushing for Austria and its allies. The army lost 4,485 casualties and over 7,000 prisoners of war, as well as leaving behind 50 artillery pieces. The French losses numbered approximately 3,000. After the battle, the Austrian commanders looked to transfer the blame, and the Archduke John saw the defeat in the failure of his leaders to move quickly.[37]

The calamitous defeat at the hands of Moreau in the battle was an anticlimactic and rather predictable end for the Austrian war effort during the wars of the French Revolution. Having reluctantly entered the war in 1792, the monarchy's army soldiered through a string of tactical and strategic defeats. Yet that same army remained intact and would enter into a reform period in 1801, the first of two, under the promising leadership of the Archduke Charles. As has been often noted in the numerous works of the late premier English-language historian of the Habsburg military, Gunther E. Rothenberg, the Austrian army was what it could be.[38] It was impossible for the army to reform in any fashion similar to the French army because it lacked the potential for the necessary radical social changes. To have changed in such a matter would have negated the monarchy itself. Rather, the army remained a pillar of the empire, if badly beaten, guaranteeing the House of Habsburg's rule, the reason it had been created 150 years earlier.

Notes

1. "Habsburg Monarchy" is a nominally standard term. However, works on the topic also make use of the terms "Austria," "Austrian Empire," "Habsburg Empire," and the "Dual Monarchy." All are essentially correct.
2. Walter C. Langsam, *Francis the Good: The Education of an Emperor, 1768–1792* (New York: Macmillan, 1959), 143.
3. These included Upper and Lower Austria, Vorarlberg, Carinthia, Carniola, Styria, Bohemia, Moravia, and the Tyrol.
4. C. A. Macartney, *The Habsburg Empire, 1790–1918.* (London: Weidenfeld and Nicolson, 1968), 165–78.
5. Charles W. Ingrao, "Habsburg Strategy and Geopolitics during the Eighteenth Century," in *East Central European Society and War in the Pre-Revolutionary Eighteenth Century*, ed. G. E. Rothenberg, B. K. Király, and P. F. Sugar (New York: Columbia University Press, 1982), 62.
6. Golo Mann, *Wallenstein* (Frankfurt am Main: Fischer, 1971), 45.
7. Oskar Regele, *Der Österreichische Hofkriegsrat, 1556–1848* (Vienna: Österreichische Staatsdruckerei, 1972), 24–32.
8. Eduard Wertheimer, "Erzherzog Carl als Präsident des Hofkriegsrathes 1801–1805," Austrian reprint (1880; Vienna: Archiv für österreichische Geschichte, 1972), 202–203.
9. Oskar Regele, *Generalstabschefs aus vier Jahrhunderten* (Vienna: Herold, 1966), 52.
10. Gunther E. Rothenberg, "The Habsburg Army in the Napoleonic Wars," *Military Affairs* 37 (February 1973): 2.
11. H. Meynert, *Geschichte des k.k. österreichischen Armee*, vol. 2 (Vienna, 1853), 161.
12. Gunther E. Rothenberg, "Nobility and Military Careers: The Habsburg Officer Corps, 1740–1914" *Military Affairs* 40, no. 4 (December 1976): 183.
13. Christopher Duffy, *The Army of Maria Theresa: The Armed Forces of Imperial Austria, 1740–1780* (Doncaster, UK: Wise, 1990), 43.

14. Manfried Rauchensteiner, "The Development of War Theories in Austria at the End of the Eighteenth Century," in Rothenberg, Király, and Sugar, *East Central European Society and War*, 49.

15. Gunther E. Rothenberg, *The Military Border in Croatia, 1740–1881* (Chicago: University of Chicago Press, 1966), 68.

16. Gunther E. Rothenberg, *Napoleon's Great Adversaries: The Archduke Charles and the Austrian Army, 1792–1814* (Bloomington: Indiana University Press, 1982), 26.

17. Arthur Paget, *The Paget Papers: Diplomatic and Other Correspondence of the Right Honorable Sir Paget, GCB, 1794–1807*, ed. A. B. Paget, with notes by J. R. Green (New York: Longmans, Green, 1896), 26.

18. Mortiz von Angeli, "Die Heere des Kaisers und der Französischen Revolution in Beginn des Jahres 1792," *Mitteilungen des k.k. Kriegsarchiv*, n.s., 4 (1889): 18.

19. Anton Dolleczek, *Geschichte der österreichischen Artillerie* (Vienna, 1887), 362–65.

20. Rothenberg, *Napoleon's Great Adversaries*, 32–33.

21. Lee W. Eysturlid, *The Formative Influences, Theories, and Campaigns of the Archduke Carl of Austria* (Westport, Conn.: Greenwood Press, 2000), chap. 3.

22. William O. Shannon, "Enlightenment and War: Austro-Prussian Military Practice, 1760–1790," in Rothenberg, Király, and Sugar, *East Central European Society and War*, 90–110.

23. Kurt Peball, "Zum Kriegsbild der Österreichische Armee und seiner geschichtlichen Bedeutung in den Kriegen gegen die Französische Revolution und Napoleon I in dem Jahren von 1792 bis 1815," in *Napoleon I. und das Militärwesen seiner Zeit* (Freiburg, Ger.: Rombach, 1975), 101.

24. J. Allmayer-Beck, "Erzherzog Carl (1771–1847)," in *Neue Österreichische Biographie ab 1815* (Vienna: Amalthea, 1956), 28.

25. T. C. Blanning, *The Origins of the French Revolutionary Wars* (New York: Longman, 1986), 60–62.

26. Carl (Erzherzogs Carl von Österreich), "Über den gegen die Nuefranken durch einen österreichischen Offizier," in *Ausgewählte Schriften*, ed. F. X. Mancher (Vienna, 1894), 5:157.

27. Eysturlid, *Formative Influences, Theories, and Campaigns*, chap. 7.

28. A. B. Rodger, *The War of the Second Coalition, 1798 to 1801: A Strategic Commentary* (Oxford: Clarendon Press, 1964), chap. 1.

29. Manfried Rauchensteiner, *Kaiser Franz und Erzherzog Carl: Dynastie und Heerwesen in Österreich 1796–1809* (Vienna: Verlag für Geschichte und Politik, 1972), 140.

30. Philip Longworth, *The Art of Victory: The Life and Achievements of Field Marshal Suvorov, 1729–1800* (New York: Holt, Rinehart and Winston, 1965), 288–89.

31. Rothenberg, *Napoleon's Great Adversaries*, 62–65.

32. Karl A. Roider, *Baron Thugut and Austria's Response to the French Revolution* (Princeton, N.J.: Princeton University Press, 1987), 386.

33. James A. Arnold, *Marengo and Hohenlinden: Napoleon's Rise to Power* (Barnsley, UK: Pen and Sword, 2005), 145.

34. Ernest Picard, *Hohenlinden* (Paris: H. Charles-Lavauzelle, 1909), 39.

35. Eduard Wertheimer, *Geschichte Österreichs und Ungarns im ersten Jahrzehnt des 19. Jahrhunderts*, vol. 1 (Leipzig: Duncker and Humblot, 1890), 246–47.

36. Arnold, *Marengo and Hohenlinden*, 245.

37. Rodger, *War of the Second Coalition*, 220.

38. For any complete understanding of the Habsburg army in the wars of the French Revolution or the Napoleonic era, it is essential, at least in English, to read Gunther E. Rothenberg's *Napoleon's Great Adversaries.*

CHAPTER 4

THE RUSSIAN ARMY

JANET M. HARTLEY

Russia's participation in the French Revolutionary Wars was limited. Catherine II did not become involved in the War of the First Coalition (although she was planning to send troops to assist the Austrians against the French at the time of her death). She did, however, conduct a war against a revolutionary power, that is, against Poland after the introduction of the constitution of May 3, 1791, in that country, which inter alia was perceived to threaten Russia's control over the weak rump of the Polish state after the first partition of 1772. After the second partition of Poland in 1793, an uprising under the leadership of Tadeusz Kościuszko was crushed by Russian troops, leading to the final partition of Poland in 1795. To the extent that the Poles were regarded as rebels, the uprising could be regarded as an ideological war. It certainly involved a degree of savagery unknown in campaigns in the south, despite the fact that Russo-Turkish wars in the eighteenth century (1695–1700, 1710–11, 1735–39, 1768–74, and 1787–92) were depicted in ideological terms as a triumph of Christianity, or more strictly speaking, Russian Orthodoxy, against Islam. The license given by General Aleksandr Suvorov (the subject of the later part of this chapter) to the Russian forces to massacre not only troops but also civilians in the Warsaw suburb of Praga in 1794 resulted in the death of some 10,000 insurrectionists and civilians.[1] The campaigns against Poland if brutal were also successful for Russia but did not, however, give rise to any significant tactical, organizational, or technical innovations in the Russian army.

It was only in the reign of Paul I (1796–1801) that Russia became involved directly in the war against France. French expansionism in western Europe in 1797–98, and particularly France's ambitions in the eastern Mediterranean, which included the occupation of the Ionian Islands, pushed Paul I toward a more active foreign policy. The occupation by the French of the island of Malta in June 1798, after Paul I had set himself up as the protector of the Knights of Malta, was the final confirmation of the dangerous extent of French ambitions. Russia joined the coalition of Great Britain, Austria, the Ottoman Empire, Portugal, and Naples. But Paul's assassination in 1801 led to the accession of his son, Alexander I, and to the withdrawal of Russia from the war. Russia was a minor player in the French Revolutionary Wars; its fundamental contribution to the defeat of Napoleon and its establishment as the most important military power on the continent of Europe lay in the future.

The Russian army has not been neglected in either Russian/ Soviet or Western historiography, but there is no specific study of the army in this period, and attention has, naturally, focused on the military campaigns of the Napoleonic Wars.[2] Paul's seemingly erratic foreign policy provoked scholarly interest, but that was mainly in the context of his downfall, or even of his mental state.[3] The reign of Paul, and the role of the Russian armed forces in the French Revolutionary Wars are not, however, without interest or significance either for Russia in particular or for European warfare in general. This was, of course, not a revolutionary army in the French mold but a conscript army made up of mainly of peasants—serfs and state peasants—whose experience of military service had not altered radically from the time of the military reforms of Peter I in the early eighteenth century. It was recruited and maintained in a country that was generally regarded as the most backward state in Europe in social, political, and economic terms with the exception of the Ottoman Empire. Nevertheless, the Russian army was capable of beating French forces in northern Italy, although admittedly in a campaign that involved relatively small numbers of troops and in which, notably, Napoleon Bonaparte did not feature. The army also showed that it was capable of maintaining itself in the field far from home and the navy of supporting an invasion force in the eastern and central Mediterranean. The main purpose of this chapter, therefore, is to explain how this "unreformed" army managed to at least hold its own in European warfare in this period and to examine evidence for the foundations of Russia's future successes, and weaknesses, in the Napoleonic Wars.

The Russian army grew throughout the eighteenth century from 100,000 men in the reign of Peter I to more than 700,000 men by the end of the campaign in 1815. When Paul came to the throne in 1796, regular troops reached 279,575, according to official statistics. This number decreased to 203,228 men by 1800, partly because of Paul's deliberate reduction of grenadier regiments from fifteen to twelve and the establishment of musketeer battalions in their place. Paul's favoring of heavy cavalry resulted in the reduction in size of light cavalry troops and the abolition of jaeger regiments and grenadier horse regiments. He replaced these forces with dragoon regiments, which increased from eleven to sixteen regiments in 1798, and cuirassiers, expanded from five to fifteen regiments in the same year. Levies took place regularly throughout his reign—a "take" of 3 men in every 500 in 1797, 1 in 500 in 1798, and 1 in 350 in 1799.[4]

The Russian army had outstripped other European armies by the 1780s. But the onset of the French Revolutionary Wars, and in particular the levée en masse, saw the deployment of far larger armies in the field. In order to compete, Russia had not only to carry out regular levies of troops but also to maintain the armies both in the field and at home. In the Russian case, the growth of the army coincided with a significant expansion of the population, from 28.4 million in 1782 to 37.2 million in 1795 and 41.7 million in 1811.[5] The population growth allowed the state to increase the size of the army without significantly increasing the burden on the population and gave Russia an advantage vis-à-vis its competitors on the continent of Europe. Indeed, the American historian Walter Pintner argued that the "cost" in terms of manpower for Russia was considerably less than in Prussia and became marginally less than in Austria and France by the late eighteenth century and the turn of the nineteenth century. By his calculations, Russian conscription comprised 1.3 percent of the Russian population in the mid-eighteenth century and dropped to 1.2 percent in 1800; comparative figures for Prussia were 4.2 and 1.9 percent, for France 1.5 and 1.2 percent, and for Austria 1.1. and 1.5 percent.[6]

Statistics, however, only tell a limited story. The Russian army made little use of mercenaries. Mercenary *soldiers* were almost unknown; the officer corps was largely drawn from the Russian empire, if not from ethnic Russians, by the late eighteenth century, although there were more foreign nationals in the navy.[7] The burden of conscription, however, was borne more directly by the population. Recruitment of ordinary soldiers, and sailors, within the empire almost certainly fell more heavily on the Russian population within the empire because some non-Russian territories, which were acquired over the course of the seventeenth and eighteenth centuries, retained privileges of this nature. The Jewish population, mostly acquired as a result of the three partitions of Poland-Lithuania in the late eighteenth century, was excluded from the levy. The statistics only relate to the number of men serving in the army in any given time and are themselves unreliable and were often deliberately faked in order to justify higher expenditure. The number of men *conscripted* into the army, as opposed to the number on the books at any given time, was of course, much higher. It has been estimated that 1,616,199 recruits were levied in Russia between 1796 and 1815.[8] This gap between the number of men conscripted and the number serving in the army was due largely to the high mortality rate. One estimate, based on statistics for 1802, estimated that the mortality rate in the army in a normal year was about three times the average for males between twenty and forty.[9] One of Alexander I's officials claimed that the army renewed itself in terms of manpower every five to six years.[10]

Of course, statistics showing that proportionally fewer Russians served in the army than Prussians was of little consolation for the unfortunate individual conscript, not least because one of the distinctive features of the Russian army was that soldiers were conscripted for life in the eighteenth century. In 1793, this term was reduced to twenty-five years, but this was, in effect, still life, not least because at the point of conscription the soldier severed all ties with his village, or town, not only economically and socially but also legally as he was now counted as a member of the military social estate. Funeral-style laments accompanied the departure of recruits from the village, because recruits were, in effect, regarded as "dead" by those they left behind. Indeed, were a soldier to return to his village, the chances were that he would be most unwelcome. A maimed soldier, or one who had survived twenty-five years of service, would be unlikely to contribute greatly to the economy of the village. In particular, his legal separation from his original social estate meant that he was no longer included in the collective responsibility of the village/town for taxation or other state obligations and was therefore a liability to the community.

Who were these recruits? Members of all the non-privileged classes were conscripted—meaning peasants above all, that is, both serfs (seigneurial peasants on noble land) and state peasants.[11] Artisans and ordinary members of the urban community were liable for conscription on the basis of the same "takes" as peasants. Clergy who had not been ordained, including sons of parish priests (Orthodox priests had to marry), were eligible for conscription and were unceremoniously culled from parishes and seminaries; the last levy of excess clergy took place in Paul's reign in 1796.[12]

Regular population censuses established the number of males (from old men to babies) in every community, and it was on this basis that the "take" was made. Usually, there was only one levy in a year, but at times of war levies could be more frequent. Recruits had to satisfy basic requirements of age, from seventeen to thirty-five years in Paul's reign; a height requirement of normally 1.60 cm; and health stipulations, including having front teeth, which were needed to bite cartridges. But these requirements were lowered in wartime and, in any event, could often be overridden by bribery at the recruitment station.[13] In practice, conscripts could be younger or older than the law specified; boys as young as fifteen were recruited in practice, as were men over fifty.[14] The law did not specify that recruits had to be bachelors, although some individual serf owners did attempt to exclude married serfs from the levy. In practice, married men, with or without children, were conscripted, often leaving their wives and families in a precarious state. The selection of recruits was made almost entirely at the local level—by peasant communes, urban self-governing institutions, etc. The result was that the least valuable members of the community were conscripted. These men could include the drunkards, the work-shy, and the troublemakers (rural and urban) and, as such, the system was an important mechanism of social control in the community. The levy was also used as a mechanism to rid the community of the least economically viable members, and their households, if they made an inadequate contribution to the tax and other state obligations borne by the community.

The Russian army, however, did not only comprise regular forces. By 1800, the army was supplemented by some 70,000 irregular troops and roughly the same number of garrison troops.[15] The main body of irregular troops were Cossacks, supplemented by smaller units of Bashkirs and other non-Russian tribes. Cossacks were ethnically Russians or Ukrainians who settled on the southern, Caucasian, and Siberian frontiers of Russia and who had formed semiautonomous military communities. They had a deserved reputation for skilled horsemanship and bravery, and a rather less commendable reputation for ill-discipline and savagery both in battle and toward prisoners and the local population. But in addition to active service, the whole Cossack community was supposed to defend the empire's vulnerable frontiers against raids—by Tatars and Turks in the south, by Chechens in the northern Caucasus, and by indigenous tribesmen in Siberia. These supplementary forces could be used to bolster Russian military strength at times of crisis—Kalmyk warriors and Bashkir tribesmen fought in the Napoleonic campaigns.

The performance of the Russian army in the French Revolutionary Wars has to be assessed in the context of its social composition described above. Although the Russian army took the disreputable and often the most vulnerable members of society into its ranks, it also had the opportunity to train soldiers over many years as service lasted, in effect, until death. The officer corps was predominantly noble, and almost exclusively so in the prestigious guards regiments. Service to the state became the raison d'être of the Russian nobility, particularly after 1762 when service became *voluntary*, something that distinguished the nobility from the unprivileged classes, which were obliged to provide recruits, tax, or services for the armed forces. Military service (the navy was the junior branch) was always more prestigious, more popular, and more glamorous than the civil service, and the problem for Russia was always the oversupply of potential officers. Wartime gave some the opportunity to enlist and thus escape from the tedium of administrative posts in the provinces. In fact, the majority of Russian nobles needed military service for basic survival because their income from their estates was too small to sustain them.[16] Elite military schools trained future officers, but many were simply educated at home and learned in the field.[17] The coup against Paul in 1801 involved 188 officers, some of whom were in the guards, and many of whom felt some personal grudge against the tsar. These grudges often concerned the hated new foreign uniforms and drills and showed nostalgia for what the officers regarded as the easygoing regime of Catherine II. It has been estimated that some 3,500 officers resigned in Paul's reign, while some 340 generals and 2,261 officers were either sacked or pushed to resign.[18]

Paul I came to the throne determined to rectify what he saw as the general slackness in government and standards at court, which he believed had become a feature of the last years of the reign of Catherine II. He was also determined to rule, after many frustrating years during which he had been physically kept away from the court and excluded from any role in government. Catherine, who as a woman was obviously unable to command the troops in person, had delegated decision making as well as command to her protégés, such as Grigorii Potemkin (her former lover), Petr Rumiantsev, and Aleksandr Suvorov. Paul assumed, in the words of one historian, that "he inherited a system of military administration grown flabby and corrupt under the administration of a series of favorites, several of whom came to regard the structure as their own satrapy."[19]

Paul did not attempt to play the role of military leader himself. Paul's genuine interest in military affairs while being an armchair general may go some way to explain his obsession with minutiae. This preoccupation went beyond the details of parade-ground displays, where Paul could spend two or three hours a day, and of uniforms and the physical appearance of his soldiers. The tsar also wanted to know details such as quartering arrangements for all his army and monthly reports on expenditures, had a personal interest in all aspects of military punishments and court resolutions, and approved minor changes to such things as ceremonial drums and flags.[20] The attraction of Prussian-style drills and standardized uniforms may also be reflect his desire to bring a "strong dose of Prussian order" to what he regarded as an over-personalized and ill-disciplined system of Catherine as much as an attempt to make fundamental changes in military activities.[21] Paul did, of course, recall Suvorov to command the campaign in Italy in 1799 despite the latter's open opposition to Prussian-style changes. This suggests that Paul was not so rigid to let such disagreements override military considerations. Personal motivations, however, probably accounted for Paul's attempt to diminish the exclusiveness of the prestigious guards regiments, because of the role played by some members of the guards regiments in Catherine's coup and in the murder of his father, Peter III; he expanded their numbers, dismissed some prominent individuals, and imposed changes to their uniforms and drills.

Paul's military reforms, however, extended beyond acts that reflected his personal dislikes and sensitivities and did go some way to establish a more efficient basis on which to support the enormous armies that the warfare of the late eighteenth and early nineteenth centuries came to require. He attempted to centralize and standardize military administration while retaining power in his own hands and in those of a few trusted ministers. In 1798, Paul remodeled the War College and divided its functions more effectively into six new divisions. The general staff was replaced by a "suite" of trusted individuals and was re-termed the "military expedition." At the same time, he established a new organization for the supervision of military orphans and new regulations and structural organization for military chaplains.[22] At the operational level, Paul reduced the number of light cavalry regiments and replaced them with heavy cavalry regiments. He changed the names of some regiments from a regional designation to the personal names of generals, something that Soviet historians have criticized as an inappropriate and mechanical copy of an alien Prussian system and as a deliberate attempt to diminish earlier glorious *Russian* deeds.[23] In fact, there is little evidence of loyalty to regional regimental names at the time. Recruits were not normally dispatched to their local regiments, and regional loyalties evolved slowly for noblemen as they commonly held lands in more than one region and frequently changed regiments during their careers.

Effective provisioning and quartering were of fundamental importance in maintaining a large army. In this respect, Paul made significant improvements, which may have contributed to the ability of the state to support the enormous armies of the revolutionary and Napoleonic periods without significant social unrest at home. Paul restructured and clarified the roles of the provisioning departments of the War College and subordinated their activities to the war minister.[24] He also attempted to regulate the prices and amount of supplies allocated to the armed forces. Of particular importance in a territory the size of the Russian empire, he decreed that provisioning stores must be set up at a reasonable distance from the regimental garrisons.[25] The Russian state was slow to build barracks for troops. Troops were scattered among towns and villages often a great distance from their headquarters, with the inevitable negative effects on military discipline and on military-civilian relations. Paul attempted to regulate quartering regulations in 1797 with the establishment of a separate Military-Field Chancellery.[26] He also authorized the construction of more barracks in Courland, Moscow, and Saint Petersburg.[27] Extensive barrack construction did not, however, take place until the early nineteenth century, and even then the majority of soldiers remained quartered on a reluctant urban and rural population, particularly in the borderlands.

Paul's military reforms have been portrayed rather more sinisterly as an attempt to militarize state and society.[28] At one level, this

was a question of image. Paul's obsession with uniforms was manifested by preserving the exclusiveness and, by extension, the superiority of the armed forces by forbidding those in civilian occupations
to wear uniforms. This ban applied not only to officials holding civil
and nonmilitary rank but also to retired officers, who were often
employed in civilian posts in local administration and for matters
of social status had normally continued to wear their military uniforms.[29] The image of the tsar and the court certainly became more
military in Paul's reign. The Winter Palace took on the appearance
of a barracks with the heavy presence of soldiers. The parades could
override traditionally nonmilitary ceremonies. In 1798, Paul combined a review of regiments with the traditional ceremony of the
Blessing of the Waters. After Paul became protector of the Knights
of Malta, ceremonials and rituals concerned with the knightly order
were featured at court.[30] Parades themselves became symbolic rituals in which tsarist power was displayed.

The performance of the Russian army also has to be seen in the
wider context of the industrial base for the supply of weapons, gunpowder, and uniforms. The low level of technology and limited
degree of technical innovation required for weaponry in this period
meant that industrial sophistication was not a prerequisite for military success. In fact, Russian iron factories—state and private—in
the Urals and its arms factories, based in the town of Tula, southwest of Moscow, were able to compete with the West both in terms
of quantity and quality of production in this period. Iron factories,
whose growth had been stimulated initially by the state in order
to meet the military needs of the Great Northern War in the early
eighteenth century, continued to expand throughout the century.
In 1798, Paul directly encouraged further growth by allowing merchants to purchase serfs, who could be used as a labor force in these
factories. Iron factories, however, remained largely in state, rather
than private, hands by century's end. By the late eighteenth century, Russia was the greatest producer of iron in the world. In 1803,
Russia produced 163,000 tons of cast iron, compared with 156,000
tons in England and 80,000–85,000 tons in France.[31] The Tula arms
factories increased the output of weaponry from 24,438 pieces in
1797 to 43,388 pieces in 1799.[32] Paul I took a personal interest
in the artillery, consolidating it into eight artillery field regiments.
He established new ratios of field guns to battalions and personally

inspected new weapons. Western and Soviet historians are in agreement that by 1801 "Russian field artillery was technically equivalent to the best in Europe,"[33] and the basis had been laid to support the army in the campaigns of the Napoleonic Wars.

Cloth and wool factories were able to provide uniforms for the army without imports, and leather factories supplied sufficient leather for boots and harnesses. The changes in uniform introduced by Paul led to increased demand in the late 1790s. The number of cloth factories rose steadily over the eighteenth and early nineteenth centuries to meet the demands of war as did the number of workers in the factories from some 273,000 people in 1764 to 496,000 in 1795 and 759,000 in 1806.[34] The main problem for cloth manufacturers was not meeting the demands of the army but the committing to supply goods at a fixed price below that which they could command in export markets. In 1797, the government had to pass a decree forcing these factories to release cloth at the stated price for the military by forbidding exports.[35]

Debate within Russian/Soviet historiography, however, has centered not so much on technological matters but on the tactical changes employed by the Russian army in the late eighteenth century. The debate has been bitter at times of East-West tension, particularly during the Cold War period, as it contrasted nativist, superior, Russian tactics and traditions against imported, foreign, usually Prussian tactics. Part of the sensitivities were concerned with borrowing from the West and the suggestion of Russian backwardness; part was also due to an assertion of the native individual genius and flexibility of Russian commanders contrasted with the slavishly mechanical military tactics of the West. The debate was not narrowly focused on the period of the French Revolutionary War, or, for that matter, on the Napoleonic period, but had deeper historical roots, which can traced back at least to military reforms in the reign of Peter I (1682–1725) and to some extent back to the conflict with Poland at the beginning of the seventeenth century. The ill-fated reign of Peter III (1762) was associated with tactics, drills, and uniforms of the Prussia of Frederick the Great. Catherine the Great (1762–96), herself of German origin, deliberately projected herself as the protector of the traditions of the guards regiments when she overthrew her husband's rule and restored the more comfortable and practical Russian uniforms. In the same way, at least part of the unpopularity of Paul stemmed from what was perceived as an attack on Russian military traditions and style as soldiers were forced to adopt tight Prussian uniforms, to tie their hair in uncomfortable wigs, and to learn the minutiae of the Prussian drills.

In fact, Russian armies had been flexible throughout the eighteenth century in both their borrowing from foreign armies and their adaptability to local military conditions. It was flexibility of approach, rather than a particular Western or native style that accounted for their military success. Thus, Catherine may have rejected Prussian-style uniforms as part of a deliberate projection of herself as the embodiment of Russian military traditions, but the military manual of 1763 was a copy of the Prussian manual because it was Prussian soldiers who at the time provided the best, and most successful, examples of precision and rapid firing. Russian armies in Catherine's reign, however, were not so much tested by central and western European forces as by the armies of the Ottoman Empire in the two Russo-Turkish Wars of 1768–74 and 1787–92. The American historian Bruce Menning has made a convincing case for attributing the changes in Russian tactics to the particular conditions of campaigning in the underpopulated and inhospitable terrain of southern Russia and the northern Balkans against mobile irregular Turkish troops. These included: the flexibility of the use of the military square; the use of the bayonet as a shock tactic rather than as purely firepower; the favoring of offensive tactics; the deployment of mobile units on the flanks; the increased use of light cavalry; the dispensing of baggage trains in favor of distribution of individual rations to soldiers; and the adoption of loose-fitting uniforms, which allowed for speed of movement on the battlefield and more rapid marching.[36] Such tactics also made excellent use of the Russian army's own irregular mounted forces—the Cossacks. Thus, in the Russian case, the success of the French forces raised by the levée en masse in the War of the First Coalition, a war in which Russian forces were not involved of course, was of far less influence on tactics than was their earlier experience of fighting the Turks.

The treatment by Russian and Soviet historians of Suvorov's "military genius," is itself part of this larger "nativist versus foreign" debate over Russian military tactics.[37] Suvorov is portrayed by Russian and Soviet historians as a prime example of the Russian flexible commander, whose success was based on his understanding of the psyche and strengths of the Russian soldier. In an account published in 1951—that is, at a time of heightened Soviet sensitivities

in the Cold War period—the historian Tsvetaev claimed that it was
the unique national composition of the Russian armies that enabled
Suvorov to instill a "moral soul" into Russian soldiers, which in
turn allowed him to motivate his men in offensive and concentrated attacks so successfully.[38] Suvorov has been credited by both
Soviet and Western historians with anticipating many of the tactical changes that occurred during the French Revolutionary and
Napoleonic Wars—particularly the emphasis on mobility and flexibility and the importance of offensive tactics—and with being an
important influence on Napoleon himself.[39]

Suvorov's own writings and aphorisms on battle give some
credence to this view.[40] In particular, Suvorov was credited with
instilling the cult of the bayonet and the importance of the decisive encounter: "The bullet is a fool, but the bayonet is terrific,"[41]
"Columns, cold steel, attack, blow—that's my reconnoitring,"[42] and
"One minute decides the fate of a battle."[43] Suvorov clearly established a rapport with ordinary soldiers, partly perhaps through his
eccentricity (he is supposed to have habitually gone around dressed
in only a shirt and to have roused his troops with a rooster call),[44]
and partly because he could communicate with them in familiar,
and sometimes earthy, language. Soldiers are supposed to have said
of him: "None of us was a stranger. . . . He shared his *kasha* [buck-
wheat porridge] with us soldiers."[45] His heroic, and not so heroic,
deeds were commemorated in soldiers' and folk songs.[46] Suvorov's
cult status remained throughout the Soviet period and is still present today. Stalin created a decoration in his honor in the Second
World War.[47]

Certainly, Suvorov made his opposition to Paul's introduction
of Prussian-style drill clear, and this led to his internal exile to his
estates in Smolensk until he was recalled for the Italian campaign.
At this point, Suvorov deliberately, and symbolically, reinstated
Russian loose-fitting uniforms for his troops and cut off the hated
Prussian-style pigtails.[48] But in fact, Suvorov, who was aged seventy
at the time of the Italian campaign in 1799, had developed his tactic firstly during the Seven Years' War of 1756–63, but then more
significantly during the Russo-Turkish wars in Catherine's reign.
The conflict with the Ottoman empire was crucial because Suvorov
learned the importance of offensive encounters, both in the field
and in the assault of Izmail, the tactical refinement of the use of
the square, the increased use of irregular troops, and the importance

of mobility both in the march to and in battle itself. Nevertheless, Suvorov's ability as a commander lay in his flexibility in the field and his acceptance that tactics had to adapt to circumstances. In his own words, he favored different tactics according to the enemy: "against regular forces the linear order as in the Prussian war [the Seven Years' War]; against irregulars as in the last Turkish War."[49]

Russian troops joined Austrian forces in northern Italy in April 1799, where the French armies, under Napoleon, had proved so successful in the previous campaign in 1796–97. The Russian army numbered some 30,000 men. Suvorov was given command of the allied troops—comprising some 86,000 Austrians—and was characteristically eager to force a decisive battle to defeat the French, who numbered some 100,000 in Italy, 62,000 of whom were in Lombardy.[50] Suvorov was impatient for action. Moving swiftly, he advanced on 18 April, forced the French from Brescia on 21 April, inflicted a heavy defeat on some 30,000 French troops at the River Adda, where the French lost some 10,000 men compared with allied losses of 2,000, and entered Milan on 28 April to an enthusiastic welcome. In part misled by poor Austrian intelligence, Suvorov moved his troops first southward and then north to occupy Turin (26 May), where after his tumultuous welcome he proclaimed the restoration of the House of Savoy much to the annoyance of the Austrians. This diversion allowed the French forces to regroup under General J. E. J. A. Macdonald. The two armies met at the battle of Trebbia, in which the French were not annihilated but were forced to retreat.

The allied forces were now in control of the plains of Lombardy but were potentially threatened by French forces to the north and south. On 26 May, Suvorov entered Turin and was greeted with even more enthusiasm than he had been in Milan. Suvorov suffered from poor military intelligence in northern Italy, but when he received news that Macdonald's army was moving swiftly to join French forces to the northwest at Tortona, he had to act decisively to back his advance. Macdonald moved through Parma toward Piacenza, brushing small Austrian units out of the way. The Russian forces had to move at great speed (through Casteggio and Stradella) to prevent the union of French forces and to prevent smaller Austrian forces from being overrun by Macdonald's troops: in a day and half the advance troops covered fifty-three miles and were rushed straight into battle, pushing the French forces back to the River Trebbia.

The battle of Trebbia took place on 17–19 June (6–8 June by the Russian calendar). Some 22,000 Russian and Austrians and 28,000 French troops ultimately took part in the battle. It was not one of Suvorov's dramatic and speedy military triumphs, as fighting lasted three days. On the first day, a ferocious Cossack charge almost destroyed the Polish troops in Macdonald's forces. The allied cavalry attacked the French flanks and forced the French to retreat some miles to the River Trebbia. On the second day, as the Austrian troops had now arrived, Suvorov's attack continued as three columns of Russians and Austrians forced the French back but were, at great cost, repelled by the French cavalry and effective sharpshooters as well as by the timely arrival of reinforcements, which again shifted the balance of force in favor of the French. On the third day, a French attack on the Russian positions was met with fierce resistance.[51] But this was ultimately a clear-cut Russian victory as the extent of losses meant that the French were forced to retreat and leave Suvorov in control not only of the field but in effect of northern Italy. Casualty figures are hard to estimate accurately, but it is clear that the French suffered far greater losses. Suvorov's own figures were that the French suffered over 6,000 deaths, including 4 generals, 8 colonels, 502 other officers, and 11,766 soldiers.[52] It was only the lack of allied troops who could follow up the victory that prevented French losses from being greater. According to one estimate, the Russians only lost 850 dead, although some 4,000 were wounded.[53]

Hagiographic accounts overstate both the genius and significance of the event, given that Suvorov was not, firstly, pitted against Napoleon in Italy and, secondly, that the overall number of troops involved in battle was relatively small. Writing in 1950, the Soviet historian Osipov, stated,

> In the year 218 B.C. Hannibal had routed the legions of Rome on the same Trebbia. Now the two best armies in the world, the army of Suvorov and the army of the French Republic, met on the same spot. . . . Both armies had been hitherto invincible and both had very high standards of military achievement. This was the chief reason for the unusual bitterness with which the battle of Trebbia was fought.[54]

A recent (2003) Russian popular biography reproduces the Osipov analysis including the quotation concerning Hannibal.[55]

Nevertheless, the battle demonstrated both Suvorov's strengths as a commander and the ability of the Russian army to more than hold its own against the French. These strengths were a combination of the tactics Suvorov had learned in previous campaigns, particularly against the Turks, and the flexibility imposed by new circumstances. First, the forced march to the River Trebbia, in which Russian troops covered fifty-three miles in one and a half days and then plunged immediately into battle, demonstrated both Suvorov's belief in speed and mobility—as well as demonstrating that he could encourage his men personally by kind words which encouraged them en route and on the eve of battle.[56] One memoirist wrote after the event that "Suvorov's army did not walk, but ran."[57] Second, the speed and boldness of the attack on the first day, despite the Russian troops being outnumbered by French infantry regiments, by some 19,000 against 12,000–15,000 men, was also typical of Suvorov's desire for a quick and decisive battle. The fierceness of the assault by Cossacks demoralized the Polish troops and saw the loss of six hundred French troops and four hundred prisoners.[58] The willingness of Suvorov to commit regiments in waves of assaults even when the enemy was more numerous in part explains the fierceness of the battle. In his own words: "This battle was the most torrid; the whole River Trebbia was on fire, and only the great courage of our army enabled us to beat the enemy."[59]

Third, Suvorov made good use of his reserve troops of 6,000 men, particularly when he had to resist French attack on the third day of the battle.[60] Fourth, Suvorov demonstrated his ability to inspire the soldiers personally in battle as well as on the march. One contemporary at the battle wrote that "he was the father of soldiers . . . elderly, thin, saddled, small, in a grey-coat, not on a cavalry but on a Cossack horse, turning in the saddle to the right and the left."[61] On the third day of the battle, when things looked desperate, Suvorov joined his fleeing men, got them to reform round a Russian battery, and then led them back in a charge against the enemy. "Back" he cried, "God is with us! Hurrah!"[62]

Finally, the battle also demonstrated that Suvorov was flexible in his tactics. He was not able, in fact, to beat the enemy through decisive action in the first two days. Even here he attempted two forms of attack: a cavalry assault on the first day and close fighting on the second day.[63] But he was then able to change tactics and move to the defensive when the French attacked on the third day, and postponed his planned attack. The inability of the French forces to break down Russian resistance forced them to cut their losses and to retreat. It was the only three-day battle that Suvorov fought in his whole career. He acknowledged that different tactics had to be used against French forces in Italy than against the Turks.[64] This flexibility was recognized at the time by contemporaries. The Austrian chief of staff J. G. Chasteler commented, "It was necessary to change the system of war in Italy, in order to obtain different results from 1796–97: that is what the Field Marshal [Suvorov] has done."[65]

Suvorov's instincts were to use this advantage to the full and push for an invasion of France and a decisive defeat of French forces. He was held back, partly by Austrian caution, but also by the limited size of his own forces and problems of provisioning and extracting goods from the local population.[66] In fact, Suvorov and the Austrians were at complete odds: while the former sought total victory, the latter had the more limited aim of wanting to secure northern Italy.[67] Austrian policy has been characterized as "timid" and even "jealous" of Suvorov's success, but the reality was that Austria's aims were always more cautious, conservative, and limited than those of Russia and were focused more on limited territorial gains than on the overthrowing of the French regime.[68] As the historian Paul Schroeder has commented, Austrian policy "aimed to push France back, not to destroy the French army or overthrow the revolution, and the first priority was preserving its own army and defending the hereditary Austrian domains."[69]

Austrian pressure prevailed, leading Suvorov to concentrate on taking a number of fortresses in northern Italy, which again gave Macdonald time to regroup. By June 1799, with the campaign in Italy seemingly won, Russian concerns began to center on Switzerland as a 45,000-strong Russian army under General A. Rimskii-Korsakov was approaching from the east. Suvorov was able to inflict a further defeat on French forces under General B. C. Joubert at Novi (14 August), which left some 7,000 French dead, 4,600 captured, and 5,000 wounded, and some 6,000 allied casualties. However, before he was able to follow up this victory Suvorov was ordered north into Switzerland to link up with Rimskii-Korsakov's forces, a decision that one historian has stated "made the final failure of the Coalition inevitable, as far as anything can be inevitable in history."[70] There then followed a crossing of the Alps by Suvorov and his Russian forces, heroic in its daring and implementation, but ultimately pointless militarily and diplomatically as the Second Coalition collapsed. As Rimskii-Korsakov fell out with the Austrians, a joint Anglo-Russian invasion of Holland ended in ignominious failure. Suvorov was recalled by Paul I in January 1800.

The victories in northern Italy were due at least in part to Suvorov's skill. The impressive performance of the Russian armies was also a testimony to the strengths of Russian, nonrevolutionary, methods of conscription, training, and organization. Russian soldiers showed physical strength, resourcefulness in tactics, flexibility in battle, and motivation against the enemy despite their very traditional forms of recruitment and their low educational levels. The irregular Cossack troops were as effective in northern Italy as they had been on the southern Russian steppes against Turkish forces. The recruitment, education, and training given to Russian officers produced at least a number of able men who could implement Suvorov's orders. General Petr Bagration fought with Suvorov at the battle of Trebbia. The Russian army was able to both equip itself with weapons and supply itself with foodstuffs and fodder at least adequately enough to remain effective in the field and disciplined in the rear. In this respect, the model of the "old" army, as opposed to the "new" armies of revolutionary France, showed that it had the capacity to at least hold its own in late eighteenth-century warfare and that it was built on secure enough foundations to face a greater challenge in the early nineteenth century. Russia's military weakness, in fact, lay in its *financial* structures, and in the social and economic conditions that underpinned those finances, and not in its military organization or tactics; however, this subject is beyond the scope of this chapter.

Notes

1. B. W. Menning, "Paul I and Catherine II's Military Legacy, 1762–1801," in *The Military History of Tsarist Russia*, ed. F. W. Kagan and R. Higham (Basingstoke, UK: Palgrave, 2002), 99.
2. More specific references can be found in this chapter, but the main works include L. G. Beskrovnyi, *Russkaia armiia i flot v XVIII veke (ocherki)* (Moscow: Voennoe izdatel'stvo, 1958); J. L. H. Keep, *Soldiers of the Tsar: Army and Society in Russia, 1462–1874* (Oxford: Clarendon Press, 1985); W. C. Fuller, *Strategy and Power in Russia, 1600–1914* (New York: Free Press, 1992); D. Beyrau, *Militär und Gesellschaft in Vorrevolutionären Russland* (Cologne: Böhlau, 1984). Further analysis of the composition of the armed forces and the cost to maintaining the enormous standing army, and navy, can be found in my *Russia,*

1762–1825: Military Power, the State, and the People (Westport, Conn.: Praeger, 2008).

3. See H. Ragsdale, ed., *Paul I: A Reassessment of His Life and Reign* (Pittsburgh: University Center for International Studies, University of Pittsburgh, 1979), and H. Ragsdale, *Tsar Paul and the Question of Madness: An Essay in History and Psychology* (New York: Greenwood Press, 1988).

4. Beskrovnyi, *Russkaia armiia i flot*, 297.

5. J. M. Hartley, *A Social History of the Russian Empire, 1650–1825* (London: Longman, 1999), 9.

6. W. M. Pintner, "The Burden of Defense in Imperial Russia, 1725–1914," *Russian Review* 43 (1984): 246–47.

7. Iu. P. Shchergolov, "Inostrantsy na russkoi voennoi sluzhbe pri Ekaterine II," *Problemy otechestvennoi istorii* 8 (2004): 65–76.

8. E. K. Wirtschafter, *From Serf to Russian Soldier* (Princeton, N.J.: Princeton University Press, 1990), 3.

9. A. Kahan, *The Plow, the Hammer, and the Knout: An Economic History of Eighteenth-Century Russia* (Chicago: University of Chicago Press, 1985), 9.

10. Keep, *Soldiers of the Tsar*, 196.

11. That is, peasants who lived on state and crown land, including former church land after secularization of church land in 1764, inhabitants of remote parts of northern Russia and Siberia where there were few noble properties, and various other categories of unprivileged people including minor servitors, coachmen, and peasants in non-Russian territories such as Old Finland, the Crimea, and parts of the land acquired in the partitions of Poland.

12. G. Freeze, *The Russian Levites: Parish Clergy in the Eighteenth Century* (Cambridge, Mass., Harvard University Press, 1977), 40.

13. Keep, *Soldiers of the Tsar*, 153–55.

14. J. M. Hartley, "The Russian Recruit," in *Reflections on Russia in the Eighteenth Century*, ed. J. Klein, S. Dixon, and M. Fraanje (Cologne: Böhlau, 2001), 37.

15. Beskrovnyi, *Russkaia armiia i flot*, 321.

16. J. L. H. Keep, "The Origins of Russian Militarism," *Cahiers du monde russe et soviétique* 26 (1985): 13.

17. N. N. Aurova, *Sistema voennogo obrazovaniia v Rossii: kadetskie korpusa vo vtoroi polovine XVIII—pervoi polovine XIX veka* (Moscow: Institut rossiiskoi istorii RAN, 2003).

18. J. L. H. Keep, "The Russian Army's Response to the French Revolution," *Jahrbücher für Geshchichte Osteuropas* 28 (1980): 500, 506–507, 510.

19. Menning, "Paul I," 77.

20. M. V. Klochkov, *Ocherki pravitel'stvennoi deiatel'nosti vremeni Pavla I* (Saint Petersburg: Senatskaia tipografiia, 1916), 289–90.

21. Menning, "Paul I," 82.

22. V. N. Voronov, ed., *Sistema voennogo upravleniia v Rossii (XVIII—nachalo XX v.)* (Moscow: Voennyi universitet, 2003), 63–66.

23. Beskrovnyi, *Russkaia armiia i flot*, 328–29, 430.
24. J. P. LeDonne, *Absolutism and Ruling Class: The Formation of the Russian Political Order, 1700–1825* (New York: Oxford University Press, 1991), 100; Voronov, *Sistema voennogo upravleniia*, 64.
25. *Polnoe sobranie zakonov Rossiiskoi imperii* (hereafter *PSZ*), vol. 24, no. 17835 (February 25, 1797), 423.
26. Voronov, *Sistema voennogo upravleniia*, 63–64.
27. *PSZ*, vol. 24, no. 18086 (August 11, 1797), 679; vol. 25, no. 18505 (28 April 1798), 224–25; vol. 25, no. 18664 (September 12, 1798), 382–84.
28. For a sophisticated and sensible discussion of this, see J. L. H. Keep, "Paul I and the Militarization of Government," *Canadian-American Slavic Studies* 7, no. 1 (1973): 1–14.
29. *PSZ*, vol. 24, no. 17951 (May 2, 1797), 604.
30. R. S. Wortman, *Scenarios of Power: Myth and Ceremony in Russian Monarchy* (Princeton, N.J.: Princeton University Press, 1995), 1:172, 181–83, 185.
31. J. Blum, *Lord and Peasant in Russia from the Ninth to the Nineteenth Century* (Princeton, N.J.: Princeton University Press, 1961), 295.
32. Beskrovnyi, *Russkaia armiia i flot*, 356, 348, 354–55.
33. Quote from Menning, "Paul I," 78; see also Beskrovnyi, *Russkaia armiia i flot*, 324.
34. Beyrau, *Militär und Gesellschaft*, 104–105.
35. Kahan, *The Plow*, 102.
36. B. Menning, "Russian Military Innovation in the Second Half of the Eighteenth Century," *War and Society* 2 (1984): 23–41.
37. For a hagiographic account of Suvorov's genius, see M. Kurmacheva, "Polkovedets A. V. Suvorov v otsenke russkogo obshchestva," in *Russia and the West in the Eighteenth Century*, ed. A. G. Cross (Newtonville, Mass.: Oriental Research Partners, 1983), 271–80.
38. V. Tsvetaev, "Takticheskoe nasledstvo A. V. Suvorova," in *A. V. Suvorov. Iz materialov, opublikovannykh v sviazi so 150-letiem so dnia smerti* (Moscow: Voennoe izdatel'stvo, 1951), 45. This view was supported by Beskrovnyi, the most significant Soviet author of works on eighteenth- and nineteenth-century military history, in a specific study of Suvorov's "national" tactics in the same year. See L. G. Beskrovnyi, "Strategiia i taktika Suvorova," in *Suvorovskii sbornik*, ed. A. V. Sukhomlin (Moscow: Izdatel'stvo Akademii nauk SSSR, 1951), 34.
39. Tsvetaev, "Takticheskoe nasledstvo," 55; Beskrovnyi, *Russkaia armiia i flot*, 10; Menning, "Russian Military Innovation," 30.
40. Suvorov's *Instructions* on military tactics of 1764 have been analyzed in a recent book, and the link with earlier Prussian instruction models has been demonstrated: N. G. Rogulin, *"Polkovoe uchrezhdenie" A. V. Suvorova i pekhotnye instruktsii ekaterinskogo vremeni* (Saint Petersburg: D. Bulanin, 2005).
41. Quoted in Fuller, *Strategy and Power*, 165.
42. Quoted in *Istoriia russkoi armii i flota*, ed. A. S. Grishinskii and V. P. Nikol'skii (Moscow: Obrazovanie, 1911), 2:153.

43. Quoted in K. Osipov, *Alexander Suvorov: A Biography*, trans. E. Bone (London: Hutchinson, 1949), 135.

44. Fuller, *Strategy and Power*, 157.

45. Quoted in Keep, *Soldiers of the Tsar*, 211.

46. J. L. H. Keep, "Soldiering in Russia," in *Transformation in Russian and Soviet Military History*, ed. C. W. Reddel (Washington, D.C.: United States Air Force Academy Office of Air Force History, 1990), 14; Keep, *Soldiers of the Tsar*, 216.

47. Fuller, *Strategy and Power*, 157.

48. P. Longworth, *The Art of Victory: The Life and Achievements of Generalissimo Suvorov, 1729–1800* (London: Constable, 1965), 238.

49. Menning, "Russian Military Innovation," 37.

50. T. C. W. Blanning, *The French Revolutionary Wars, 1787–1802* (London: Arnold, 1996), 235; Longworth, *Art of Victory*, 237.

51. See accounts in Longworth, *Art of Victory*, 251–54; official (1912) Russian account in Grishinskii and Nikol'skii, *Istoriia russkoi armii i flota*, 2:129–32; and a recent, detailed, military account in Russian: M. A. Presnukhin, *Bitva na Trebbii. Tri dnia A. V. Suvorova* (Moscow: Reittar, 2001).

52. Suvorov to S. R. Vorontsov, 19 (O.S.)/30 (N.S.) June 1799, in *Zhizn' Suvorova, rasskazannaia im samim i ego sovremennikami*, comp. V. S. Lopatin (Moscow: Terra-knizhnyi klub, 2001), 492.

53. Grishinskii and Nikol'skii, *Istoriia russkoi armii i flota*, 2:131.

54. Osipov, *Alexander Suvorov*, 149.

55. A. V. Shishov, *Generalissimus Suvorov* (Moscow: Olma Press, 2003), 351.

56. Longworth, *Art of Victory*, 250–51, 434.

57. Extract from the memoir of Iakov Starkov in *Zhizn' Suvorova*, 479.

58. Osipov, *Alexander Suvorov*, 150; Presnukhin, *Bitva na Trebbii*, 25, 112.

59. Quoted in Shishov, *Generalissimus Suvorov*, 362; Leshchinskii, "Ital'ianskii i shveitsarskii pokhody—vershina polkovedcheskogo iskusstva A. V. Suvorov," in *Suvorovskii sbornik*, 112.

60. Leshchinskii, "Ital'ianskii," 113, Tsvetaev, "Takticheskoe nasledstvo," 47.

61. Quoted in Presnukhin, *Bitva na Trebbii*, 41.

62. Longworth, *Art of Victory*, 253.

63. Leshchinskii, "Ital'ianskii," 112.

64. Beskrovnyi, "Strategiia i taktika," 46.

65. Quoted in M. Dean, *Austrian Policy during the French Revolutionary Wars, 1796–99* (PhD diss., University of Cambridge, 1988), 135.

66. Leshchinskii, "Ital'ianskii," 107.

67. Dean, *Austrian Policy*, 133.

68. Longworth, *Art of Victory*, 264; Leshchinskii, "Ital'ianskii," 104.

69. P. W. Schroeder, "The Collapse of the Second Coalition, *Journal of Modern History* 59 (1987): 249–50. See also R. E. McGrew, *Paul I of Russia, 1754–1801* (Oxford: Clarendon Press, 1992), 291–92 and

H. Ragsdale, "Russia, Prussia, and Europe in the Policy of Paul I," *Jahbücher für Geschichte Osteuropas* 31 (1983): 90–91.
70. A. B. Rodger, *The War of the Second Coalition, 1798 to 1801: A Strategic Commentary* (Oxford: Clarendon Press, 1964), 166.

CHAPTER 5

THE BRITISH ARMY

EDWARD J. COSS

During a dinner party in 1791, Edmund Burke—conservative Whig member of Parliament and vocal advocate of Britain's need to struggle against the French, their Revolution, and its related Jacobin ideals—warned Prime Minister William Pitt about the extreme peril of the Revolution as he saw it. Pitt responded in a way that exemplified the determination and the method that eventually led to success over the French: "Never fear, Mr. Burke: Depend on it, we shall go on as we are [resisting the French] until the Day of Judgment."[1]

Keen leadership, organizational changes in government and related efforts to assess and channel national funds to the armed forces, a burgeoning economy (enhanced by the first surge of the Industrial Revolution), alterations in the army administrative and tactical systems, and fortune—in many forms, including miscalculations, large and small, made by the French—allowed Britain to weather the rise of French revolutionary armies. Looking forward from any point over the final two decades of the eighteenth century, however, one would be hard pressed to find a linear correlation between the variables in this grand equation and the events that transpired; predicting, with any degree of certainty, the Albion triumph that culminated with the Battle of Waterloo was beyond the soothsaying skills of anyone on either side of the channel.

Enormous forces were at work, shaping the fundamental ways Britain prepared for and waged war. Challenges regarding revenue collection and allocation, manpower, force structure, logistics, intelligence, leadership, discipline, operations, and battlefield tactics washed like waves over the government. The infrastructure that was tasked to address these tribulations was not particularly sophisticated or functional, but it was certainly complex, a quality that created its own set of difficulties. The magnitude of the trials and the relative unpreparedness of the army and the government to meet these challenges makes the final triumph over the French that much more remarkable.

The stakes were certainly high enough. David Bell, citing army size and casualty numbers, calls this prolonged conflict between the French and the numerous coalitions "apocalyptic" and the "first total war." He offers as evidence that

> More than a fifth of all major battles fought in Europe between 1490 and 1815 took place in the twenty-five years after 1790. Before 1790, only a handful of battles had involved more than 100,000 combatants; in 1809, the battle of Wagram, the largest yet seen in the gunpowder age, involved 300,000. Four year later, the battle of Leipzig drew 500,000 with fully 150,000 of them killed or wounded. During the Napoleonic period, France alone counted close to a million deaths related to war, possibly including a higher proportion of its young men than died in World War 1.[2]

It must be noted, though, that the British army in the field (at any given place and time, excluding allies) never numbered much over 50,000 soldiers (Vitoria in 1813), making it smaller than the armies of Austria, Prussia, Russia, and the French juggernaut.[3] The army, in totality, still expanded eightfold in twenty years. This great fluctuation in army size, from the reduction to 40,000 men in 1792 to a peak of over 320,000 men (of all ranks) by 1813, acted as a catalyst for change and demanded immediate action and results from governmental mechanisms given more to conservative, often glacial, rates of transformation.[4]

The financial expenditure needed to support such an expansion was staggering: for the army, navy, and ordnance, the vast sum of £830 million was required to cover outlays during the two decades of warfare against the French, 1793–1815.[5] Expenses progressively exceeded income; by 1810, this deficit was almost £16 million. The budget gap rose to £19 million by 1811 and to £27 million the year after that. By 1811, the interest on the national debt, alone, was £35 million annually.[6] Moreover, Britain could not hope to see victory without major military efforts by and diplomatic cooperation from its continental allies—Prussia, Austria, Russia, Spain, and Portugal, among others—which Britain funded directly in order to continue its proxy war against the French. Subsidies paid to these allies over the twenty-two years of conflict amounted to nearly £66 million, a substantial figure.[7] All in, it is estimated that the wars against the

French may have cost the British three times the expense of all their wars, combined, since the Glorious Revolution of 1688.[8]

The complexity of issues facing Britain and its martial ability to combat French threats during the period in question makes identifying only a few key leaders as the primary catalysts of change problematic. In untangling the cumulative impact of scores of political and military leaders, departments, regulations, and innovations, there is a tendency to see order where there was little, oftentimes oversimplifying or misidentifying the reactants and the processes that resulted in significant change. Nevertheless, it appears that many of the reforms initiated by William Pitt (the younger, 1759–1806) during his years as prime minister (1783–1801, 1804–1806) so profoundly influenced British governmental mechanisms to finance and conduct war that to ignore his contributions is equally misguided.[9] "Honest Billy," as he was later to be called, formed a government during a time of political chaos following in the wake of the loss of the American colonies. Pitt won general elections in 1784, 1790, and 1796, the first when he was yet twenty-four years old, a notable achievement and streak of political success by any standard.

First and foremost, Pitt was noteworthy in that he had no personal agenda to profit from his office.[10] In a governmental system often troubled by sinecures, patronage, inefficiency, and corruption, Pitt's independence and forthrightness provided him both insight and freedom of action.[11] As a former chancellor of the exchequer, Pitt had expertise in finance and navigating the mainstream governmental bureaucracy with all its meandering tributaries. He blended this skill set with a discerning eye for talent. He appointed men such as Robert Stewart (Viscount Castlereagh), George Canning, Henry John Temple (Lord Palmerston), Harry Calvert, and Henry Addington, who were as industrious, earnest, and honest as himself.[12] He then allowed them the freedom to carry out reforms within their spheres of influence. By selecting and influencing key ministers throughout the government, Pitt was able to establish personal and ongoing relationships that permitted him to guide departmental affairs in ways usually beyond the direct reach of the prime minister.[13]

The numbers of bureaucrats needed to address the complex French and Napoleonic challenges mushroomed, nearly tripling the number of public servants: those needed in the various navy, army, and ordnance departments in London grew from 569 men in 1797 to almost 1,500 by the time of Waterloo. By the end of the conflict, the number of civil servants in all public offices was 24,598, with combined salaries totaling £3.2 million.[14]

Pitt's intellect, integrity, redoubtable work ethic, and dynamism—which likely led to his struggles with illness, depression, alcohol, and early demise at age forty-six, possibly due to a peptic ulcer[15]—drove the reorganization of the expanding, yet still dysfunctional, governmental machinery that inhibited Britain's capacity to face, head on, the growing menace of France. As William Hague contends, "The war [with America] had revealed that the British state was ill-equipped to deal with the growing military, political and financial complexity of major conflict."[16] The reforms of Pitt's administration (the one that ended in 1806) continued after his death and were instrumental in Britain's cathartic transformation from a nation reeling from the loss of its American colonies to a dominant power with an unmatched naval and military reputation.

Pitt's efforts to make the government accountable and efficient were many, most of which require more pages than would be justified in this analysis, so only a select few will be highlighted. First, Pitt approved and attempted to implement the conclusions of the Committee on Public Accounts, which advocated that all government workers be considered "servants of the state," answerable to the state, and, with salary increases, immune from fees and gratuities, which were previously the method by which most public business was resolved.[17] Actual transformation and modernization, as a result of this shift in perception regarding public service, took many years to complete; nevertheless, it was an important initial step. Pitt then turned his attention to reducing the national deficit and raising capital. When he began his administration, Britain had a national debt of £234 million, and, with yearly revenues of £13 million, the country was allocating £8 million just to pay off the interest on the loans.[18] In response, Pitt established a "Sinking Fund" into which £1 million (£1.2 million from 1792 on) was placed and the accrued interest allocated to lowering the loan principle; by 1792, money in arrears was trimmed to £170 million, no small achievement.[19] Pitt also cut naval debt by converting the primary debt into stocks that were then sold on the London exchange; within three years, from 1783 to 1786, the total fell from £15 million to £1.5 million. He then managed to convince Parliament to increase naval expenditures.[20] In 1789, there were about 16,000 sailors in the service of the king; by 1812, the Royal Navy provided work for over 140,000 seamen.[21]

Balancing revenues and expenditures is a difficult endeavor for any nation; in Britain, raising funds through taxation in an effort to balance the books, while at the same time allocating appropriate moneys for defense, was especially challenging since there was no hard data regarding population statistics until the population bill of 1800 resulted in the 1801 census. In the 1790s, population guesstimates for England and Wales ranged from a low of seven or eight million to a high of eleven or twelve million inhabitants.[22] Current estimates show that the population was about 8 million in 1790; the 1801 census data places the population of England and Wales at about 9.2 million people, a 15 percent increase in a decade.[23] Without such information, budget projections and allocations were tenuous and highly inexact.

Properly accounting for the money collected was a further concern that troubled Pitt. He reorganized the Treasury, redefining roles and responsibilities, reduced the generalized role of the four chief clerks (who were then to lead specific sections), created the post of assistant secretary (who was not politically appointed), and made the secretary of war accountable to the Treasury.[24] For years, payments from government offices were an expected dysfunction, while follow-up accountability was the very definition of negligence. By 1801, for example, the War Office had inspected only 460 of 9,546 supply contracts covering the period of 1798 through 1800. Slowly, though, accounts received began to bear some resemblance to expenditures.[25] One wonders whether these reforms could have been realized were it not for Pitt's personal connections and experience gained while chancellor of the exchequer.

The British capacity to build a dominating navy and a small but competent land component was reflected in the government's willingness to commit large amounts of treasury pounds to defense. In 1790, British governmental spending was £16.9 million, with £4.7 million allocated for the armed forces. By 1810, the budget had increased nearly five times to £82 million, with nearly 60 percent (£49 million/59.75 percent) apportioned to defense, a staggering expansion in just two decades.[26] None of this would have been possible without changes in taxation ushered in by Pitt's administration (and those that followed) and significant, if sporadic, national economic growth.

After the financial shock of 1797, Pitt persuaded Parliament to enact Britain's first income tax. This funding source raised £32 million in 1799 and approximately £155 million by the end of the war.[27] Even so, it was custom duties on imports and exports that filled government coffers, yielding 60 to 70 percent of government revenue. The long list of taxable articles included "beer, salt, malt, candles, leather, paper, silk, soap," etc., as well as a host of other newly taxable items available due in part to the Industrial Revolution and expanded trade routes.[28] By and large, these assessments were efficiently paid, collected, and dispersed due to the administrative changes made by Pitt, his ministers, and the small army of civil servants whose job it was to follow the money.

The connections between taxes, loans, the national debt, secure trade routes, government efficiency, and the challenge of providing adequate money to finance the endeavors of the army on the continent were not lost on Pitt and the prime ministers who followed: William Grenville (1st Lord Grenville), William Cavendish-Bentinck (3rd Duke of Portland), Spencer Perceval, and Robert Jenkinson (2nd Earl of Liverpool).[29] Neither was the essential need to grow the economy ignored.

David Landes's work on technological change in the eighteenth and twentieth centuries provides insight into the Industrial Revolution in Britain and the resulting economic growth in a great many commercial industries. He points out that in Europe, but particularly in Britain, the "spread of commercial manufacture from the towns to the countryside . . . [allowed] industry to draw on an almost unlimited supply of cheap labor . . . [producing] goods at a price that opened to it the markets of the world."[30] These rural burgs quickly grew and were assimilated by local towns. In 1751, there were only two cities with a population of 50,000 inhabitants (London and Edinburgh). By 1801, there were eight such cities; by 1851, there were twenty-nine.[31]

The dramatic shift from the "golden age of hand weaving and looming" to, as Landes phrases it, "the substitution of machines— rapid, regular, precise, tireless—for human skill and effort" over the eighteenth and nineteenth centuries transformed how work was done. This transition had a fundamental impact on the labor force that was displaced and on those who learned to run the machines, changing the social order and altering "the balance of political power, within nations, [and] between nations."[32] The early machines were not much faster than handlooms, but they were quickly improved; the mechanical advantages over handwork ranged from six to twenty-four to one for jennies and several hundred to one for frames.[33] The profit potential for these marvelous machines was enormous, especially given new markets in Asia, Africa, and the New World. The demand for cotton to feed these machines—as an indicator of capacity and profit and as a new taxation source—illustrates the growth of certain British industries. In 1760s, raw cotton imports were steady at approximately £2.5 million a year. By 1787, this total had increased almost nine times, to a yearly rate of £22 million.[34]

Other exports also soared: as an example, pig iron production, less than France's in the 1780s (68,300 long tons in 1788), grew to 258,206 long tons by 1806.[35] From the beginning of the war against the French until 1804, the total value of British exports increased by 50 percent, as did import totals.[36] Overall, according to statistician and editor John Powell, British produce and manufacture exports doubled from just under £16 million in 1793 to almost £33 million by 1815.[37] In general, industrial production in Britain was impressive and continual during this era: it grew 22.9 percent from 1800 to 1810.[38] The related increases in tax revenue, coupled with a growing population, provided the requisite capital needed for defense.

This is not to imply that economic growth in Britain was linear. There was a punctuated equilibrium aspect to industrial development, periods of stasis followed by bursts of expansion.[39] Moreover, much of the progress and profits took place in industries connected to the war effort.[40] These thrived, as has been noted in my previous work, but others stagnated:

> Copper mining and production, gun making, and shipbuilding and related dock work [prospered]. Coal mining, brick making, iron making, hardware and plate goods manufacturing, and glass making bore the brunt of curtailed trade and increased duties; these industries experienced limited growth, if any. The building industry was also depressed as a result of taxes on houses (house, window, income, and local rates) and building materials.[41]

Consecutive years of failed harvests, in 1799 and 1800, and a choking off of markets due to conflict with America combined with dramatic increases in food prices to create an unpredictable pattern of economic dislocation for a great many industries and huge swaths of society. (The British did find other markets, but it took time.) From 1797 to 1801, the cost of wheat increased 200 percent; oats rose 231 percent; and barley more than doubled in price (255 percent).[42]

Interfering with the frequency of these oscillating waves of prosperity (or at least stability) and deprivation were the demands of a growing population and the availability of foodstuffs. Agricultural production did not keep pace with population increases, the former rising 100 percent in the century from 1750 to 1850 while the latter climbed 165 percent during the same period.[43] The masses existed on cereal diets; skyrocketing bread prices, from six pence a loaf in 1797 to one shilling, five pence by 1812, created nightmarish conditions and overwhelmed communities.[44] Those at the lower end of the economic scale all too often found themselves malnourished and susceptible to disease, without much in the way of hope that their circumstances might change.

The numbers were especially stark for those in the new industrial centers in the Midlands, where machines replaced workers.[45] The demand for less expensive garments drove up profits for the industrial textile mills and their owners, but the handweaving and hand looming occupations collapsed as these skills were eclipsed by mechanization. It is here, from these same areas and occupations, that the army drew many of its recruits. The relationship between economic dislocation and enlistment appears to be beyond dispute.[46] Recruitment success was inversely proportional to economic growth and occupational opportunities. Convincing men to enlist for life was a hard sell, however. As the war wore on into the nineteenth century, even cycles of hard times, the dearth of jobs, and rising enlistment bonuses could not put enough men into the army. The increase in the daily wage for a private, from eight pence to a shilling a day in 1797, provided little incentive given the risks involved.[47]

Keeping the ranks filled was just one of the challenges facing the government and the army throughout the twenty-year struggle against the French. The army's organizational machinery presented a severe test for anyone wishing to raise, field, and sustain an army on campaign. It was a warren of convoluted structures and chains of command: some departments were independent, others shared overlapping jurisdictions and responsibilities, and all were filled with competing administrators.

The professional military posts were the commander in chief, the adjutant general, and the quartermaster general (Horse Guards). The top-level civilian roles at the War Office were secretary at war (who dealt with financial concerns) and secretary of state for war (whose concern was running the war).[48] From a practical standpoint, control of the army itself was divided between the secretary at war, the commander in chief, and the Treasury.[49] If this tripartite of power and separate channels of command were not enough, the artillery, arms, and ammunition, meanwhile, came under control of the master general of the Board of Ordnance. Pay fell to the paymaster general, while clothing and equipment were governed by the adjutant general. Movement of troops to foreign theaters of operation fell to the Transport Board. Moreover, the commissariat was a subdepartment of the Treasury, commanded by a commissary general.[50] Adding to these strata was the position of home secretary, whose responsibilities under George III put him in charge of raising the militia.[51] Disagreements were inevitable.

It should be noted that the commander in chief and his subordinates were expected to carry out the policies of the civilian government, not create strategic policy.[52] Nevertheless, the commander in chief was able to exert some power (especially in emergency defense of Britain), guiding and reining in cabinet proposals; the more details he had in hand related to troop strength and unit effectiveness, the more control he wielded. He was accountable for training, officer promotion, and placement of officers in the field. Make no mistake, though—decision making was almost always left to the two secretaries and, sometimes, to royal intercession (the king being the titular head of the army). The commander in chief had no authority over troops dispatched to foreign lands.[53] The system worked, if only barely.

Such a multilayered organization necessitated proactive men of talent who were willing to work within the bureaucracy, or even attempt to change it. Prince Frederick, the Duke of York (the second son of George III), was a professional soldier, trained by the Prussians in the 1780s, and, as the king's son, was rapidly elevated through the ranks in the kind of swift army promotion that he would later try to minimize.[54] He was appointed commander in chief of the army in 1795 at the age of thirty-two, after his return as the general in charge of British troops in the difficult two-year Flanders campaign, which ended with the evacuation of British forces in the spring of 1795.[55] This joint endeavor with the Dutch, Prussians, Austrians, and Hanoverians against the post–levée en masse French Republic was plagued by significant supply, command, coordination, training, unit cohesion, and civilian interference issues (by Henry Dundas back in London).[56] The second British brigade sent to Flanders, manned by new recruits, was labeled by Calvert as "totally unfit for service."[57] The campaign was an embarrassing and overwhelming defeat for the allies, one that had resounding consequences for each nation. For the British, the ineffectiveness of the army and the resulting 20,000 British casualties illustrated that the army was, without question, unable to deal with either the French army or the exigencies of campaign.[58] Despite the damage to his reputation as a result of this operation, York, as commander in chief, immediately began to address the failings of the army.

Described by Colonel Henry Bunbury, who served under him as an undersecretary at the War Office, as "indefatigable, energetic, and just," York recognized that radical change in the multi-headed, hydra-like machinery of Horse Guards and the War Office was a practical impossibility and, quite possibly, a political liability.[59] Instead, drawing on his experiences in Flanders and his natural gifts as a bureaucrat, York utilized his position and political clout to work within the existing structures, initiating a series of crucial reforms that positively influenced both the manner in which the army was led, organized, and trained and the fashion in which it functioned on the battlefield. This transformative effort was sorely needed because for more than the first decade of the war against revolutionary France, the British army was the least competent and least feared of all the armed forces allied against the French.[60]

York established service requirements (two years for subalterns seeking promotion to captain, and an additional six years for elevation to major), set the minimum age for ensigns at sixteen, created a system of confidential officer evaluation reports, and required letters of recommendation in an effort to mitigate the problems engendered by the promotion system.[61] These changes applied to the infantry and cavalry branches; the Board of Ordnance promoted strictly on seniority.[62] In addition, York supported the ideas of then Lieutenant Colonel John Le Marchant and helped establish a training school for subalterns, at High Wycombe, in 1799; this became the Royal Military College in 1801 (later moved to Sandhurst in 1812).[63] The training school included a staff college, the Senior Department, for training commanders and senior officers.[64] The artillery and engineering branches already had the Royal Military Academy, at Woolwich, founded in 1741.

Moreover, York instituted standards, procedures, and chains of command in an attempt to manage the complex organizational structures of the armed services, previously described.[65] He also helped the ordnance board secure a near monopoly regarding the purchase of small arms and artillery, nearly eliminating the free trade arrangement of manufacturers that often squeezed the government out of the procurement loop.[66] The concept of a government factory was proposed in 1794 and finally was initiated in 1804 with an assembly line at the Tower of London.

This measure was but the first surge of changes that altered how the army functioned. Another series of initiatives, in many ways even more transformative, modified the systems by which the army and national defense forces were established and manned. The final version emerged, however, only after several and substantial missteps. An auxiliary force was reestablished in 1802, with the passing of the Militia Acts.[67] Men, aged eighteen through forty-five, divided into classes based on the number of dependents, were conscripted for home defense; they were selected by a series of ballots in each parish and expected to be mustered for training, from time to time, and to serve as part of ongoing militia regiments meant to protect the parishes in which they were raised, though not exclusively.[68] The men were not compelled to serve beyond Great Britain's borders, and they were exempt from the ballot for the army of the reserve (discussed below). These units were supposed to be held to the same standards and discipline as the regular army; usually, however, stiff fines or incarceration, even for desertion, sufficed as penalties for misbehavior.[69]

The system, and purpose behind it, began to disintegrate almost immediately, as a man was allowed to avoid service by paying a surrogate to go in his place. Bounties generally fetched a replacement volunteer around £16 to £20.[70] This bonus was equal to half a year's wages for an unskilled laborer, which made the militia attractive to men who had fallen on hard times.[71] In practice, the numbers of proxy soldiers overwhelmed the quantities of balloted men by more than a seven-to-one ratio (22,946 substitutes to 3,129 principals), the data coming from a return after the levy was completed in 1808.[72] In Middlesex, the 4,500-man quota was filled with 4,499 substitutes and one originally drafted man. The lord lieutenant begged to keep the man because this made him such a curiosity.[73] Substitutes were not required to come from the parishes in which the militia unit was being raised; this negated, almost entirely, the local focus of the Militia Acts. The situation was the same in Scotland, where the militia draft was generally despised because signing on was erroneously believed to be linked to life service. In Bute, when the final quota was entered into the books, it was discovered that only five men came from the parish and not a single balloted man signed on.[74]

A secondary, but hugely important, corollary to this practice of militia substitution was the bounty cost, which was equal to or often higher than that offered for service in the army. The men who volunteered as militia substitutes were the same men who would have enlisted in the army had the bounty for militia service not been higher; joining the militia also allowed the men to serve at home.[75] Thus, the government unintentionally hindered recruitment for the very force the regular militia was designed to support. This self-inflicted shortcoming was in spite of Parliament passing an act in 1799 allowing men in the militia to transfer directly into the army, each volunteer earning an additional £10 bounty.[76] A provision prohibited these enlistees from serving anywhere but continental Europe. This stipulation was intended to increase the efficacy of this piece of manpower legislation; the extreme dread of being sent to the West Indies stopped many men from enlisting. Seized by the British in 1793 as a response to rebellions by locals (free and enslaved) driven by the spreading ideals of revolutionary France, this Caribbean region cost the British over 400,000 casualties during the course of the French wars, mostly due to disease (both infectious and mosquito-borne).[77]

The number of militiamen who joined the colors, taking advantage of the 1799 provision and the additional bounty, is estimated as being around ten thousand enlistees a year, which was the required level as set forth in the acts.[78] Many of the men who seized this opportunity in 1799 and 1800 also volunteered to serve in Egypt, which they were not obligated to do. Because they did so, this cadre of men was considered by Sir Ralph Abercromby to be a cut above regular recruits.[79]

The second governmental design to fashion a multilayered defense was the creation of the British Volunteer Corps, originated in 1794 as a reaction to the unrest in France. (The allied Provisional Cavalry Act was enacted two years later.) Raised locally, part-time participants were intended to be a regional, static defense force, meant to repress local radicalism and pro-revolutionary fervor and to act as coastal or internal security, as needed; if all else failed, the Volunteers Corps could operate as pockets of resistance should the French attempt to occupy Great Britain.[80] A by-product of counter-revolutionary zeal, the system raised over 100,000 men by 1801.[81] Led mostly by men of property, the enlisted ranks included many impoverished souls, eager to accept compensation for drill time.[82] Service was not compulsory, though, meaning a man could resign at any time; discipline suffered accordingly. Members were enticed with waivers, making them exempt from the militia ballot, a not insignificant attraction for any man wishing to avoid service of greater duration, possibly father away from home.[83] Within a few years, the number of men serving in the corps throughout the country was approximately 340,000, with recruits coming from much wider ranges of the social and economic spectrums than had previously been the case.[84] The sheer numbers of volunteers overwhelmed the government, though, which had neither the weapons to distribute nor a functional bureaucracy specifically tasked to organize the men properly. This haphazard system allowed Britain to give itself the illusion of security while at the same time avoiding the political and financial costs of full-scale mass conscription.[85]

Yet a further effort was made to give men a taste of army life and, thus, encourage them to transfer into line regiments. In 1802, Addington, as prime minister, pushed through legislation intended to draft men into an "army of the reserve," thereby creating fifty second battalions for existing regular army regiments. The act required that 34,000 men be raised in England—10,000 in Ireland and an additional 6,000 in Scotland.[86] These balloted men were not expected to serve outside Great Britain. This act put the reserve in direct competition for manpower with the militia, the regulars, and even the volunteers, which doomed it from the start. Drafted men scrambled, often unsuccessfully, to find substitutes who had not already been rejected by army physicians. The cost to find a stand-in soared to as high as £100.[87] Rising desertion rates, bounty jumping, and public disinterest made making monthly quotas impossible. Despite every enticement and effort, including the use of crimps (individuals of questionable characters and methods who shanghaied men by any means and presented them for the bounty), by the end of 1803 only 40,897 of the required 50,000 men could be found. Of these men, 4,278 promptly deserted, 1,301 men were found physically wanting, and 286 died after having their names inscribed in the lists; this left

35,032 men, a total that fell 30 percent short of quota. An additional 5,000 draftees turned out to be boys too young to serve.[88] Deemed unsustainable, the concept of a yearly draft was abandoned by the spring of 1804.[89] (The second battalions that were raised remained extant.)

All these changes, ushered in by Pitt, York, Addington (prime minister from 1801 to 1804), and later Castlereagh—the secretary of state for war (1805–1806 and, again, 1807–1809), characterized as "the ablest man that ever controlled the war office"—were an attempt to formalize and rearrange the army manpower system into a standing army (regulars), a local defense contingent (militia), a loosely coordinated security force (the volunteers), and, for a time, the army of the reserve.[90] These competing reforms were desperate measures intended to give the nation better access to the men it needed to fend off the threat of potential French domination, at home and on the continent.[91] These cumulative alterations, which have been described as "one of the greatest internal overhauls in its [the army's] history," sculpted the army for a long-term conflict against the French.[92]

The army of the reserve act, despite its failure to fill the ranks, had a major, if unintentional, impact on British army culture. In times of war, the government usually supplemented army numbers by raising new regiments and converting the few existing second battalions into newly numbered units. The negative effects this had on regimental association, pride, and cohesion were significant. The reserve act transformed this process, creating the fifty second battalions around a regimental construct, with one battalion readily deployable and the second acting as a core administrative, recruiting, and training entity (while offering a measure of home defense).[93] The system, much of which evolved during Castlereagh's time as secretary of state for war, had profound consequences: it altered the dynamic by which the army did business for the next century. It also transformed, for vast numbers of soldiers and for regiments, as a whole, how they perceived their affiliation with the army. Unit continuity allowed men to become comrades connected to particular regiments, with their histories, traditions, and norms. These changes, in regard to unit effectiveness and as combat multipliers on the battlefield, took time to bear fruit: the British army that took the field in Spain and Portugal against Napoleon had its genesis here, with the reforms of the late 1790s and early 1800s.

The growth of a regimental culture had a deep and meaningful effect on the army: recruiting became regimentally based; the regiment gained the capacity to exchange soldiers between the battalion sent abroad and the one(s) remaining at home, thus controlling not only the regiment's manpower numbers but also its quality; the flexibility of the system allowed for prolonged deployments even as "strategic consumption" threatened the ability of Horse Guards and the War Office to keep a viable army in the field; regimental identities were established, creating an esprit de corps that acted to tie the soldier to his battalion, affecting behaviors during times of hardship and combat. The esprit and continuity within the regiment improved unit effectiveness as standards were established and continually reinforced, the officers and enlisted men learning to trust one another over time. The resulting regimental variations that arose permitted commanders to differentiate between units, utilizing the most operationally and tactically proficient regiments as campaign demands required.[94] The professional ethos that resulted became one of the key cornerstones of British achievement in the peninsula, a direct and indirect outcome of twenty years of trial-and-error reforms.[95]

All this brings us to British tactical developments, which evolved out of battlefield experiences in the Seven Years' War (1756–63) and the war of the American Revolution (1775–83). The basic building block of the British army of the 1790s remained, as it had been for the entirety of the eighteenth century, the infantry regiment, which consisted, by and large, of one battalion. Such a unit was typically made up of eight line companies, as well as one light infantry and one grenadier company; the average battalion company was composed of three officers, two drummers, and between sixty and seventy non-commissioned officers and privates. There was almost always a difference, however, in the paper strength of these companies compared to actual numbers, due to the recruiting limitations already discussed. The 1803 army of the reserve regulation permitted the raising of a second battalion, theoretically increasing the strength of a regiment to one thousand enlisted rankers, requiring over forty officers.[96] The authorized movement of men from the home battalion to the deployed battalion allowed the latter to maintain its strength while on campaign. The establishment of second battalions was not entirely new, however. It was done on several occasions during the Seven Years' War and the American Revolution.[97]

The army's experiences in North America during both the Seven Years' War, often referred to within the colonies as the French and Indian War, and the American Revolution were particularly formative for the infantry, even if the limitations of the government and the military sometimes prevented lessons learned from having an immediate effect. Soldiers in America fighting the French during 1750s and 1760s were challenged by every type of geographical feature—from open fields to rocky, dense woods—that demanded conventional and irregular approaches to tactical problems, resulting in what has been termed "bush fighting."[98] Lieutenant Colonel Thomas Gage, then of the 44th Foot, raised the first official unit expected to act in this manner, writ large, with his 80th Regiment of Light Armed Foot in 1758.[99] The unit and its experiences acted as a catalyst, and light company experimentation was under way. This methodology was developed further during the years that followed, as the British infantry focused on open-order and quick, decisive movements in response to the topographical challenges inherent to fighting in colonial North America.[100] An instruction issued by Major General Phillips to John Burgoyne's army in 1777 represents an official expression of the high degree of tactical freedom apportioned to and expected from individual companies in America: "Every company may form a body singly, and though attached to its place in the battalion, yet always ready to act separate from it, as the nature of the ground may acquire, or the nature of local service they may be sent on make necessary."[101]

The techniques that grew out of the American experience were ad hoc alterations that were later institutionalized into the army's *Regulations for the Exercise of Riflemen and Light Infantry* in 1803.[102] Select foot regiments—the 43rd, 52nd, 68th, 71st, 85th, 90th, and a battalion of the 60th—were converted to light infantry regiments following the creation, in 1800, of an experimental light infantry regiment dressed in green. This unit, the 95th "Experimental Corps of Riflemen," was officially absorbed into the army the same year the manual was published.[103] The year 1803 also saw the creation of a light infantry division, under Sir John Moore's guidance, incorporating the 43rd, the 52nd, and the 95th. Light units learned to scout, screen, and (in pairs) hunt officers and NCOs during battle. In 1800, Ezekiel Baker produced the army's first rifle; it had seven grooves, a 30-inch barrel, and fired a .653 round accurately out to two hundred yards, double the effective distance of muskets (which lacked sights and were inaccurate at distances approaching one hundred yards).[104] This became the weapon of choice for the 95th Foot.

In the aftermath of the American Revolution, the loss of its American colonies being far more a British strategic failing than a tactical one, a series of training regulations was issued to both the infantry and cavalry of the British army as the military attempted to absorb lessons from the conflict while at the same time trying to anticipate tactical challenges posed by new European threats and plummeting budgets. The steady, decade-long reduction of the army, to a low of 40,000 soldiers by 1792, made training and doctrine revisions a lesser priority in the years following the Treaty of Paris (1783), as defense expenditures plunged from £18.6 million in 1782 to low of £3.8 million in 1787.[105]

When Colonel Sir David Dundas published his manual, *Principles of Military Movements: Chiefly Applied to Infantry* in 1788, the defense budget had inched up to a still paltry £4.4 million.[106] Dundas, who attended Prussian army maneuvers in 1785 alongside the Duke of York, was a strong believer in traditional Prussian tactics. He found little wanting in the way Frederick the Great's army approached battlefield challenges; using Prussian methods as a foundation, Dundas compiled what he believed were the essentials of tactical procedures, based on eighteen maneuvers and the three-rank line. His work was both a condemnation of the irregularity of drill in the British military and a laying bare of perceived tactical weaknesses. Prior to 1784, British battalions in Europe were utilizing different drill manuals and regulations than those in America, in part the result of variations in topography, battalion experience, officer competence, and allowed freedom of action. Open-order infantry tactics in the colonies worked well on battlefields intersected by terrain features (woods, streams, etc., as well as abrupt changes in elevations) against an enemy that had little in the way of European-style cavalry and limited avenues of fire for its artillery. Battalions remaining in Europe, however, utilized the time-honored practices of Frederick the Great and the Prussian military: strict, close-order lines, relying heavily on a combination of massed volleys and bayonet charges, preparing to traverse slowly across large, open battlefields, and facing large numbers of infantry, mounted troops, and massed artillery.

Dundas's work adopted the linear Prussian and European interpretation of the battlefield.[107] His maneuvers and drills, however, were not without their critics. His system revolved around the three-rank line, despite battalion experiences in America fighting in two-ranks as early as 1771–72, and it marginalized open-order techniques.[108] The two-rank line became the official formation in 1801, Dundas's theories notwithstanding, due to the firepower, spacing, and shock advantages it offered compared to the three-rank version (all ranks being able to engage the enemy). In addition, his eighteen maneuvers were a bit convoluted and not always practicable given the realities of the battlefield; they sometimes appear to focus far more on movement rather than on the act of engaging the enemy (combat).[109] Dundas, who later served as commander in chief from 1809 to 1811, earned his nickname "Old Pivot" due to the numerous turns required to carry out his tactical schemes. The British setbacks in Flanders at the hands of French light troops led, over time, to the blending of Dundas's regulations, to some extent, with the light infantry, open-order tactics of the American war.[110] Calvert's eventual rise to adjutant general of the army allowed him to influence the army in the years 1799–1805, helping to solidify light infantry and rifle tactics within British doctrine.[111] Despite these limitations and evolutionary spasms, in addition to opposition from veterans of the wars in American (such as Lieutenant General Charles Cornwallis and Calvert), there was much merit in the collective regulation of the infantry initiated by Dundas's manual.[112] Bunbury, later the Duke of York's undersecretary, was scornful of the army's state of readiness as late as 1793; his comments make clear why he felt that Dundas's manual of drill was necessary:

> Our army was lax in discipline [and] entirely without a system, and very weak in numbers. Each colonel of a regiment managed it according to his own notions, or neglected it altogether. There was no uniformity of drill or movement; professional pride was rare; professional knowledge still more so. Never was a kingdom less prepared for a stern and arduous conflict.[113]

Dundas's work was warmly received by York and officially sanctioned by Horse Guards, his instructions becoming the authoritative guide for British infantry (1792).[114] His regulations, in fact, became the foundation of tactical drill for British infantrymen for nearly the next sixty years, though often remodeled.[115] The value of his contribution, even considering its shortcomings, cannot be overemphasized, for when the British army faced and defeated the French in the Egyptian campaign (1801), the ranks fought in Dundas's elbow-to-elbow formations.[116]

An additional, and critical, development within the British army during the latter half of the eighteenth century shaped how the infantry fought, the emphasis placed on the volley-and-charge tactical method. Though Dundas's regulations were largely modeled on Prussian techniques that favored high and sustained rates of firepower, the fusion of such actions with skills and traits learned in North America led to a tactical theory based on short-range, destructive volleys of fire, followed by immediate bayonet charges.[117] Such a technique had its antecedents both on the continent and in the Americas, as shortcomings of the Brown Bess musket, related to both range and accuracy, mandated the need for a definitive method for closing with an enemy and putting them to flight.[118] British infantrymen who fought in North America during the Revolution became accustomed to such an assault. This evolved to be the preferred tactical practice for British regulars, one that carried into and through the Peninsular War, for it best accounted for firearm limitations while, at the same time, providing the best system for managing and making use of soldier fear. There are any number of battlefield accounts during the French wars describing British fondness regarding the use of cold steel.[119] The lore of the British "three rounds a minute" solution to tactical engagements turns out to be more fallacy than fact.[120] It was the resolve of the British redcoat and the efficacy of the close-range volley-and-charge technique that, more often than not, won the field. It was, perhaps, strikingly intuitive that British military officers and administrators realized that new developments in Europe, resulting from the French Revolution, meant that Dundas's theories and reliance on large, traditional Prussian-style formations and firepower required amending to reflect battlefield realities. This was in spite of the Duke of York's original directive that the Dundas regulations be "strictly followed . . . without any deviation whatsoever."[121]

While the British army was unquestionable infantry-centric, the cavalry and artillery branches also merit investigation. A typical regiment of cavalry was made up of four squadrons, each of which fielded two troops of eighty men; thus, a full unit would, at least on paper, consist of over six hundred men.[122] The British cavalry was composed of both heavy regiments (dragoons or dragoon guards) and light regiments, such as hussars. Thus, analysis is much influenced by definition (type) and stated purpose. There was little difference in training or intent, though, between shock cavalry, dragoons, and hussars during the 1790s as the cavalry was erratic and, according to one historian, "in as hopeless state of chaos as that of the infantry and with consequences yet more depressing."[123] As with the infantry, there was no standardized training; the greatest assets of this branch, its speed and ability to deliver shock attacks over large areas of the battlefield, thus became its greatest liabilities. Once initiated, a charge moved quickly beyond the command and control of both the officer who launched it and the one who led it. Without a common methodology and the delineation of roles, the value of the various cavalry units was diminished greatly.

Drawing on his experiences as commanding officer of dragoons in the Seven Years' War, as well as the painful lessons experienced in Flanders, Dundas composed a companion field manual to his infantry treatise: *Rules and Regulations for Cavalry*. These 1796 regulations attempted to establish uniform administrative reforms, as well as tactical evolutions, for the mounted arm of the British army. Unfortunately, like his infantry rules, they had serious shortcomings. His regulations did not differentiate between the three types of cavalry; his training treated them as one entity. Additionally, his concepts lacked practicality in battle, again being unduly complicated. As late as 1827, they were criticized by a German officer, who questioned the "complicated manoeuvers . . . which like Chinese puzzles, only engross time and labor to the undesirable end of forming *useless combinations*."[124] Nevertheless, Dundas's work provided a baseline for training and offered the hope of some general uniformity of method. It was complimented in 1796 by the issuance of the *Rules and Regulations for the Sword Exercise of the Cavalry*, a manual of swordsmanship for cavalryman compiled by then Major John Le Marchant of the 16th Light Dragoons, who also helped design a new cavalry saber.[125] This volume was a detailed guide to improving the combat swordsmanship of the cavalry trooper. An additional revised manual for cavalry, *Instructions and Regulations for the Formations and Movements of the Cavalry*, was issued in 1799 and again in 1808. Despite these attempts at homogeneity, the cavalry remained a problem (to control) in battle throughout the years of the French wars. It was, perhaps, fortunate that most of the cavalry units remained on home station in the decade following the Flanders campaign.[126] On the other hand, this circumstance likely robbed the branch of the kind of knowledge indispensable to melding innovation based on experience with the core competencies outlined in manuals.

Given the plethora of challenges facing leaders, and the speed at which shortcomings threatened to overwhelm British national defense, it is understandable that one branch might be ignored, or even misunderstood. The artillery, under the Board of Ordnance, was the most specialized of all the services; the required technological proficiency—dealing with range tables, fuse lengths, weather, distance estimations, all with non-standardized ordnance—created a complexity that often confounded civil and military leadership.[127] Ammunition consisted of round, grape, exploding shrapnel, and canister, the choice of which depended on battlefield exigencies. Artillerymen and officers required extensive training and could not be thrown into a campaign and expected to learn their jobs in the field, as was often the case with infantry and cavalry. Proficiency in this branch, more than any other, required time, something politicians, bureaucrats, or even field commanders often failed to grasp fully.[128] This was especially true given cycles of reduction and, as inevitably happened, follow-on call-ups. After the Peace of Amiens, the Royal Artillery was cut by 37 percent, from around 5,300 men of all ranks to a bit less than 3,340 gunners; this talent and experience deficit was not easily made up when the "Great French War" recommenced a year later.[129] Unlike the infantry and cavalry, which had no selection processes, the artillery branch relied on a policy of merit-based admissions to the Royal Military Academy at Woolwich; promotion, thereafter, was through seniority. The strength of this system was its reliance on expertise; its weakness was that it produced a senior officer corps that was often too old to serve on campaign. The average number of years in service for a lieutenant colonel in the artillery branch was twenty-four years.[130]

Foot artillery was divided into light cannons (3-, 6-, and 9-pound pieces, as well as a 5.5-inch howitzer), heavy guns (12-, 18-, and 24-pounders, and large howitzers), and mortars.[131] Through 1795, however, artillery was deployed in two-gun sections, directly attached to infantry battalions. These guns were mostly 3- and 6-pounders, the lightweight pieces being hand-prolonged by small contingents of gunners and soldiers.[132] This experiment in combined arms support failed to take advantage of the potential of massed fires.

Charles Lennox, the 3rd Duke of Richmond, Pitt's master general of ordnance from 1784 to 1795, helped initiate several important reforms during his time in office. He established a committee in 1788 to ascertain the best way to implement mobile artillery. This led, in 1793, to the creation of the Royal Horse Artillery.[133] The intent of this artillery subset was to support cavalry and infantry units on the move. A year later, the Royal Corps of Artillery Drivers came into being, supplanting civilian drivers and their teams.[134] Some historians have conjectured that it would have been far more effective from organizational, training, and command perspectives to integrate the artillery with its drivers (rather than having separate corps), a fair appraisal of this half measure.[135]

These modifications, while improving the performance of the artillery, never caused the branch to attain the level of tactical importance established by the French, particularly under Napoleon. The British failed to field sufficient numbers of weapons, and maintaining adequate quantities of horses to pull gun carriages proved an ongoing problem on campaign. Moreover, French fire rates were faster and ranges longer, the latter due to British guns being constructed to take a charge that was 10 percent lighter than French artillery pieces.[136] The result was that the British army leaned more heavily on its infantry than any other branch.

Perhaps the best, and most immediate, example of the synthesis of old and new tactical ideas, illustrating the inestimable, and often unintended, results of vast governmental and military reforms, is the Egyptian campaign of 1801. Coming only a half dozen years after the woefully inadequate performance of the British army in Flanders, the skills and discipline exhibited by the armed services, the infantry in particular, were more than promising. The British were fortunate, however, that French incompetence allowed the redcoats a greater margin of error than had usually been the case when fighting an army trained by Napoleon; this permitted the British army to gain much-needed experience and the time to assimilate lessons of the battlefield.

The British expeditionary force under General Ralph Abercromby landed near Aboukir Bay, on the Mediterranean coast of Egypt on 8 March 1801 in an effort to drive the remaining soldiers of Napoleon's abandoned Armée d'Orient out of the country, the emperor having returned to France in 1799. Poor intelligence and a certain degree of confirmation bias led the British to overestimate their own prowess and the available support of the Turkish army under Kapitan Pasha, while underestimating the strength of the French forces under General Jacques-François de Menou.[137] These misperceptions, however, were more than offset by French confusion and tactical reluctance.

Napoleon, believing that French possession of Egypt was vital to peace negotiations with the British, issued a proclamation to the Armée d'Orient regarding the anticipated British-Turkish assault: "Every man who disembarks must be killed or captured; the desert of Qatyeh must become the tomb of the grand vizier."[138] Menou declared that he would defend Egypt to the last man, yet he dallied, left half his available force in Cairo, and then spurned an offer of assistance from the Mamluk chieftain Murad Bey.[139] Menou's adoption of the Muslim faith put a barrier between him and his divisional officers; he favored officers who followed the teachings of Muhammed, which created unnecessary feuds among the men and affected discipline.[140] Adding to this command challenge was Menou's disregard of the British army, on the whole, and the fighting spirit of the redcoat, in particular.[141] Despite ample warning of the pending British landings, Menou's disdain led him into blunders of overconfidence: he neither reinforced existing fortifications nor built new defenses; he did not even bother to have the local forts fully supplied.[142]

Sir John Moore, leading the reserves (the 40th, 23rd, 28th, and 42nd Foot Regiments, as well as the Corsican Rangers, Hompesch Hussars, and the 11th Dragoons), was in the British flotilla as it slowly rowed to the beachhead. The approximately 5,500 British regulars landed in small, flat-bottom boats under an intense artillery bombardment, suffering severe casualties. Moore's description of this phase of the assault and the destructive effects of fire on both men and boats from fifteen French artillery pieces is almost clinical in nature, in some ways revealing the professional eye with which Moore observed the unfolding events.[143] What he captured next illustrates the discipline of the rank and file and the growing competence of leadership:

> As soon as the boats touched the land and the officers and men
> sprang out, formed on the beach, and landed. I then ascended the
> sandhill with the Grenadiers and Light Infantry of the 40th, 23rd,
> and 28th Regiments in Line. They never offered to fire until they

had gained the summit, where they charged the French, drove them, and took four pieces of artillery. . . . Brigadier-General Oakes with the 43rd, 58th Regiments, and the Corsican Rangers, which composed the left of the reserve, landed to the left of the sandhill. They found the enemy ready to receive them. They formed expeditiously, were attacked by both infantry and cavalry, both of which they repulsed, and they also followed them into the plain, taking three pieces of artillery. The Guards, who should have been upon the left of the reserve . . . got into confusion on landing and were at first in the rear of the 42nd and 58th; but as these regiments advanced, the others fell into their place on the left. . . . They [the French] made good their retreat, though with considerable loss.[144]

Moore sanguinely acknowledged the two factors aligned against the British: the enemy had eight days to prepare, and the ground was bad and suited for defense. Nevertheless, he commented, "Our attempt was daring, and executed by troops with the greatest intrepidity and coolness."[145] The rankers fought with zeal and self-control, sweeping the two thousand French defenders under General Louis Friant off the crest with a determined bayonet charge.[146]

While French mistakes certainly worked in favor of the redcoats, the capacity of leadership to coordinate and execute an amphibious attack under these conditions, adapting to the confusion while fighting uphill through the sand, demonstrates the progress the army had made since the Flanders campaign only six years past. British losses were estimated at a little over seven hundred men, including sailors, while the French suffered three hundred to four hundred casualties.[147] Waxing poetic, one historian called the landing and assault "perhaps the most skillful and daring operation of its kind that was ever attempted."[148]

This was but the first leg of the Egyptian campaign. Two weeks later, on 21 March, Abercromby led the full contingent of about 14,000 British regulars, well supported by artillery, against about 18,000 French infantry, 1,500 cavalry, and almost fifty cannon in what became known as the Battle of Canope (Alexandria). In chaotic night-fighting, the redcoats under Moore repulsed a series of French attacks with devastating, short-range volleys followed up with cold steel.[149] The acumen shown by the 28th Foot—which when attacked from both front and rear, pivoted the rear rank, volleyed at close range, then turned to face the front again—would have made Dundas proud.[150] The 42nd Highlanders performed a similar pivot under orders from Moore and helped the 28th drive off a French column.[151] The French attempted to organize one more assault, but could not muster enough men for the attack. Moore, with justifiable pride, observed that "had their infantry again advanced we have must have repelled them with the bayonet. Our fellows would have done it; I never saw men more determined to do their duty."[152] Thus began the restoration of the British army's reputation.

Moore provided a succinct description of the battlefield: "I never saw a field so strewed with dead."[153] Casualties for the French reached approximately 4,000 soldiers, with well over 1,000 dead; the British lost about 1,500 men, wounded and killed, including Abercromby (who took a shot in the thigh and likely expired because of infection).[154] Moore, who received a musket ball in the leg early in the battle, and three other generals were wounded. François Lanusse, who lost a leg to grapeshot, was one of two French generals to die that day. His supposed last words to Menou were "to the effect that Menou was not fit to be an onion peeler in the kitchen of the Republic."[155]

The meaning of the British victory in Egypt, the first such tactical and operational triumph over the French in thirty years, was not lost on Napoleon. Reflecting back after his final defeat at Waterloo, he opined to Emmanuel-Augustin-Dieudonné-Joseph, comte de Las Casas, "If instead of the expedition to Egypt, I had undertaken that against Ireland, what would England be today? . . . What would the continent be [like]? [What] of world politics?"[156]

The British display of discipline might rightly be seen as proof of the efficacy of Dundas's regulations.[157] Yet what is sometimes overlooked is that most of the British brigade commanders, notably Generals Sir John Moore and Eyre Coote, were experienced veterans of the American (1775–83) and Caribbean (1790s) campaigns. Coote served throughout the American Revolution, fighting under Cornwallis at Green Spring and Yorktown and, like Moore, was experienced in amphibious landings.[158] Therefore, it might be fair to argue that Egypt was an example of the successful combination of skirmish tactics with the kind of maneuver and firepower advocated by Dundas (followed by rushes with the bayonet); the combat effectiveness of the redcoat in Egypt was the result of an amalgamation of the American and Prussian tactical styles.[159]

Before concluding this analysis of British combat experimentation and transformation, the operational debt the British army owed to the navy must be acknowledged. Britain's control of the seas was paramount; without it, no victory over the French would have been remotely possible. What it accomplished, just logistically, for the army over the many years of war against the French—in the retreat after the defeat in Flanders; the delivery, supply, and extraction of the British expeditionary force sent to Egypt; and the long-term support of the army in Spain and Portugal—was majestic in scope. The navy provided the strategic reach that Pitt envisioned a long twenty years before. Governmental expenditures on the navy rose continuously throughout the late eighteenth and early nineteenth centuries, peaking at just over £20 million in 1813.[160]

The British army of the French revolutionary period can best be described as a service in transition, with its governmental and administrative mechanisms in a state of flux. Dedicated and insightful leaders, beginning with Pitt, but including scores of other talented civil servants and officers, directed the labyrinthian bureaucracies that governed the nation's collection and allocation of funds, logistical procurement and dispersal, and the size and readiness of the armed forces. Empowered by the monies generated through the irregular, but sometimes spectacular, spurts of mechanization that constituted advances during the Industrial Revolution, Britain fought against the French for twenty-two years (1793–1815), the conflict interrupted only briefly by the Peace of Amiens (1802). It was the sole nation to stand as part of every alliance against republican and Napoleonic France, including the seventh coalition, which eventually brought about Napoleon's demise. By the turn of the nineteenth century, the British army was better prepared, by far, for the French wars than it had been ten years earlier. The nation's continued successes were bound to the planned, and often unintended, consequences of army reform.[161]

The ensuing British triumphs over the French in the many years of war that followed were observed, no doubt with a bit of antipathy, by Swiss theorist and sometime French staff officer Antoine-Henri Jomini, who identified the Egyptian campaign as the turning point and this period of British military resurgence as, *"l'époque de sa régénération."*[162] The evolution of the British army, from an incapable force in 1795 to a proficient and dangerous instrument in Egypt and later in Spain and Portugal (in the hands of Wellington), was a genuine, if unpredictable, metamorphosis.

Notes

1. Roger Knight, *Britain against Napoleon: The Organization of Victory, 1793–1815* (New York: Allen Lane, 2014), 386.
2. David Bell, *The First Total War: Napoleon's Europe and the Birth of Warfare as We Know It* (New York: Houghton Mifflin, 2007), 7. Bell's casualty numbers for Leipzig appear to be high. David Chandler puts the total at 129,000, but notes that such figures "are extremely hard to calculate." David Chandler, *The Campaigns of Napoleon* (New York: Macmillan, 1966), 936. In total, it is estimated that the British army lost approximately 225,000 soldiers on the continent over the years 1803–14, when the army averaged about 144,000 regulars (worldwide) and the navy, 64,000 sailors. That is a higher casualty rate, comparing fatalities to numbers serving, than that of the Great War. Rory Muir, *Britain and the Defeat of Napoleon, 1807–1815* (New Haven, Conn.: Yale University Press, 1996), 14. These numbers do not include men lost in the West Indies. Patrick O'Brien estimates that the armed services included somewhere between 11 to 14 percent of the male population of Britain, ages fifteen to forty. Patrick O'Brien, "The Impact of the Revolutionary and Napoleonic Wars, 1793–1815, on the Long-Run Growth of the British Economy," *Fernand Braudel Center for the Study of Economies, Historical Systems, and Civilizations* 12, no. 3 (1989): 335–95.
3. Stephen Conway, "The Eighteenth-Century British Army as a European Institution," in *British Soldiers: Rethinking War and Society, 1715–1815*, ed. Kevin Linch and Matthew McCormack (Liverpool: Liverpool University Press, 2014), 19. It is interesting to note that Prussia, with a smaller population than Britain and Ireland, put a larger army in the field. The Vitoria information is from "The Battle of Vitoria," BritishBattles.com, accessed September 6, 2014, http://www.british-battles.com/peninsula/peninsula-vitoria.htm. Rory Muir lists the British army at 52,000 men for Vitoria. Muir, *Britain and the Defeat of Napoleon*, 15.
4. Linch and McCormack offer 250,000 soldiers as the peak of army strength, Linch and McCormack, *British Soldiers*, 6. Robert Burnham and Ron McGuigan provide data showing the British army at its pinnacle (in 1813) as having 287,869 men. Robert Burnham and Ron McGuigan, *The British Army against Napoleon: Facts, Lists, and Trivia, 1805–1813* (Barnsley, UK: Frontline, 2010), 2. This is rank and file, only. As Burnham and McGuigan point out, an additional 12.5 percent (approximately) is needed to include noncommissioned officers and officers. This produces a figure of slightly more than 320,000 men (323, 853).
5. Knight, *Britain against Napoleon*, 386, 388, 410. Knight states that "£578 million of new funded debt was created to add to the national debt" during this period (386, 410).
6. For a breakdowns of these loans, see Charles Esdaile, *Napoleon's Wars: An International History, 1803–1815* (New York: Viking, 2007), 157.

7. Knight, *Britain against Napoleon*, 391. In the years 1797 to 1810, government loans totaled £400 million.
8. Linda Colley, *Britons: Forging the Nation, 1707–1837* (1992; repr., London: Pimlico, 2008), 150. For data comparison, Colley cites Paul Kennedy, *The Rise and Fall of the Great Powers: Economic Change and Military Conflict from 1500 to 2000* (New York: Vintage, 1988), 105. For a look at how British society responded to both the French Revolution and the long crises against the French, see Mark Philp, ed., *The French Revolution and British Popular Politics* (1992; repr., Cambridge: Cambridge University Press, 2002).
9. Pitt was the second son of William Pitt, the 1st earl of Chatham and the prime minister during much of the Seven Years' War.
10. William Hague, *William Pitt the Younger* (London: HarperCollins, 2004), 228. What makes Pitt's probity that much more astonishing is that he was frequently in personal financial distress, often due to negligence and sometimes due to outright theft on the part of his employees. While he attempted to balance the government's books with exactness, he was less successful managing his own money (213–16).
11. While Pitt was not a particularly organized man, there being no apparent system to his correspondence, he was incredibly thorough. He tended to disregard communications on subjects he was not currently exploring, which often irritated individuals whose topics were ignored for months on end. His tendency to analyze and solve one problem at a time, given his energy and his focus, was the source of his brilliance, however, and he was frequently forgiven by those he had put off once he turned his considerable talents to their once-neglected issues. Ibid., 210–11.
12. Canning, in fact, served as treasurer of the navy, as foreign secretary, and, briefly, as prime minister in 1827. Addington, later the 1st Viscount Sidmouth, became prime minister from 1801 to 1804, then foreign secretary. His excellent work on the income tax system, nearly doubling its efficiency, was offset by his defensive and unsuccessful war policies, the latter causing his government to fall in 1804. There were a great many other efficient and effective ministers appointed by Pitt, including Charles Jenkinson (Lord Hawkesbury and later the Earl of Liverpool) and Spencer Perceval, who also became a prime minister in 1809. These selectees of Pitt collaborated to reform and run the government. They also brought appointees of their own, as Rory Muir puts it regarding Canning: "He collected round him a group of talented followers and friends." Muir, *Britain and the Defeat of Napoleon*, 10. Muir identifies Canning, Castlereagh, Hawkesbury, and Perceval as the "four most important ministers in government" by the time of the Peninsular War (ibid.).
13. This praise is not meant to convey any sort of omniscience on the part of Pitt. His misjudgment of the strategic value of the West Indies, designating it the as the primary area of concern and operations in the early years of the long conflict with the French (ignoring, for the most

part, events on the continent), was certainly a great misstep. The loss of manpower was staggering, with perhaps as many as 75,000 soldier deaths and 420,000 casualties over the course of the war, most due to disease. One-seventh of the Jamaica garrison, for example, died every year. Roger Buckley, *The British Army in the West Indies: Society and the Military in the Revolutionary Age* (Tallahassee: University Press of Florida, 1998), 276, 220; and Buckley, "The Destruction of the British Army in the West Indies 1793–1815: A Medical History," *Journal of the Society for Army Historical Research* 56, no. 226 (1978): 79–80. Richard Glover also condemns Pitt for allowing the army to "rot, in the decade of peace from 1783–1793," failing to appoint a commander in chief for the entire decade. As is sometimes the case, Glover's best tool is hyperbole. He seems to assume that the reforms related to training and standardization implemented by the Duke of York in 1795 could or would have been put in place sooner with the selection of any commander in chief, an assumption not borne out by the conduct of previous leaders. Nevertheless, the neglect of systematic battalion training was a debilitating oversight. Richard Glover, *Britain at Bay: Defence against Bonaparte, 1803–1814* (New York: Barnes and Noble, 1973), 40. Buckley, however, more astutely recognizes that Pitt, despite his personal abhorrence of slavery, failed to put his "considerable talents and extensive political influence to persuade government supporters to vote for [its] abolition" due to his concerns regarding its effects on trade with the West Indies. This is a much more damning assessment. Buckley, *British Army in the West Indies*, 142.

14. Knight, *Britain against Napoleon*, 315.
15. Hague, *William Pitt the Younger*, 577. Colley lists several more work-related demises, including Canning and Castlereagh. Colley, *Britons: Forging the Nation*, 151. The details regarding Castlereagh's duel with Canning, resignation, later return to politics, tragic decline, and suicide can be found in John Bew, *Castlereagh: A Life* (Oxford: Oxford University Press, 2012), 257–67, 298–310, 537–57.
16. Hague, *William Pitt the Younger*, 83.
17. The U.S. Army concerns itself today with the distinction between an *organization* and an *institution*, with the former being an association of individuals with a common purpose and the latter being an organization based on existing, and particular, norms or laws. Thus, it would seem that Pitt, by trying to establish mores, with related behavioral expectations, was attempting to form institutions within the government, writ large. Richard Tracy, strategic intelligence analyst, United States African Command, U.S. Armed Forces, interview by author, 17 October 2014. U.S. Army briefing, 7 July 2014, "Encouraging Effective African Defense Governance: A Planning Framework," author's collection.
18. Hague, *William Pitt the Younger*, 180.
19. Michael Turner, *Pitt the Younger: A Life* (London: Hambledon and London, 2003), 94. Knight, *Britain against Napoleon*, 25.
20. Knight, *Britain against Napoleon*, 4.

21. Colley, *Britons: Forging the Nation*, 287. She cites numbers from Clive Emsley, *British Society and the French Wars, 1793–1815* (London: Macmillan, 1979).
22. Knight, *Britain against Napoleon*, 118.
23. "Key Dates in Census, Statistics and Registration Great Britain 1000–1899," Education Resources, accessed 30 September 2014, http://www.thepotteries.org/dates/census.htm.
24. George Harrison, who held this role of assistant secretary and spend over twenty years at the Treasury, made key contributions to further reforms within his department. See J. R. Torrance, "Sir George Harrison and the Growth of Bureaucracy in the Early Nineteenth Century," *English Historical Review* 83, no. 326 (January 1968): 52–88. William Grenville (Baron Grenville) was Pitt's cousin and a close confidant; he was both home secretary and foreign secretary under Pitt (and later first lord of the Treasury, then prime minister following Pitt's death). He continued Pitt's Treasury restructuring.
25. Knight provides evidence that upon taking the office of secretary of war in 1809, Lord Palmerston discovered that "40,000 regimental accounts were in arrears, stretching back to 1783." Knight, *Britain against Napoleon*, 335.
26. "Total Public Spending in the United Kingdom Central Government and Local Authority," UK Public Spending, accessed 24 September 2014, http://www.ukpublicspending.co.uk/breakdown_1790UKmt_14mc5n, and http://www.ukpublicspending.co.uk/breakdown_1810UKmt_14mc5n.
27. Knight, *Britain against Napoleon*, 94. According to Knight, "Whereas taxation in Britain had accounted for roughly 20 percent of national income, in France it ranged from 10 to 13 percent" (387).
28. Colley, *Britons: Forging the Nation*, 65. The list of taxable items was quite extensive, to include, "hats, ribbons, . . . linens, calicoes, coal, gold and silver plate, imported silk, exported lead, postage rates, and shooting certificates." Hague, *William Pitt the Younger*, 181.
29. Grenville was a key player in these reforms, relied upon by Pitt, as was Henry Dundas. Also see Knight, *Britain against Napoleon*, 386, regarding these connections.
30. David Landes, *The Unbound Prometheus: Technological Change and Industrial Development in Western Europe from 1750 to the Present* (Cambridge: Cambridge University Press, 1969), 18.
31. Eric Hobsbawm, *Industry and Empire: The Birth of the Industrial Revolution* (New York: New Press, 1999), 64.
32. Landes, *Unbound Prometheus*, 41. Hobsbawm also notes the regularity and never-ending grind of such work, which ran counter to the cycle of labor to that point. Hobsbawm, *Industry and Empire*, 64. For a more detailed analysis of British reactions and protests to industrialization, see John Archer, *Social Unrest and Popular Protest in England 1780–1840* (Cambridge: Cambridge University Press, 2000), particularly his chapters on food riots and industrial protests. He comments that as time

progressed, the former had the tendency to meld into, or even emerge concurrently with and emerge from, the latter. These struggles, in various forms (from letter writing and petitions to rioting, arson, and property damage) were against the distinct disintegration of the standard of living and the new evolving status quos that minimized the voice and the value of the individual worker and his/her substratum of society. The rioters wanted a return to the past, which was something forever beyond their power. Also see Emsley, *British Society and the French Wars*, and Emsley, "The Military and Popular Disorder in England 1790–1801," *Journal of Army Historical Research* 61, no. 245 (1983): 10–21.

33. Two boys on a power loom with a technical advantage of 7.5 to 1 could do the work of fifteen handcraftsmen. Landes, *Unbound Prometheus*, 85–87.

34. Ibid., 41–42. In the decade after Waterloo, British industrial textiles consumed nearly £366 million worth of cotton.

35. Ibid., 95. Also see Hobsbawm, *Industry and Empire*, 47, 54.

36. Knight, *Britain against Napoleon*, 392.

37. According to John Powell, the population of Britain and Wales grew from 8,872,980 to 11,997,663 between 1801 and 1821. John Powell, *Statistical Illustrations of the Territorial Extent and Population, Rental, Taxation, Finances, Commerce, Consumption, Insolvency, Pauperism, and Crime, of the British Empire* (London, 1827), 37. Powell shows a different total on page 44, increasing the value to almost £42 million by 1815. For a breakdown by type and location for exports, see page 54 on.

38. Hobsbawm, *Industry and Empire*, 46.

39. For an illustration of the oscillating nature of the economy, see the "Statement Exhibiting the Total value of Merchandize Annually" (quantity and value of exports over imports, 1710–1821), Powell, *Statistical Illustrations*, 55.

40. Best wonders aloud at the relationship between the war and industrial growth in Britain, noting their symbiotic ties. Geoffrey Best, *War and Society in Revolutionary Europe, 1770–1870* (Leicester: Leicester University Press, 1998), 143.

41. Edward Coss, *All for the King's Shilling: The British Soldier under Wellington, 1808–1814* (Norman: University of Oklahoma Press, 2010), 66–67.

42. Roger Wells, *Wretched Faces: Famine in Wartime England, 1793–1801* (Gloucester, UK: Sutton, 1988), 51. Theodore Ropp, over fifty years ago, noticed the catalytic and beneficial effect that Napoleon's blockade had, long-term, on Britain's economy, arguing that it forced Britain to find alternative markets overseas, resulting in greatly expanded trade. Theodore Ropp, *War in the Modern World* (Durham: North Carolina University Press, 1959), 122–23. Nevertheless, the social disorder created by shifting markets, changes in methods of production, and rising food costs should not be underestimated.

43. B. A. Holderness, "Prices, Productivity, and Output," *Agrarian History of England and Wales*, vol. 6, *1750–1850*, ed. G. E. Mingay (Cambridge:

Cambridge University Press, 1989), 174. According to John Powell, the population of Britain and Wales grew from 8,872,980 to 11,997,663 between 1801 and 1821. Powell, *Statistical Illustrations*, ix, 33 (by county).

44. H. V. Bowen, *War and British Society, 1688–1815* (Cambridge: Cambridge University Press, 1998), 37. Douglas Hay argues that in "good years" about 10 percent of the population could not afford bread over an entire year; in "bad years," that number rose to 20 percent; and in very hard years, perhaps as much as 45 percent of the country could not afford bread. Douglas Hay, "War, Dearth, and Theft in the Eighteenth Century: The Record of the English Courts," *Past and Present* 95, no. 1 (1982): 131. During the first decade of the nineteenth century, poor rates increased over four times the rate of population growth (65 percent compared to 15 percent). Frank Darvall, *Popular Disturbances and Public Order in Regency England* (New York: Augustus M. Kelley, 1969), 19–20.

45. Powell, *Statistical Illustrations*, 28.

46. Coss, *All for the King's Shilling*, 264–71.

47. It has been argued that after deductions for food, clothing, certain supplies for maintaining equipment, and required contributions to the soldier homes at Chelsea and Kilmainham, something in the order of between only six and eighteen shillings actually made it into a private's pocket over the course of an entire year. That was about the weekly wage of a silk worker at the time. John Fortescue, *A History of the British Army*, vol. 4, *1789–1801*, pt. 2 (London: Macmillan, 1906), 935; Richard Glover, *Peninsular Preparation: The Reform of the British Army, 1795–1809* (London: Cambridge University Press, 1963), 215; and Coss, *All for the King's Shilling*, 74.

48. Andrew Bamford, *Sickness, Suffering, and the Sword: The British Regiment on Campaign, 1808–1815* (Norman: University of Oklahoma Press, 2013), 5. This latter post was created by Pitt in 1794. The first appointee was the difficult and forceful Henry Dundas (later Lord Melville), previously home secretary, president of the India Board of Control, the treasurer of the navy, and, in 1804, first lord of the Admiralty. It is easy to understand why Pitt might appoint a friend through whom so much power ran: there was a great potential for efficiency and getting something done in a timely manner. The Duke of York also relied upon him, however reluctantly. Knight, *Britain against Napoleon*, 26. Haythornthwaite records that, in 1806, Dundas was impeached for "misappropriation of public funds and though acquitted never again held office." Philip Haythornthwaite, *The Armies of Wellington* (London: Arms and Armour, 1994), 14.

49. Correlli Barnett, *Britain and Her Army, 1509–1970: A Military, Political, and Social Survey* (London: Allen Lane, 1970), 239.

50. Ibid., 239.

51. Glover, *Peninsular Preparation*, 16.

52. Bamford, *Sickness, Suffering, and the Sword*, 6.

53. Haythornthwaite, *Armies of Wellington*, 15.
54. York began his career as a lieutenant colonel at seventeen and progressed to major general two years later and lieutenant general another two years after that. He was a full general by 1793. He was rewarded by his father after returning from the Low Countries with a promotion to field marshal and was named the army's commander in chief. It was good to be the king's son. York was felled in 1809 by a scandal involving his former mistress, Mary Ann Clarke, centered on a promotion-for-a-sum bribery scheme, supposedly happening under his watch. After investigation, the House of Commons concluded that York was immoral (regarding his relationship with Clarke) but not corrupt, as there was no evidence that he was aware of the ploy or profited from it. He resisted Clarke's efforts to blackmail him over the incident and was reappointed in 1811. Also see Haythornthwaite, *Armies of Wellington*, 15.
55. A shortage of maps and local knowledge (and available references) stymied the army; during his retreat in Flanders in 1794, the Duke of York urgently requested from Horse Guards military surveys and maps, something apparently not considered important or readily available to him before the campaign. This was the kind of unpreparedness within the officer corps and the army that York hoped to eliminate. Glover, *Britain at Bay*, 19. Moreover, Glover comments that despite the repeated scares of invasion during the late 1790s, local troops in England still lacked reliable maps. Glover, *Peninsular Preparation*, 19. The intelligence service was equally as challenged.
56. Sir Henry Bunbury provides a detailed account of the Flanders campaign. Lieutenant-general Sir Henry Bunbury, *Narratives of Some Passages in the Great War with France, from 1799 to 1810* (London, 1854).
57. Harry Calvert to John Calvert, 26 April 1793, in *The Journals and Correspondence of General Sir Harry Calvert, bart: Adjutant-general of the Forces under H. R. H. the Duke of York. Comprising the Campaigns in Flanders and Holland in 1793–4*, ed. Sir Harry Verney (London, 1853), 67.
58. Robert Harvey, *War of Wars: The Epic Struggle between Britain and France, 1789–1815* (New York: Carroll and Graf, 2006), 140. Fortescue points out the hazards of the British command structure, noting that, among his many directives, Henry Dundas withdrew troops from York's command and sent them to the West Indies, overriding York's authority and compromising the effort in Flanders. Fortescue, *British Campaigns in Flanders, 1690–1794: Being Extracts from "A History of the British Army,"* 302–304, among many references. Fortescue estimates the losses just during the final retreat at about six thousand men (401–402).
59. Knight, *Britain against Napoleon*, 273.
60. Glover, *Peninsular Preparation*, 2.
61. Barnett, *Britain and Her Army*, 240. York also kept track of talented officers who lacked the means to buy their ranks and attempted to find

empty command slots for them. Nevertheless, as Barnett observes, the purchase system allowed men of means to recommend individuals of similar affluence and standing, with family connections trumping merit. (Wellington was especially careful to seek well-bred men as subordinates.) Harry Calvert wrote, "We want a stop put that most pernicious mode of bestowing rank on officers without even the form of recommendation . . . and to relieve deserving officers from the intolerable grievance of seeing men without merit, without family, or the smallest pretension to any military ability, pass over their heads." Harry Calvert to Sir John Hamilton-Dalrymple, 12 October 1794, in Verney, *Journals and Correspondence of General Sir Harry Calvert*, 360.

62. Glover contends that had the Duke of York the freedom to manage the army as he desired, he would have abolished the purchase system, substituting seniority promotion to the rank of captain and advancing on merit thereafter. This idea he shared with Castlereagh. Glover, *Peninsular Preparation*, 154.

63. Le Marchant was a skilled cavalry officer. He died as a major general, leading a charge at Salamanca in 1812. For an overview of the creation and evolution of British army education, see Glover, *Peninsular Preparation*, 187–213.

64. Barnett, *Britain and Her Army*, 240.

65. Glover, *Peninsular Preparation*, 164–65.

66. Ibid., 51–54. York also ensured that firearms were distributed according to a regiment's actual, not full-strength, numbers, which helped eliminate both need for some units and overabundance for others (56).

67. Previous militia acts, such as the one of 1757, generally had the same purpose. While passed during the lull in the wars against France (1802), the later militia bills were intended to protect the nation in times of war, which, given the continued tensions between Britain and France, seemed on the immediate horizon.

68. John Fortescue, *The County Lieutenancies and the Army, 1803–1814* (London: Macmillan, 1909), 15, 18. Fortescue also lays out all the differences between the regular and local militias.

69. Ibid., 20. One bonus of serving in the militia, rather than in the regulars, was the Crown's support for the militia man's family, which was entitled to "parochial support" during the man's absence. There was no such assistance for families of men in the regular army (33).

70. As the years passed and militia duty appeared too uncomfortably close to the potential of real fighting, bounties rose to outrageous sums, £44 in Anglesey, £45 in Monmouth, and £50 to £80 in Forfar, for example. Ibid., 197, 255.

71. Coss, *All for the King's Shilling*, 74.

72. Fortescue, *County Lieutenancies and the Army*, 196.

73. Ibid., 47.

74. Ibid., 49. Fortescue argues, "It was assumed in every quarter that substitutes would be provided in every case; and, in fact, in 1803–05, the

ballot was simply an instrument for compelling the parishes to reorganize at their own expense recruiting depots for the Militia" (40).
75. Ibid., 4.
76. Ibid., 5.
77. Buckley, *British Army in the West Indies*, xviii.
78. Fortescue, *County Lieutenancies and the Army*, 5–6, 254. In 1811, 11,453 transferred (1,453 more than required), driven no doubt by the second consecutive failed harvest of 1811 (257).
79. Ibid., 5–6.
80. In many ways, it seems as if the Volunteer Corps might have been utilized as local insurgents, defying French occupation should the invasion have taken place. J. R. Western describes the organization's purpose as "giving able-bodied civilians the rudiments of military training" with the units functioning as "perfect cadres for political clubs." With that as the metric for success, it is hard to see volunteer units as being very useful in open or sustained conflict. J. R. Western, "The Volunteer Movement as an Anti-Revolutionary Force, 1793–1801," *English Historical Review* 71 (1956): 605, 607.
81. J. E. Cookson, "The English Volunteer Movement of the French Wars, 1793–1815: Some Contexts," *Historical Journal* 32, no. 4 (1989): 867.
82. Bowen, *War and British Society*, 14. For an overview of the volunteer system, see Western, "The Volunteer Movement as an Anti-Revolutionary Force," 603–14. Men of status, nevertheless, played a part. Pitt was a colonel of the Royal Trinity House Volunteer Artillery and the Cinque Ports Volunteer Corps, despite his ill health. As was almost always the case, Pitt threw himself into the task, raising and training men and making plans. Hague, *William Pitt the Younger*, 520.
83. Cookson argues that for many reasons, including financial, "volunteering most suited the poor." Cookson, "The English Volunteer Movement of the French Wars," 866.
84. There was, apparently, some parliamentary confusion as to which cohort of volunteers qualified for the exemption when the group was reformed in 1803. Fortescue, *County Lieutenancies and the Army*, 65.
85. J. E. Cookson, "British Society and the French Wars, 1793–1815," *Australian Journal of Politics and History* 31, no. 2 (1985): 196. Napoleon's later failure to control the English Channel, however, and exigencies in Austria required the French invasion army to be marched eastward toward Ulm in 1805. By the time of the British naval victory at Trafalgar in the autumn of that year, the threat of invasion had already dissipated, and so did the Volunteer Corps.
86. Fortescue, *County Lieutenancies and the Army*, 27, 35.
87. Ibid., 70.
88. Ibid., 73. While the numbers varied slightly the next year, the final tally was nearly identical. The idea of recruiting boys, however, survived: those deemed to be of sufficient height (around sixty inches tall) were often accepted directly into regimental ranks. A. W. Cockerill estimates that, by 1811, there were likely as many as 3,600 young men under the

age of sixteen in the army. A. W. Cockerill, *Sons of the Brave: The Story of Boy Soldiers* (London: Cooper, 1984), 74.

89. The Militia Amending Act of 1811 allowed up to one-quarter of militia recruits to be fourteen to sixteen years old, if of a minimum height. Fortescue's data shows about 1,500 boys joining the army every year, with a high of 3,800 in 1807. Fortescue, *County Lieutenancies and the Army*, 292. He never defines with any exactness, however, the category of "boy." Also see Coss, *All for the King's Shilling*, 248.

90. Fortescue, *County Lieutenancies and the Army*, 234. The government initiated an additional measure for home defense through the creation of temporary fencible regiments of infantry and cavalry in the mid- and late eighteenth century. Assigned mostly garrison duties, these volunteer units were assessed by Glover as being the "last, and possibly the most useless, auxiliary force." Poor training and equipment limited their value; the Duke of York disbanded most of the regiments in 1799–1800. Men from these units were encouraged to join the regulars, although the numbers doing so are unclear. Glover, *Peninsular Preparation*, 217–18.

91. It is highly unlikely that the militia or the Volunteers Corps could have stood against Napoleon's troops for any appreciable time had the French invaded.

92. Bamford, *Sickness, Suffering, and the Sword*, xx.

93. Ibid., 13.

94. Ibid., 12, 59, 61, 63, 143, 287, 292. Bamford's fine work is marred only by his refusal to acknowledge the human cost of British logistical shortcomings. There was nothing abstract about prolonged nutritional deprivation on campaign, even if it was punctuated by short periods wherein barely adequate rations were provided. Whether or not the harrowing demands of campaigning without sufficient food "criminalized" the British regulars, as Charles Esdaile has opined, is an argument worthy of a session at a future Wellington congress. Charles Esdaile, "Incorrigible Rogues: The Demobilization of the British Army in the Wake of Waterloo" (paper presented at the final meeting of the Peninsular War 200 Committee, Apsley House, London, 17 June 2014).

95. Bamford, *Sickness, Suffering, and the Sword*, 301.

96. Peter Lloyd, *The French Are Coming! The Invasion Scare, 1803–1805* (Tunbridge Wells, UK: Spellmount, 1992), 119–23.

97. For example, the 71st Regiment of Foot was raised in 1775–1776 in Scotland by volunteers and received so many recruits that it was necessary to form them into two battalions. Lawrence Babits, *Devil of a Whipping: The Battle of Cowpens* (Chapel Hill: University of North Carolina Press, 1998), 45. Also see J. A. Houlding, *Fit for Service: The Training of the British Army, 1715–1795* (New York: Clarendon Press, 1981), 91–94, 120–25. In the case of the 71st Foot, the second battalion was created out of organizational and campaign need; as a result, both battalions saw extensive combat. Stephen Conway, "British Mobilization in the War of American Independence," *Historical Research* 72, no. 177 (1999): 58–76.

98. Stephen Brumwell, *Redcoats: The British Soldier and War in the Americas, 1755–1763* (New York: Cambridge University Press, 2002), 192. Matt Spring's chapter on the subject of bushfighting is especially informative as it applies to this type of fighting during the period of the American Revolution. Matthew Spring, *With Zeal and with Bayonets Only: The British Army on Campaign in North America, 1775–1783* (Norman: University of Oklahoma Press, 2010), 245–62.

99. Ibid., 229.

100. For the best study of British tactical evolutions during the American War of Independence, see Spring, *With Zeal and with Bayonets Only*, 76–102.

101. Ibid., 183.

102. *Regulations for the Exercise of Riflemen and Light Infantry and Instructions for Their Conduct in the Field* (London: War Office, 1803). The book's preface describes the manual as an original work by a German officer and claims that George III gave directions that the guide be translated and distributed as official doctrine. The German author was Major General Baron de Rottenburg.

103. Charles Esdaile, "Wellington Triumphant: An Analysis of British Battlefield Invincibility in Spain and Portugal, 1808–1814" (unpublished paper), 22. I am indebted to my longtime friend for sharing this paper with me.

104. For Baker's perspective, see Ezekiel Baker, *Twenty-three Years Practice and Observations with Rifle Guns*, 2nd ed. (London, 1804). He observes that, after extensive testing of his rifle, two hundred yards proved to be "the greatest range I can fire with any certainty. At 300 yards I have fired very well at times, when the wind has been calm" (8).

105. "Total Public Spending in the United Kingdom Central Government and Local Authority," UK Public Spending, accessed 15 November 2014, http://www.ukpublicspending.co.uk/total_spending_1782UKmn. See also http://www.ukpublicspending.co.uk/total_spending_1787UKmn. While Glover makes a good case that current perception of the lax training of eighteenth-century armies is, perhaps, too skewed by modern military standards, it is worth considering that American political and budget arguments led in 2013 to the U.S. Army reducing and then, for all practical purposes, canceling training, army-wide, due to sequestration cuts. This allegedly left only two of the army's forty-two combat brigades ready for battle. Sydney Freedberg, Jr., "Sequestration Cuts Leave Army With Only 2 Brigades Ready To Fight: CSA Odierno," *Breaking Defense* (21 October 2013), accessed 15 November 2014, http://breakingdefense.com/2013/10/army-of-two-sequesters-training-cuts-leave-only-2-brigades-combat-ready/.

106. Colonel David Dundas, *Principles of Military Movements: Chiefly Applied to Infantry. Illustrated by Manoeuveres of the Prussian Troops, and by an Outline of the British Campaigns in Germany, during the War of 1757* (London, 1788). "Total Public Spending," UK Public

Spending, accessed 15 November 2014, http://www.ukpublicspending .co.uk/total_spending_1788UKmn.

107. Glover, *Peninsular Preparation*, 119; Haythornthwaite, *Armies of Wellington*, 89.

108. Spring, *With Zeal and with Bayonets Only*, 139.

109. Dundas, *Principles of Military Movements*, v–vii.

110. General John Money, a participant in the campaign, observed that the British army had suffered "owing to our having only small bodies of irregulars to meet large ones." Glover, *Peninsular Preparation*, 125.

111. Mark Urban, *Fusiliers: How the British Army Lost America but Learned to Fight* (London: Faber, 2008), 307–19. The importance of light infantry became largely solidified by the 1803–1804 specialized light infantry camp established at Shorncliffe by Sir John Moore, which resulted in the conversion of several line battalions into true light infantry and rifle regiments. Houlding, *Fit for Service*, 250–52, 336–38.

112. Cornwallis opposed Dundas's directives and stood strongly in defense of the loose-file tactics utilized in America, especially in the southern colonies, where he spent a great deal of the war. His posting to India as governor, however, meant that he was too far removed to offer significant opposition. Urban, *Fusiliers*, 299–310.

113. Bunbury, *Narratives of Some Passages in the Great War*, vii. He summed up the subsequent 1794–95 campaign in Flanders as "disheartening" (xvii).

114. Given similar experiences observing Prussian methods during their formative years as soldiers, it is unsurprising that Dundas and York came to agreement on Dundas's recommendations. Dundas was also an aide-de-camp under Major General George Eliot in Cuba, where he witnessed what he believed was the ineffectiveness of light troops fighting on open ground. Brumwell, *Redcoats*, 262. For a detailed analysis of this development, see also David Gates, *The British Light Infantry Arm, c. 1790–1815* (London: Batsford, 1987).

115. Houlding, *Fit for Service*, 238–50; Mark Urban, *Fusiliers*, 300–306.

116. These were the same formations the British army utilized against Napoleon. Brumwell, *Redcoats*, 263.

117. Spring, *With Zeal and with Bayonets Only*, 216–44. Spring highlights that the regulars received no actual training "to fence with their bayonets" because defenders rarely stood their ground (222–23).

118. Brent Nosworthy, *With Musket, Cannon and Sword* (New York: Sarpedon, 1996), 202–18.

119. Coss, *All for the King's Shilling*, 167–74. Only at the Battle of Albuera, 16 May 1811, was a short-range, extended musketry duel attempted. The casualties were so high that both British and French units faltered. Rory Muir, *Tactics and the Experience of Battle in the Age of Napoleon* (London: Yale University Press, 1998), 86–89.

120. Nosworthy, *With Musket, Cannon and Sword*, 219–41.

121. York quoted in Glover, *Peninsular Preparation*, 121.

122. Gunther Rothenberg, *The Art of War in the Age of Napoleon* (Bloomington: Indiana University Press, 1981), 183.

123. Glover, *Peninsular Preparation*, 135.

124. Ibid., 137. Italics in original.

125. For an intimate biography, see Denis Le Marchant, esq., *Memoirs of the Late Major-Genl. Le Marchant* (London, 1841).

126. The Marquess of Anglesey, *A History of the British Cavalry, 1816 to 1919*, vol. 1, *1816–1850* (London: Cooper, 1973), 47. Arguably, the best single volume work on the British cavalry of the Napoleonic period is Ian Fletcher, *Galloping at Everything: The British Cavalry in the Peninsula and at Waterloo, 1808–15* (Staplehurst, UK: Spellmount, 1999).

127. Nick Lipscombe, *Wellington's Guns: The Untold Story of Wellington and His Artillery in the Peninsula and at Waterloo* (Oxford: Osprey, 2013), 24.

128. Ralph Adye's *The Bombardier, and Pocket Gunner* (London, 1804) became the manual of choice for junior artillery officers attempting to increase their aptitude.

129. Lipscombe, *Wellington's Guns*, 17.

130. Ibid., 24.

131. Ibid. William Congreve's rockets were first tested in 1804.

132. Ibid., 18.

133. Glover, *Peninsular Preparation*, 86.

134. Ibid.

135. Ibid., 88; Lipscombe, *Wellington's Guns*, 21–22.

136. Esdaile, "Wellington Triumphant," 5.

137. Fortescue, *History of the British Army*, 4:808. J. Christopher Herold, *Bonaparte in Egypt* (1963; repr., Barnsley, UK: Pen and Sword, 2005), 375. Menou, though unpopular among his fellow officers, took control of Egypt after the assassination of Jean-Baptiste Kléber in June of 1800. Perhaps the most interesting outcome of Menou's period of command was his forced surrender of the Rosetta Stone to the British after the French surrender of Egypt. Menou initially refused to part with the object, claiming it as personal property. Max Sewell, "The Discovery of the Rosetta Stone," The Napoleon Series, accessed 21 January 2015, http://napoleon-series.org/research/miscellaneous/c_rosetta.html>.

138. Napoleon, *Correspondance de Napoléon Ier publiée par ordre de l'empereur Napoléon III* (Paris, 1858–70), 7:40. Sent 20 February 1801. Napoleon further encouraged the men: "So many achievements attest to future centuries the glory of our great nation, and you are deserving of new evidence of the recognition of the homeland" (40).

139. Herold, *Bonaparte in Egypt*, 378–79. Bey, a cruelly vicious leader, died of the plague a month after the landings.

140. Fortescue, *History of the British Army*, 4:815–16.

141. Oddly, Fortescue blames William Pitt as being responsible for this interpretation and for the fall of the army's reputation. As has been

shown, however, Pitt's efforts had, in fact, resuscitated all branches of the armed services. The British victory in Egypt was the first of many battlefield triumphs over the next two decades.

142. Ibid., 816.
143. Sir John Moore, *The Diary of Sir John Moore*, ed. Major General Sir J. F. Maurice (London: Arnold, 1902), 2:3–4.
144. Ibid., 4.
145. Ibid.
146. Fortescue, *History of the British Army*, 4:823. Moore, *Diary of Sir John Moore*, 2:15–18.
147. Fortescue, *History of the British Army*, 4:823.
148. Ibid.
149. See Fortescue for a detailed account of the battle. Ibid., 835–38. Also see Moore, *Diary of Sir John Moore*, 2:15–18.
150. The deed earned the regiment the honor of wearing a sphinx emblem on the rear of the men's shakos. "1801—The Battle of Alexandria," Soldiers of Gloucestershire, accessed 21 November 2014, http://www.glosters.org.uk/textonly_timeline/3.
151. Moore, *Diary of Sir John Moore*, 2:14.
152. Ibid., 16.
153. Ibid.
154. For a detailed breakdown of casualties, see Fortescue, *History of the British Army*, 4:840–43.
155. Herold, *Bonaparte in Egypt*, 379.
156. Las Casas wrote his recollections of conversations with Napoleon after the latter's exile to Saint Helena. Emmanuel-Augustin-Dieudonné-Joseph, comte de Las Casas, *Mémorial de Sainte-Hélène* (Paris, 1842), 592.
157. Piers Mackesy, *British Victory in Egypt, 1801: The End of Napoleon's Conquest* (London: Routledge, 1995), 100–101.
158. Stephen Brumwell, *Redcoats*, 227.
159. Huw J. Davies, "'A Wandering Army': Tactical and Operational Development in the British Army before the Peninsular War" (paper given at the fifth Wellington Conference, Southampton, UK, April 2013).
160. Muir, *Britain and the Defeat of Napoleon*, 17. In the years of the Peninsular War, alone, the navy provided the army and its allies in Spain and Portugal food, reinforcements, ammunition, and all sorts of stores in four hundred escorted conveys numbering 13,500 individual ships, an endeavor of breathtaking proportions. Knight, *Britain against Napoleon*, 425.
161. All of this, of course, was assisted by Napoleon's propensity for overreach. Had Napoleon's intertwined ambitions in Spain and Russia not exceeded his grasp, British efforts to contain his continental dominance, more likely than not, would have fallen short.
162. Antoine-Henri Jomini (baron de), *Histoire critique et militaire des guerres de la Révolution* (Paris, 1837), 203. Pitt, likely more so than

any other principal, might have nodded, with sage understanding, at Brutus's spoken reflections on timing and urgency, summing up his reasons for attacking Mark Anthony at the conclusion of William Shakespeare's *Julius Caesar*:

> There is a tide in the affairs of men,
> Which, taken at the flood, leads on to fortune;
> Omitted, all the voyage of their life
> Is bound in shallows and in miseries.
> On such a full sea are we now afloat;
> And we must take the current when it serves,
> Or lose our ventures.
>
> > Act 4, sc. 3, lines 249–55 (original portfolio),
> > ca. 1599 (London: Athenaeum Press, 1904), 149.

CHAPTER 6

THE SPANISH ARMY

CHARLES ESDAILE

The Spanish army of the Revolutionary Wars is not a subject that is particularly well known to anglophone audiences. With the exception of the brief coverage it was accorded in the author's own *Spanish Army in the Peninsular War* (Manchester, 1988), there is almost nothing on it in English, and the few comments that it has attracted have, to put it mildly, been less than complimentary. Yet the general lack of esteem in which it is held is not justified by the reality. No foreign armies penetrated very far into France even in the terrible crisis of 1793, but the army of General Ricardos got farther than most, whilst the Spaniards also remained in occupation of their conquests longer than any other power. Few battles on the Pyrenean front are remembered—Steven T. Ross's *Historical Dictionary of the Wars of the French Revolution* (Lanham, Maryland, 1998) has just three entries relating to the Spanish war—but at Trouillas the Spaniards dealt the French a blow that was the equal of anything they suffered in Flanders or the Rhineland. None of this is to say, of course, that the Spanish army was a particular paragon of virtue in military terms when war broke out between Spain and France in 1793. On the contrary, it had many deficiencies, and no modern writer could feel comfortable echoing the sentiments of the nineteenth-century military historian the Conde de Clonard. For example, writing of the infantry of the army of Carlos III, Clonard says, "The state which our infantry had attained in such a short time really was worthy of envy: the principles of discipline had been considerably reinforced; tactical training had been greatly improved; and the internal organization of the corps left noting to be desired."[1] However, the army's deficiencies were problems shared by many other European armies in the 1790s, and there is no reason not to believe that with better fortune they might have in the end been overcome. By the same token, meanwhile, it is more than time that the troops who fought for Spain between 1793 and 1795 received a greater degree of attention than has been habitual in the past.

Organization

In the moment that war broke out between France and Spain in March 1793, the Spanish army was in many ways typical of the armed forces that were to confront the armies of the French Revolution in the 1790s. Let us begin, for example, with its origins. In the Europe of the so-called age of reason, the professional standing army was the cornerstone of the state and, indeed, the very bedrock of absolute monarchy. Without such forces, no state could prosper in the hurly-burly of contemporary international relations and no dynasty impose its authority on the powerful forces—above all, the Catholic Church and the great magnates—that were everywhere determined to oppose the rise of the modern centralized state that was the central trend of government in the eighteenth century. In Spain, meanwhile, this was particularly true, for the ruling Bourbon dynasty had only come to the throne at the cost of a bloody conflict—the War of the Spanish Succession—in which victory had depended on the ability of the rival candidates to the throne to fashion a new army from the wreckage of the old tercios of the seventeenth century. Given that the chief Spanish adherents of the Habsburg pretender were to be found in Catalonia—a province that had waged a long war against the Spanish throne only fifty years before in defense of its traditional rights and was in consequence deeply suspicious of anything that might boost the authority of the monarchy—it is hardly surprising that it was Louis XIV's candidate, Felipe V, that in the end won out. Nor, meanwhile, is it surprising that the army should have become uniquely important in the governance of Spain. With the commanders—captains general—who headed the military regions into which the country was divided at the same time the presidents of the regional councils of administration-cum-courts of law known as *audiencias* or *chancillerias* on which much of the business of government devolved, and the military governors of such towns and cities who had them also their chief magistrates or corregidores, few European states could boast such an integration of the army into the machinery of the state. Indeed, even Prussia had nothing to equal it.[2]

This symbiosis of army and state was to play a dramatic role in the events of May 1808 when Spain rose against Napoleon. This, however, is not a matter that need concern us here. Far more important are the structure of the army and the forces that it could put into the field. At the summit of the military estate, of course, was the monarch, but the latter's authority as commander in chief was in practice exercised through the medium of the Supreme Council of War, which comprised the minister of war, the senior officers of the various arms of combat, and a number of other officers who were appointed by the king to represent military opinion as a whole. Originally this body had been the supreme authority in all matters pertaining to the army, as well as the highest court in the system of military justice. However, by the late eighteenth century, most of its administrative functions had been taken over by the ministry of war. Moreover, it was through the minister of war that the orders of the sovereign were communicated to the military commanders of the army—in peacetime the captains general, and in wartime the general officers commanding the various field armies into which Spain's forces might be divided. And it was to the minister of war, also, that the inspectors general who headed the different branches of the army—the line infantry, the Swiss infantry, the line cavalry, the dragoons, the artillery, the engineers, the provincial militia, the Guardias de Corps, the Guardias de Infantería, and the Carabinieros Reales—reported, the task of these officers being to implement the decisions of the ministry of war, preside over the workings of the code of military law, deal with all personnel matters, and watch over the internal economy of the units for which they were responsible.[3]

These arrangements concealed many disadvantages. The continued survival of the Supreme Council of War ensured that the minister of war was constantly at risk of being undercut, whilst his authority was further undermined by the facts, first, that his authority was not total—the army's finance, for example, was entirely in the hands of officials responsible to the ministry of finance—and, second, that the ministry for which he was responsible simply did not have the resources to fulfill all the functions that was expected of it. The rigid division of the army into independent corporations (of which, incidentally, there were far too many, the proliferation of inspectorates in the royal guard being particularly noticeable) promoted factionalism and was disproportionately expensive; the relationship between the army's territorial and military commands was left very vague;

and no use was made of the captain-generalcies either as a basis for the organization of the army into permanent divisions or a reconstitution of the inspectorates. Nor, of course, was there any general staff, the result being that all military planning was completely ad hoc, as were the arrangements that would have to be made whenever the army went to war: on the outbreak of hostilities, each field commander, who might or might not be the captain general of the region in which he was operating, and could in theory very easily be some court favorite who owed his prominence solely to his aristocratic lineage, would in consequence have to improvise both his own headquarters and the organization of his forces.[4]

In consequence of all this, it was inevitable, first, that the army would be even more expensive than might otherwise have been the case, and, second, that its military operations were certain to be marred by poor staff work. Yet there was nothing unique in these problems, and with common sense they could to some extent be subverted; in 1793, as we shall see, not only was the chief command given to one of Spain's foremost soldiers, but also it was ensured that he possessed both military and territorial authority in the region in which he was operating.[5] And in other respects, the Spanish army was far less deficient. With the accession to the throne of the Bourbons in 1700, the cumbersome Hapsburg tercios had finally disappeared (though the name, as we shall see, survived to serve as a title for some of the volunteer and irregular units raised in the period 1794–95). Needless to say, the original model had been the French army, but the victories of Frederick the Great had switched attention to Prussia, and in 1768 the Spanish forces had acquired new ordinances that were characterized by a slavish devotion to Prussian military practice. Nor was there much deviation from this thereafter; whilst the French army was experimenting with the column of line and column that produced the devastatingly effective tactical regulations of 1791, the Spaniards remained loyal to the concept of the linear warfare that had served Der Alte Fritz so well. Thus, when Carlos III dispatched a commission of officers to report on the armies of Europe in 1787 with a view to establishing whether military reform was needed, the report that his emissaries produced consisted of nothing more than a hymn of praise to the Prussian army.[6]

In 1793, then, Spain possessed an army that was no more old-fashioned than those of most of the other powers of Europe. Of what, though, did its forces consist? Let us begin with the infantry, or rather the line of battle that was the bedrock of all armies when the French Revolution burst upon the scene in 1789. On the death of Carlos III in 1788, there were twenty-seven Spanish and eight foreign regiments of line infantry, each of which were supposed to consist of two battalions (the foreign units numbered three Flemish, three Irish, and two Italian regiments). Each battalion was divided into eight musketeer companies and one grenadier company, but in wartime the former were drawn off to form separate elite battalions. To this array, meanwhile, there could be added the two regiments of guard infantry, which numbered six battalions apiece, the four regiments of Swiss infantry (these again numbered two battalions), and the forty-three regiments of provincial militia, a supplementary force raised by conscription that was only mobilized in time of war. As in Prussia, the three-deep line was the standard tactical formation, its role being steadily to advance upon the enemy, firing repeated volleys as it did so, before charging with the bayonet (when fighting cavalry, the array adopted was either the square or the *sólido*, a variant of the battalion-column in which companies doubled their ranks and closed up very tightly on one another). As was normal, fire was generally delivered not by entire battalions all firing at once, but rather by files, companies, or half-companies, the general effect being to ensure that no unit was ever completely unloaded. To help them in this task, in 1789 a new model of musket had been given to the infantry, of whom the latter carried sixty rounds of ammunition (the cavalry and artillery, meanwhile, got new pistols and carbines as appropriate). Equivalent to the latest European models, these were equipped with iron ramrods and had a caliber of 18mm as opposed to the 15mm of the previous model, whilst they appear to have been weapons that were at least as serviceable as the firearms that were in use everywhere else; the bayonet was shorter than that in use in some other armies, the hammer easily broken, and the trigger action notoriously stiff, but, in an important innovation, the steel was grooved, thereby increasing the chances of striking a spark.[7]

If the Spanish infantry was very much a conventional force, so was the Spanish cavalry. Of cavalry proper, there were twelve line regiments in 1793, each of which was composed of four squadrons, in addition to which we must also remember the two guard-cavalry regiments: the highly privileged Guardias de Corps, who normally mounted guard on the royal household, and the rather more mundane Carabinieros Reales. Dressed in blue rather than the white of the line infantry, these forces relied entirely on Frederician-style shock action instead of the French system of volleys of carbine and pistol fire that had been favored in the first half of the eighteenth century: when attacking the enemy, soldiers were to charge home at speed "with sword in hand and much courage." According to the army's tactical regulations, meanwhile, regiments were to be able to move and change formation at the trot or even the gallop, to maneuver in column, and to fight in line, whilst by the time the war broke out there were strong suggestions that the carbines that the men carried should be thrown away as an encumbrance.[8] If mobile firepower was required, this was supposed to be the work of the eight regiments of yellow-uniformed dragoons. Organized in four squadrons like the cavalry, dragoons were in theory trained to use firepower both in the saddle and on foot—indeed, in the latter case, they were even supposed to form line of battle like the infantry—and this may explain why they came to enjoy such an evil reputation as mounted troops.[9] But in general neither Guardias de Corps nor Carabinieros Reales nor line cavalry nor dragoons were much to be relied upon; by the late eighteenth century, centuries of mule breeding (which has the effect of destroying the fertility of the mares employed for the practice) had gravely weakened Spain's horse herds in both numbers and quality.

Supplementing these serried ranks of musketeers, grenadiers, heavy cavalrymen, and dragoons were several units of light troops. To be precise, in 1788 these forces consisted of three regiments of light infantry and two of light cavalry. Owing their origins to the constant need to safeguard Spain from the depredations of its own native bandits on the one hand and the Barbary corsairs on the other, these units were dressed in a more comfortable fashion than the troops of the line, and in the case of the infantry were from 1792 onward equipped with a modified musket that had a slightly longer barrel that made for improved accuracy and a cutaway stock that made for reduced weight. Needless to say, the primary task of these troops was not action on the battlefield, but rather the raiding and other forms of *petite guerre* that typified eighteenth-century warfare away from the major field actions, and in these last the Spaniards—like the Prussians—were to be badly outclassed by the French, who were increasingly thinking about the development of fresh tactical doctrines for such troops and moving toward the integration of line and light infantry. In this respect, perhaps, it is interesting that the first mention of the use of light infantry on the battlefield that we see in print in Spain is a translation of Grandmaison's famous treatise that appeared in Madrid in 1794.[10]

Finally, we must speak of the artillery. This force—in 1793 a single regiment of six battalions, each of seven companies—was at least well-equipped, having in 1783 been supplied with the so-called Nueva Ordenanza—a standardized range of 12-, 8-, and 4-pounder guns and 7- and 9-inch howitzers mounted on French-pattern Gribeauval carriages.[11] All accounts agree that the crews of this force were of the highest quality, but this was somewhat nullified by a serious lack of mobility; there was no permanent artillery train, and the guns were therefore pulled by a variety of horses, oxen, and mules that were hired from civilian sources on the outbreak of war along with their drivers. To expect such men to expose themselves on the battlefield was optimistic in the extreme, and all the more so in the event of the fighting going the way of the enemy, and the result was that defeats such as Peyrestortes and Le Boulou always saw the loss of many valuable cannon.[12]

In addition to its regular components, the Spanish army could also draw upon the support of considerable numbers of irregulars. Thus, in the Basque provinces, Navarre, and Catalonia, in time of invasion the authorities could mobilize local home guards. Organized in parish companies under the command of local worthies of various sorts, it was the task of these forces to harass the invaders by every means available and in effect to engage in guerrilla warfare, although it was accepted that they might also engage in such tasks as picket duty and general garrison work. Taking the Basque provinces and Navarre first of all, bands of armed civilians certainly turned out against the French when they raided the Pyrenean valleys of the Baztán and the Roncal in 1793, whilst the Conde de Clonard talks of a general mobilization that produced as many as 60,000 combatants.[13] This number, however, is almost certainly an exaggeration. In April 1793, the official *Gazeta de Madrid* reported that Vizcaya had ready a force of fifty-eight companies of sixty militiamen apiece, whilst in 1794 three tercios of volunteers—say 3,000 men?—were raised from the province. In 1794 the authorities of Navarre claimed to have 16,000 men under arms. And at the beginning of the war, Guipúzcoa raised a home guard of 4,600 men by means of a forced levy. In all, then, it is doubtful that the whole amounted to even as many as 25,000 men.[14] So concerned was the government at the French penetration of the Basque provinces in the summer of 1794 that an attempt appears to have been made to extend the system beyond its traditional boundaries; in November of that year, the authorities of the province of Burgos were ordered to organize the enlistment of all males between the ages of eighteen and forty with the exception of sole breadwinners (very interestingly, it was even laid down that there should be no exemption for the nobility).[15]

As yet, little research has been conducted into the extent of popular resistance in the Basque provinces. Much better documented, by contrast, are the *somatenes* of Catalonia (the name, incidentally, comes from the Catalan word *som atent* which means "to be alert"; a translation familiar to American readers would therefore be "minutemen"). In so far as the war of 1793–95 was concerned, given that these forces played no part in the struggle until Spain was invaded by the French in the second year of the conflict, the regulations that matter are those contained in an order of the day dated 6 May 1794 that was circulated among the justices and town councils of Catalonia. In brief, the order laid down the principle of universal military service for all men aged between fifteen and sixty, but proceeded to alleviate the immense burden that this would have supposed by a long series of qualifications. Catalonia's manpower was divided into two age groups—men aged from fifteen to forty formed the first cohort, and men aged from forty-one to sixty the second—whilst the province was split into three strips of territory, the first of which consisted of all those towns and villages within ten leagues of the French frontier, the second of all those towns and villages between ten and twenty leagues from the French frontier, and the third of all those towns and villages farther than twenty leagues from the frontier (n.b.: a Spanish league was the equivalent of about three English miles). This done, service was then imposed by means of a quota system based on a sliding scale; settlements located in the first band of territory were expected to produce half the men they had available in the first cohort and one-quarter of the men available in the second; settlements located in the second band, one-third of the first and one-sixth of the second; and settlements located in the third band, one-quarter of the first and one-eighth of the second. In addition, men in the older category who could claim noble status or who occupied positions that were "incompatible with a career of arms"—a term that was all too obviously open to abuse of every sort—could buy themselves out for a fixed sum should they draw an unlucky number in the municipal ballots that decided who should actually serve as somatenes. Once conscripted, meanwhile, the men were to serve for a fixed period of time, whilst they were to receive both pay for themselves and allowances for their families. In theory, then, any invasion of Catalonia would be faced by a very considerable force of irregular combatants; in 1794 the present-day province of Gerona alone appears to have provided some 16,000 men. Nor was this an end to it, for Catalonia also possessed a tradition of voluntary enlistment in time of war. We come here to the so-called *migueletes* (in Catalan, the term used is *miquelets*, just as "somatenes" is rendered *somatens*; for a variety of reasons, however, preference will be given to the Castilian forms in this chapter). Named after the followers of a sixteenth-century Catalan soldier of fortune named Miquel de Prats, migueletes were not conscripts, but rather men who volunteered for the duration of the war and in exchange received preferential conditions of service. Thus, rather than having to join regiments of the regular army, they could serve in special units that were raised in Catalonia alone and officered entirely by Catalans. Known as *tercios de migueletes*, these were traditionally never employed outside Catalonia, whilst, like the somatenes, they were also only organized in time of war and guaranteed their freedom at the close of hostilities. However, unlike the somatenes, migueletes were not primarily intended to play the role of irregulars; at times they were certainly employed in this fashion, but their main job was rather to reinforce the regular armies and fight with them on the battlefield. As such, however, they in theory represented a considerable force; when the formation of tercios de migueletes was authorized in the closing months of 1794, the aim of the authorities was to produce no fewer than twenty battalions of some 1,500 men apiece.[16]

There is, finally, one more source of troops that needs to be examined. In the eighteenth century, it had been common practice for armies to recruit gangs of freebooters in times of war to engage in what was commonly known as "la petite guerre." Usually referred to by the German name of *Freikorps*, such units were deemed to be particularly useful in mountain regions, and it is therefore not surprising to find the Spanish government succumbing to this tendency. Indeed, at least two such forces were formed. Thus, in Navarre the émigré Marquis de Saint Simon was permitted to form the so-called Legión Real from French deserters, at the head of which force he conducted a number of raids on French villages, whilst in Catalonia an officer of a somewhat wild stamp named Pedro Agustín Echavarri, who had been employed hunting down bandits in Andalucía, was given command of a band of repentant smugglers. Neither force, however, seem to have been much use; indeed, it is alleged that Echavarri's men—the so-called Compania de Contrabandistas Indultados—caused more harm to the local inhabitants than they did to the enemy.[17]

Before moving on, we must say something specific about the officer corps. On the whole, this body has not enjoyed a good reputation. This is, perhaps, a little unfair; in the war of 1793–95, there is no doubt that many Spanish officers showed both skill and courage. However, what cannot be gainsaid is that the officer corps did suffer from a number of serious problems. In the first place, training was clearly inadequate. A number of small military academies had been established in the course of the eighteenth century, but by 1793 almost all of them had ceased to exist whilst they had only ever catered to a minority of the men involved. Most officers, then, received such instruction as they received on the job, and this was often all too often barely adequate. And, in the second place, promotion was often extremely slow. Paradoxically, the Spanish army was much more egalitarian in its approach to granting commissions than many other forces of the epoch. Thus, no fewer than one-third of its numbers was supposed to come from men promoted from the ranks, and this implied, in turn, that many officers were non-noble (although it has recently been argued that the proportion represented by ex-rankers fell steadily as the eighteenth century wore on). But for such men, promotion, which rested on a complicated mixture of favor and seniority, did not come easily, and they generally languished for many years in the lower ranks, the most that they could aspire to being a captaincy. In practice, high rank was reserved for men who entered the army as officer cadets, the usual age of entry being around fourteen. Such candidates had to be both noble and sufficiently monied to be able to support their expenses. This was not quite as socially exclusive as it sounds—around one-tenth of the population could claim to be noble—but in terms of the officer corps' internal dynamics it was disastrous. Particularly if they enjoyed the favor of the court, such men could rise very rapidly—sometimes extremely rapidly—and thus it was that important commands sometimes fell into the hands of men who were both very young and very inexperienced. But precisely because of this court favor, not to mention a variety of other problems, which are too complicated to go into here, for most officers there was little reward in the way of advancement. Nor, meanwhile, was pay especially good, and all the more so as the fixed salaries enjoyed by the officer corps were by 1790 being eroded by galloping inflation. As to the effects of all this, they were only to be expected. Boredom, cynicism, and disillusion were all too common, whilst indiscipline, too, was a constant problem. Hence the very large number of officers who were absent from their regiments when the war broke out: of 112 officers serving with the four battalions of Guardias Españolas, for example, no fewer than 71 were missing, whilst the single battalion of the Regimiento de Infantería de Línea de Málaga that was present on the frontier was in even worse straights with just two officers present out of twenty-four. Yet at the same time there was no lack of generals. Every time that the Spanish army had engaged in significant military action in the reign of Charles III, the regime had marked the occasion by large numbers of promotions to, and within the ranks of, the *generalato*, and the result was that this had roughly doubled in terms of both size and cost.[18]

Such, then were military resources that Spain possessed on the accession to the throne of Carlos IV in 1788. What we see is in many respects a typical army of the eighteenth century, and one that, it has to be said, did not have a particularly good record as a fighting force: setting aside, the unsuccessful siege of Gibraltar in the American War of Independence, an expedition to Algiers in 1775 had collapsed in complete chaos. Add to this the negative effects that result from Spain's diplomatic situation (see below), and it can be seen that the army was not ready for a major European war in 1793. Some reform was carried out at the last minute; the number of foreign line infantry regiments was halved, and the reformados that resulted were used to bring the remaining four units up to strength, whilst several new regiments were formed, including one regiment of Spanish line infantry and—interestingly—three regiments of light infantry. But in the end much would depend upon whether the strength of the army could be increased after the outbreak of war, and it is to this question that we must now turn our attention.

Recruitment

Perhaps the worst problem faced by the army in 1793 was that of manpower. In theory, the rank and file of each line infantry regiment consisted of 1,377 men, but, with the regime of Carlos III committed to building a new battle fleet to fight the British, the amount of money available for the army was extremely limited; in 1770, the navy absorbed 12.1 percent of the annual budget; in 1782, twenty percent; and in 1785, 27.8 percent. To put this another way, given that defense spending overall remained roughly stable, in 1770 the army had been taking roughly twice as much money as the navy, whereas by 1790 the proportions had been reversed.[19] Moreover, Spain was secure on land; with the Pyrenean frontier covered by the permanent alliance between the French and Spanish Bourbons known as the Family Compact, the only enemies whom the court of Madrid was likely to have to deal with in a land campaign were Portugal and Morocco. In consequence, there was nothing to stop the ministry of war from sanctioning a series of defense cuts that saw the strength of the army steadily reduced. Seventy-seven strong according to the regulations of 1768, in 1771 each musketeer company was reduced to fifty-three men, whilst the following year it was decreed that in time of peace no regiment should have more than four hundred rank and file (at the same time, it was also laid down that, every four months, half the infantry should be sent on leave).[20] Still worse, indeed, many units in effect disappeared altogether; according to one account, in the 1770s only six line infantry regiments could muster the two battalions laid down by the regulations.[21] In theory, of course, the gaps in the ranks were to be made up as soon as war broke out by fresh volunteers or, more likely, conscripts, but when hostilities erupted with France there was simply no time to find the men required, and so the army found itself marching off to war desperately understrength; in the first forces that invaded Rousillon, for example, the Regimiento de Infantería de Línea de Saboya numbered 884 men; the Regimiento de Infantería de Línea de Granada, 870; and the Regimiento de Infantería de Línea de Valencia, just 508.[22]

How, then, were these gaps to be made up? In answering this question, let us first look at the issue of conscription. Spain had been subject to various forms of compulsory military service ever since the seventeenth century, and in 1793 there were in fact two different systems in operation. Of these the first and most arbitrary was the so-called *leva*. In brief, as codified by an ordinance of 7 May 1775, the aim of this measure was both to provide men for the army and to purge society of ne'er-do-wells and the destitute alike. Periodically, then, the authorities were authorized to arrest all those men aged between seventeen and thirty-six who could not show that they were in permanent employment, or who had in one way or another earned a reputation as a *vago*—a layabout or drifter—been causing trouble by, say, drinking or brawling, or were suspected of criminal activity, and to march off those deemed capable of military service to the nearest regiment, the last such roundup having taken place in 1787.[23] So brutal, arbitrary, and open to abuse was this system, which obviously bid fair to criminalize poverty and made the numerous class of day laborers vulnerable to enlistment at almost any time, that it was much feared, but there is some evidence to suggest that the authorities believed that it was less unpopular than the more regular system of recruitment that had joined it in 1770. Known as the *sorteo* or *quinta*, this was essentially a ballot. In brief, the government was supposed to announce the number of recruits that it required, it then being the job of the provincial authorities to share the quota that had been assigned among the various municipalities contained within their jurisdiction. Having first established who was liable for military service, and whether or not they were physically fit to take up arms, the names of all those concerned would be read out one by one by the local justice of the peace, whilst a child drew a series of different colored balls out of an urn, black meaning that the man whose name had just been called would have to go into the army and white that he could remain free. Great efforts were made in the regulations to ensure that the whole process was seen to be aboveboard, but the opportunities for corruption were enormous, and it is quite clear that abuses of various sorts were very frequent (with the aid of a little money, for example, it was always possible to obtain a doctor's note testifying to some suitably incapacitating medical condition). But even should no such chicanery take place, the system was unfair in itself. Nobles and members of the clergy were exempt, as were a long list of what in the Second World War would have been termed "reserved occupations," whilst there were also a few geographical exemptions, including the city of Madrid and the Basque provinces. On a brighter and more egalitarian note, the regulations did show a laudable concern to protect those who were especially poor and vulnerable; married men and, in addition, those who could genuinely

show that they were the sole support of their families in theory had
nothing to fear, whilst the purchase of substitutes was prohibited. But
this attempt to sweeten the pill in practice counted for very little; in
the end, the burden of conscription fell on a very reduced section of
the populace, and, what is more, on its very poorest elements. In this
respect, figures that we have for the district of Burgos in 1773 tell
their own story. In Orbaneja del Castillo, for example, the age group
liable to compulsory military service contained sixteen unmarried
men, but of these nine were exempt on account of their occupation,
social class, or personal circumstances, and another six were medically unfit, with the result that there remained just one name for
the ballot; meanwhile, in Herrera del Río Pisuerga, nine men were
deemed both medically fit and liable for military service as opposed
to twenty-three men who were categorized as invalids and another
twenty-four who were covered by other types of exemption. In the
district as a whole, what all this meant was that of 939 unmarried
men of military age, only 231 were actually subjected to the sorteo.[24]

Not surprisingly, then, the sorteo was hated (as, for that matter,
was the rather similar system that was used to make up the ranks of
the provincial militia). Nor was the reason for this just that the system of recruitment was unfair. Soldiers had a very low reputation in
society and were perceived as criminalized and drunken brutes who
invariably ended up as beggars or bandits (in fact, the state did try to
make provision for ex-soldiers through the maintenance of numerous companies of "invalids" who were employed in garrison duties,
but these do not appear to have been able to absorb all the men
concerned). Even serving soldiers were not well looked after; with
money for the army extremely short, they often went unpaid and
unfed, one British observer describing them as "dirty, melancholy
dwarfs."[25] To poor conditions, meanwhile, were added the physical
brutality typical of many eighteenth-century armies, as well as a
long series of more-or-less petty and humiliating restrictions and regulations. Soldiers, for example, were not allowed to smoke in public
and were banned from streets and squares liable to be frequented by
polite society.[26] However poor and desperate they were, meanwhile,
few members of the rural populace—the overwhelming majority of
the population—had any desire to leave their native towns and villages. And, finally, the loss of a son to the army meant the loss of
a useful pair of hands on the family small holding or an equally
useful contribution to the family's income. Anti-conscription riots,

then, were fairly frequent—there was a particularly serious example in Barcelona, for example, in April 1773—whilst many men went into hiding, fled their homes, and even mutilated themselves rather than risk being called up.[27] To make matters worse, meanwhile, this discontent was reflected in the propertied classes; whilst landowners, clergymen, men of letters, local magistrates, and town councilors might not have had to worry about the sorteo themselves, they were understandably concerned at the threat that it posed to public order and even believed that it was injurious to public health (in order to avoid the risk of conscription, for example, many men got married very young, and this was supposed to increase the risk of having handicapped children; equally—and with more veracity—military service was seen as carrying with it very high risks of venereal disease).[28]

In the face of this massive hostility, the regime of Carlos III was in 1777 forced to abandon its preferred policy of the annual imposition of the sorteo—in favor of more traditional methods. Setting aside the leva—itself a measure that was not to be imposed lightly—this decision implied a reliance on voluntary enlistment. However, as a system this carried with its own difficulties. Thus, the only available sources of recruits were all likely to increase hostility to military service. Like many other states of the period, Spain strained every nerve to recruit foreign manpower for its armed forces, whether it was by means of contracting with the Catholic cantons of Switzerland for the upkeep of the army's four Swiss regiments, or by encouraging the recruitment of foreign deserters and draft evaders. However, attitudes to military service being much the same in most of the states of Europe, the trouble with such recruits was that they were "a most wretched crew."[29] Nor was the situation much better with regard to those few soldiers who could be obtained on the home front, for, as the Frenchman Laborde observed, fresh blood was only to be found in spots that abounded in "dupes and libertines."[30] In short, in 1793 Spain's soldiers were the proverbial "scum of the earth," the result being that the whole system appeared to be caught in a vicious downward spiral from which there seemed to be no escape.[31]

Or, at least, so it seemed. With the outbreak of the War of the Convention, according to the traditional view of events, all was resolved in an instant. Thus, following a long period in which the authorities had discouraged discussion of events in France, the

coming of hostilities were greeted by a torrent of propaganda in which
generals, officials, ecclesiastics, and men of letters competed with
one another to hurl abuse at the Revolution and call Spain to arms.
In this, of course, they were joined by the thousands of French émigrés, whose number included many priests, who had fled across the
Pyrenees since 1789. Such newspapers as there were, were soon full
of stories of riot, disorder, and attacks on the interests of property and
the Church, not to mention scornful depictions of Robespierre's Cult
of the Supreme Being, whilst pastoral letters, pamphlets, articles, and
poetic odes united in portraying the Revolutionaries as *sacrilegios*,
impios, the spawn of Satan, and outright madmen, and the events
of 1789–92 as the fruit of some devious masonic or even Protestant
plot. Nor was the war against the Revolution conducted solely on
paper; well aware that levels of literacy in Spain were very low, the
ecclesiastical authorities sent out hundreds of friars to proclaim
the need for a holy war in *plazas mayores* all over the country, whilst
many parish priests, too, preached sermon after sermon in which
the message was driven home still further. In Catalonia, at least,
meanwhile, recruiting agents entitled *promotores de la defensa de la
religión y de la patria* were sent out to encourage recruitment. And,
or so it is claimed, no sooner was a crusade preached, than a crusade
was embarked upon. All over the country volunteers came forward,
or so it is said, by the thousand, whilst the actual arrival of French
troops on Spanish soil turned torrent into tidal wave, the whole of
Spain being energized by the horror stories—many of them all too
justified—that emanated from Catalonia, Guipúzcoa, and Navarre.[32]

A whole series of facts militates against this picture, however.
In Catalonia, for example, despite the fact that they were offered
copious booty, good rates of pay, and ten years' exemption from
certain taxes, the much vaunted migueletes never recruited more
than 14,500 men, whilst they proved so indisciplined and prone to
mutiny, desertion, and pillage that in May 1795 a special code of
discipline had to be drawn up to put an end to their excesses. This
was exceedingly draconian: moving more than 100 paces from the
battalion without the written permission of an officer was pun-
ishable by fifty lashes, whilst the cost of outright straggling was
running the gauntlet twenty times followed by twenty years' ban-
ishment to the dreaded Moroccan fortresses of Ceuta and Melilla.[33]
Also interesting here are the details that we have of the frontier
town of Berga. This last produced 245 volunteers for the migueletes,

but, of these, something more than 200 were residents of settlements on the French side of the Pyrenees who had fled conscription and sought refuge in Spain and now found themselves with no
means of support.[34] Nor were the somatenes much better; as well
as being extremely ill-disciplined, they were also inclined to reject
the authority of the Spanish generals and, in an early demonstration of Catalan regionalism, much given to complaining about the
inadequacies of the Spanish war effort.[35] Meanwhile, of course,
the very fact that special conditions of service had to be introduced
to encourage the Catalans to take up arms suggests that not even the
fact of French invasion was sufficient to persuade the inhabitants
to participate in the war effort with any enthusiasm. The migueletes, indeed, were formed after a special conference of Catalonia's
local authorities that was held in Barcelona in 1794 at the behest
of the then captain general of the region, General José de Urrutia,
after the latter had heard that Catalan recruitment to the regular army was not going well.[36] And that this was the case is clear
enough; perhaps 18,000-strong at the start of the war, the Spanish
field army that fought in Roussillon and Catalonia still numbered
no more than 40,000 men at the beginning of 1794.[37] There had
been some voluntary enlistment, certainly, but the lists of patriotic contributions that appear in the Spanish press of the epoch
suggests that the motivation of the men concerned had little to do
with either love of Spain or hatred of the French. Let us here consider, for example, one such list that relates purely to the efforts of
Catalonia. The escribano de marina, Josep Antoni Font, we read,
provided one volunteer for the army; Bernabé González Chaves, a
knight of the Order of Carlos III, Antonio Casamores, and Antonio
Arnaldo presented three more in the person of their sons; José
Bosque and Jaime Estévez, both of whom were residents of Lérida,
contributed one more apiece; the magistrate of Batea offered fifteen more; and so on. Also notable are the many references that are
made to the provision of bounties for the recruitment of common
soldiers: the Barón de Castellnou, for example, laid down a golden
onza to recruit two soldiers. There are a few examples of men offering their own persons for service in the army, but one suspects
that this was as much as anything an attempt to secure a commission—traditionally, men of noble origin unable to obtain a position as a cadet could enlist as soldados distinguidos in the hope of
becoming an officer later on—the fact being that the "voluntary"

enlistment that took place was often not voluntary at all. Thus, what we see is almost certainly prominent citizens of Barcelona and other cities pressurizing dependents of various sorts—tenants, employees, servants, sons—into taking up arms, and, beyond that, the rural and urban poor being cajoled into enlisting in exchange for a handful of reales.[38] This pattern is also visible in examples that can be found from the province of Valencia. When we are told, for instance, that the monastery of Valldigna supplied fifty soldiers for the cause, one can only suppose that they were drawn from the families of men working their lands as peasant farmers, and that it was again economic pressure that was used to ensure compliance with the demands of the abbot.[39] And where men did come forward voluntarily, they often offered themselves for service not in the army but in the navy, which in the circumstances of 1793–95 was hardly a central pillar of the Spanish war effort (Blas Carbonell, indeed, informs us that the majority of the province of Valencia's 2,192 volunteers went to the navy).[40] Also from Valencia comes a home guard that was set up in 1794 on the initiative of the Duque de la Roca. Supposedly composed of twenty-eight battalions of one thousand men apiece, this force undoubtedly attracted substantial numbers of recruits. Yet given that service in this corps brought with it freedom both from conscription to the regular army and military service anywhere beyond the frontiers of Valencia—a region that never came within hundreds of miles of a French invasion—this is hardly surprising.[41] Nor is it especially reassuring that in Madrid, Barcelona, and other cities, there were serious disturbances that in one case saw the massacre of one hundred French prisoners of war who had joined one of the émigré units raised on the Pyrenean front and then had been dismissed on the grounds that they were politically unreliable. If women wearing their hair in French-style fashions were jeered and assaulted on the streets of the capital by members of the populace, one suspects it was not so much the result of antirevolutionary feeling as the product of the resentment stirred up by the various social reforms introduced during the reign of Carlos III. Equally, if mobs ran amok in Barcelona and elsewhere, it was because mobs were always liable to run amok in a situation where large parts of the population were living on the verge of destitution. In so far as genuine enthusiasm for the war was concerned, it was in fact confined to representatives of the *antiguo régimen*—in other words, to the Church, the nobility, and the representatives of the state. That such elements were a useful source of finance there is no doubt: the archbishop of Valencia donated 1,000,000 reales; the cathedral chapter, 1,500,000; the Barón de Manuel, 500,000; and the landowner Felix Pastor, 300,000.[42] As for the minority of the 17,456 recruits whom the authorities of the Kingdom of Valencia claimed to have produced after the war who actually ended up in the regular army, the majority almost certainly came from the quinta, and this, we know, was deeply unpopular; when Godoy attempted to extend the levy for the provincial militia to Valencia in 1801, he was confronted by a major peasant insurrection that had to be put down with the help of regular troops.[43] And, above all, traditional forms of resistance everywhere remained all too visible; after the war, the Spanish chief minister and royal favorite, Manuel de Godoy, reported that at least 24,000 men deserted in the course of the fighting.[44]

How many men, then, did what Herr is pleased to call "Spain's levée en masse" actually produce for the army?[45] In terms of genuine volunteers, the answer almost certainly has to be "not many." According to the rather unreliable returns available to us from the censuses conducted in Spain in 1787 and 1797, it is clear that there was some increase in the size of the military estate; in the first year 77,884 men laid claim to such a title, whereas in the second, the number who did so was 149,340.[46] Rather more reliable, perhaps, are the revised figures offered by the Spanish historian José Cepeda Gómez, who puts the totals at 85,843 and 132,037 respectively.[47] Whatever the exact figure was, however, the number of men who were actually bearing arms, or had borne them at some time in the past, certainly grew, and all the more so given the many dead of the war of 1793–95, which Godoy again placed at about 24,000.[48] And, if one is to look for more concrete evidence of an increase in Spain's military potential, one might point to the fact that in the course of the war Godoy was able to add five regiments of line infantry, five regiments of light infantry, and two regiments of hussars to the army's order of battle (interestingly, several of these units took the title "volunteers").[49] That said, despite all this evidence of expansion, these figures beg many questions. Contained in the increase were many foreigners, for several units of French émigrés—in theory, enthusiasts for the royalist cause, but in practice either prisoners of war who did not fancy long spells of imprisonment in Spanish fortresses or deserters who had found shelter with the

Spanish army—had been formed in the course of the war, whilst Godoy also recruited two fresh regiments of Swiss mercenaries.[50] At the same time, it appears more than likely that all those men who had served in the *somatén* and the various Basque provinces raised in Navarre and the Basque provinces would also have claimed the right to be included in the military estate in the census of 1797, and yet many of these men were in effect nothing more than conscripts.

In short, when everything else is stripped away, the number of men who actually came forward to fight the French on a voluntary basis was probably no more than a few thousand. From this it follows that the "people's war" of 1793–95 in large part rested on conscription. Knowing, as we do, that the sorteo was immensely unpopular, it speaks volumes that the Spanish government had recourse to it at all. But so it did; both a sorteo and a leva were ordered as early as February 1793, whilst a further sorteo was imposed two years later after a call for 40,000 volunteers made the previous year had proved a complete failure, and that despite the fact that all those who came forward enjoyed generous bounties as well as higher rates of pay than the soldiers of the old army. By 1795 the constant demand for manpower had become deeply unpopular with the population, and a variety of measures were resorted to in an attempt to placate the growing anger. It was promised, for example, that the number of men taken in any pueblo would amount to no more than one in every fifty of those eligible for military service, and, further, that none of those taken would have to serve for any longer than the duration of the war (the normal term of service for conscripts was eight years). In addition, meanwhile, a series of amnesties promised generous terms to any deserters who were prepared to rejoin their units, the hope here being, of course, that this would reduce the number of men that would have to be taken by force.[51]

In view of what is now known of the response of the Spanish people to the infinitely more acute and threatening situation that they experienced in the Peninsular War of 1808–14, none of this should surprise us. Thus, in that conflict, too, the inhabitants did not rush to take up arms, but rather had to be compelled to serve amidst the same scenes of mutiny, fraud, self-mutilation, desertion, and draft evasion that had always greeted the sorteo.[52] Why this was so is not something that can be gone into in any detail here, but, in brief, modern research—one thinks here particularly of the work of Linda Colley and José Alvarez Junco—has shown that the sort of nationalism that is the foundation of a true people's war is something that, first, has to be manufactured over a long period of time, and, second, can only emerge in the wake of a complex series of social, political, and economic changes. As yet these changes had not been seen in Spain—indeed, they did not really begin to take effect until the early twentieth century—and so there was nothing to underpin the crusade against France that the authorities and their allies in the Church and the nobility struggled so determinedly to launch. To talk, then, of a Spanish levée en masse—a concept, incidentally, that Godoy himself described as being hopelessly impracticable—is therefore wildly inaccurate, what one sees in the "War of the Convention"—the term given in Spain to its participation in the French Revolutionary Wars—actually being very much an eighteenth-century state at war.

Military Performance

The War of the Convention began on 7 March 1793 when the French assembly, driven by a mixture of revolutionary ardor and fear of attack, precipitated hostilities against Carlos IV. A this point, however, very few French troops were available on France's southern frontiers, and thus it was that it was left to Madrid to take the initiative. Nor was it long before the Spaniards had evolved a plan of operations. Whilst 8,000 troops under General Ventura Caro covered the Basque provinces and Navarre from invasion and another 5,000 performed a similar function in the high mountains that delineated the central section of the Pyrenean frontier, 24,000 men would cross the rather less difficult terrain offered by the eastern Pyrenees and strike into the province of Roussillon. This, however, was not the most effective of plans. In theory, an offensive in Roussillon was fine, and all the more so as a few short months were to prove that, next to the district known as the Vendée, the Rhone valley and the Mediterranean coast were the areas of France that were ripest for revolt. But 24,000 men were simply not enough to do the job—they would be unlikely to penetrate much beyond the city of Perpignan, if, indeed, they got that far—and it is therefore clear that it was only the political imperative of being seen to take effective action against the Revolution that persuaded the Spaniards to cross the frontier.

These reservations notwithstanding, the Spanish commander in Catalonia (and that province's captain general), the sixty-six-year-old General Antonio Ricardos y Carillo, was a soldier of considerable experience, energy, and courage. Having got together forty-one squadrons of cavalry, thirty-eight battalions of infantry, and some 150 guns, he managed to outflank and rout the first French troops that were sent against him. By the middle of May, indeed, his troops had got through the line of mountains that marked the frontier and had penetrated the valley of the River Tech. On 20 May there followed the first serious battle of the war. Dividing the 12,000 troops he had available into four columns, Ricardos launched an attack on the newly formed Army of the Eastern Pyrenees. Commanded by General Charles de Flers, this force was entrenched in a strong position south of Perpignan between the villages of Mas Deu and Thuir. Having marched through the night, the Spanish troops arrived on the field somewhat scattered, and the French commander therefore seized his opportunity and struck at the Spanish left with all his strength. Hastily reordering his line, Ricardos counterattacked, and there followed a fierce struggle. Even then the French, who fought very well, might have prevailed, but Ricardos sent the Duque de Osuna to outflank their right wing whilst he himself distracted their attention by advancing at the head of his cavalry on the other side of the battlefield. Perceiving that they were caught between two fires, the French began to waver, and, much battered by the superior Spanish artillery, they finally broke and fell back on Perpignan in a state of rout.

This affair was beyond doubt a considerable victory, and it is possible that had Ricardos pushed on he might conceivably have taken Perpignan in one fell swoop. But the battle had been fierce and bloody, and his men were utterly exhausted, whilst he also had to contend with the fact that French troops were still manning the fort of Bellegarde high in his rear. Before doing anything else, then, the Spanish general decided to secure his communications with Spain. This, however, was easier said than done. In the first place, there was the issue of bringing up the necessary siege train from Barcelona, this being something that presented Ricardos with many difficulties. And in the second, there was the problem of the target itself. Bellegarde was not a modern fortress, but it was almost inaccessible to attack, whilst the garrison was strong and enthusiastic. It was not, then, until 15 June that siege operations began, whilst the defenders endured nine days of ferocious bombardment before they finally hoisted the white flag.

With Bellegarde in his hands, Ricardos could again turn his attention to Perpignan. Having long since recovered from his defeat at Mas Deu, however, Flers was in a fighting mood. A preliminary attack on the coastal town of Collioure was beaten off with heavy casualties, and, thus encouraged, on 7 July 4,000 French troops hurled themselves upon the Spaniards holding the entrenched camp that had been established at Mas Deu. But this was not Flers's wisest move; the attackers initially drove back the defenders, but in their excitement they pursued them too far, and were cut down in large numbers by a Spanish cavalry charge. Much chastened, the Army of the Eastern Pyrenees in consequence dug in around Perpignan, covering the main approaches to the city with a series of entrenchments that the French christened the Camp de l'Union. Attacked in these positions on 17 July in an action known as the battle of Perpignan, the army's 12,000 men succeeded in beating off the Spaniards with heavy losses. Yet, despite the fact that his exhausted troops were now down to half-strength and were faced not just with the need to contain the French troops in Perpignan but to blockade the bypassed coastal towns of Collioure and Vendres, Ricardos was still not finished. Thus, undeterred by a French riposte that saw General Luc Dagobert seize the Spanish border town of Puigcerdà far beyond his western flank, on 29 August he sent two columns of troops across the River Têt (the river on which Perpignan stands) by means of a pontoon bridge. Four days later, meanwhile, these forces seized control of a range of hills some miles to the north of the city centered on the village of Peyrestortes, thereby all but cutting Flers's communications with the rest of France.

With matters in this state the fall of Perpignan looked assured. Indeed, many officers and officials abandoned the city, whilst the troops were in a state of complete disorder. Yet, for all that, it was never taken. Fresh heart was put into the defenders by the rhetoric of the local *représentent en mission*, Claude Fabre de l'Hérault, whilst the news of Dagobert's capture of Puigcerdà also did much to boost morale, and all the more so when news arrived that he had been placed in command of the Army of the Eastern Pyrenees. With Ricardos's army now spread out in a great semicircle around Perpignan, the result was not long in coming. On 16 September the troops to the north of the city tried to occupy a small village called Vernet that stood just beyond its walls. However, on reaching their goal they were attacked by 2,000 French troops commanded by Eustache d'Aoust and were driven back in great disorder. Much encouraged, the victors pressed on to Peyrestortes, where they were joined by fresh troops coming from the north. Attacked in flank and rear, the commander of the Spanish forces, an officer of Flemish extraction named Juan Courten, was overwhelmed and was forced to order the evacuation of all the posts held by the Spaniards on the left bank of the Têt. Their assailants having fallen into disorder as soon as they occupied the Spanish camp at Peyrestortes, most of Courten's men got away, but even so it was a signal defeat, the Spaniards having lost 850 men and many guns. Still worse, they also had to abandon all thoughts of taking Perpignan, with Ricardos leading his men back to the new entrenched camp that had been built as a forward base at Ponteilla.

There followed a lull in the fighting that saw the French receive substantial reinforcements. With no more than 30,000 men, Ricardos now faced perhaps 40,000 French, whilst the Army of the Eastern Pyrenees had now been taken over by the aggressive Dagobert. Though the Spanish general had truly achieved much with little, it was all too clear that his bolt was shot, and that the initiative had now passed to the French. On 22 September 1793 there followed the battle of Trouillas, of which an account is given below. Great Spanish victory though this was, it solved none of Ricardos's problems, and a few days later he fell back from the vicinity of Perpignan to a safer position some miles farther south at Le Boulou. Protected by fresh entrenchments that made excellent use of the terrain, the Spanish army then turned at bay, and for the rest of the year fighting raged to and fro as Dagobert launched attack after attack on the Spanish positions. On each occasion, however, the French were driven back by gallant counterattacks, whilst the Spaniards were even able to take Collioure and Port-Vendres. Among the French dead was Fabre de l'Hérault, who thus became the only représentent en mission to fall on the battlefield. As the Spanish troops in the Basque provinces and Navarre, who had won a number of skirmishes in the course of the summer, had just repelled a major French attempt to cross the River Bidasoa and invade Spain, it would not have been such a bad end to the campaign had Ricardos not died of illness on 13 March 1794.

Before proceeding with our account of the war in the Pyrenees, we need to pause to make some mention of the only theater of war

in which Spain's forces were involved outside the Pyrenean frontier. This was none other than the port of Toulon. France's chief
naval base in the Mediterranean, in July 1793 Toulon had joined the
so-called federalist revolt and had invited the powers involved in
the First Coalition to secure the city. By August, then, some 18,500
foreign troops were lining the walls including 2,500 British, 7,000
Spaniards, and 9,000 Piedmontese and Neapolitans. Not long afterward—on 7 September to be precise—the inevitable siege began. In
the fighting that followed, the Spaniards distinguished themselves,
most notably at the fort of Saint Louis, where four hundred Spanish
soldiers put up a fierce fight under the command of a colonel named
Luis de Ariza. Other points held by the Spaniards, meanwhile, were
the bastions of Saint Phillippe and Saint Charles. As is well known,
however, thanks in part to the influence of the young Napoleon
Bonaparte, who distinguished himself at the head of the French
artillery, the defenders were overcome, and on 18 December the surviving allied forces pulled out. According to Spanish sources, the
Spaniards were the last to embark, but that may simply be patriotic
invention. What is not in doubt, however, is that, as in Roussillon,
the Spanish army had proved itself to be a gallant opponent.

To return to the Pyrenean front, the death of Ricardos was
beyond doubt a serious loss to the Spanish cause. As decisive as he
was aggressive, he had done more than anyone could have expected
and had shown genuine skill in the fighting round Perpignan.
Though brave and active, moreover, the officer who took his place—
the Conde de la Unión—was lacking in talent and, as a proverbial
"sprig of the nobility" who had soared to high rank at a very early
age, much disliked by his fellow generals. With the army ravaged
by sickness in the wake of a miserable winter of cold and rain, it
was also simply too weak to hold the lines of entrenchments that
protected its positions. In these circumstances, the arrival of a
5,000-strong Portuguese division commanded by an English general named Forbes could do little more than plug some of the gaps.
With the French much reinforced, the result was inevitable. Leading
his men out of winter quarters, on 30 April 1794 Dagobert threw
the whole of the Army of the Eastern Pyrenees against La Unión.
Known as the battle of Boulou, the action that followed was a rout.
For a full day, the Spaniards and Portuguese managed more or less
to hold their own, but when Dagobert resumed the attack on the
following morning, he broke through on the Spanish right. With

their flanks exposed, regiment after regiment fell back, whilst matters were made worse by the fact that many of the Spanish generals failed to react to the changing situation with the vigor that had served them so well under Ricardos. Seeing that all was lost, La Unión ordered a retreat, but order was now breaking down on all sides, and by the end of the day the Spanish army was in complete flight. Many battalions were in a state of disintegration, whilst left behind in the redoubts around Le Boulou was much of La Unión's artillery, its civilian drivers having fled with their animals as soon as the day had turned against the Spaniards. Small Spanish garrisons still hung on in Collioure, Port-Vendres, and Bellegarde, but the Spanish invasion of France was at an end.

There followed the campaign of Catalonia. Faced by the likelihood that the French would follow up their success and cross the Pyrenees, the Spanish government, as we have seen, mobilized the somatenes, whilst La Unión regrouped his battered army around the major fortress of Sant Ferran, a powerful citadel that stood on a hilltop above the town of Figueres.[53] Nor were their fears unfounded. Having first cleared the last Spanish troops from French soil, in July 1794 the Army of the Eastern Pyrenees, which was now commanded by General Jacques Dugommier, a creole officer from Guadeloupe who had left the Bourbon army as a captain in 1772 and had just headed the French recapture of Toulon, invaded Spain and on 13 August gained a victory at Sant Llorenç de la Muga. However, the invaders proved surprisingly slow to follow up their advantage, and the decisive battle did not come until 17 November when Dugommier attacked the Spaniards in their lines just to the north of Figueres. With 46,000 men and 250 guns dug in in no fewer than ninety-seven redoubts, La Unión was in a strong position, and at first the French made little progress other than to drive back the Spanish left. But Dugommier was not a man to be put off, and the next day he pressed home his advantage. Commanded by Courten, the Spanish left fought hard, whilst Dugommier was slain by a cannon shot, but by the end of the day the defenders had been driven back almost to the gates of Figueres. Now commanded by the future Marshal Perignon, at dawn on 19 November the French attacked the Spanish center. Spearheading the attack was a division headed by another future marshal, Pierre Augereau. Supported by the numerous heavy cannon mounted on the walls of Sant Ferran, the Spaniards again showed much courage, but in the midst of the fighting La Unión was struck down by a musket ball whilst trying to lead a counterattack. With his death, Spanish morale collapsed, and, apart from a sacrificial rearguard commanded by Courten and another Flemish officer named the Vizconde de Gand, the survivors fled the field, leaving behind them 8,000 casualties.

The battle known to the French as Montagne Noir and to the Spaniards as Muntanya Negra brought with it the capture of the fortress of Sant Ferran; despite the fact that he had 9,000 men and plentiful supplies of food and ammunition, the governor was so demoralized by what he had witnessed that on 28 November that he surrendered without firing a shot. But the French did not pursue the Spaniards, who, now commanded by the weak and indecisive Marqués de las Amarillas, were able to rally their forces at Girona. Constantly harassed by the somatenes of the Pyrenees, the invaders were also open to attack from the sea, in consequence of which they turned aside to besiege the small coastal fortress of Roses. Possessed only of the most defective fortifications and completely dominated by hills lying just outside the walls, this place ought to have been easy meat for the 30,000 French troops who now descended on it, but, constantly reinforced from the sea and supported by a naval squadron under Admiral Gravina, the governor, Domingo Izquierdo, managed to hold out for sixty days. Thanks to a staunch rearguard action by three hundred troops who manned the ruined walls to the end, meanwhile, the wounded, the sick, most of the surviving members of the garrison, and a considerable amount of munitions were got away by sea before the end came on 2 February 1795.

With the fall of Roses, the way was clear for the French to march on the Spanish army that still clustered around Girona under a new commander in the person of General José de Urrutia. However, before we look at the last stages of the Catalan campaign, we must first turn to events in the western Pyrenees. Here, the first months of 1794 had been marked by the same inconclusive skirmishing that had characterized the campaign of the previous year, but in late July the French Army of the Western Pyrenees, which was now 57,000 strong and commanded by the future Marshal Moncey, launched an offensive that took it across the frontier on a wide front between Hendaye and Les Aldudes. Whilst some forces cleared the valley of the River Bidasoa, others pushed west along the coast, capturing the towns of Fuenterrabía and San Sebastián, of which the latter surrendered without the slightest attempt to defend itself despite its formidable fortifications. With their rear secure, the French turned south and by 9 August they had reached Tolosa, where they inflicted a serious defeat on the Spaniards, whose commander on this front was now the less than inspiring Conde de Colomera. Operations then came to a stop for two months, but on 16 October Moncey began a drive on Pamplona. This began well; all but cut off, the Spanish forces holding the area around the pass of Roncesvalles were forced to retreat in disorder. However, autumn in the Pyrenees is not the best time for campaigning, and the advance petered out in a welter of rain and mud a few miles north of the Navarrese capital, leaving Moncey with no option but to go into winter quarters.

By the time that the year 1794 came to an end, then, the Spanish army had shown itself unable to prevent the French from penetrating the frontier at both ends of the Pyrenees even if the amount of territory the latter occupied was not in fact very great. In the invaders' rear, many bands of irregulars were active, but war weariness was growing on the home front, whilst a half-baked republican conspiracy was uncovered in Madrid. With little real hope on offer from its British allies, Spain clearly needed peace as soon as possible, and negotiations were duly opened with the French at Basel. It should be noted, however, that the Spanish army was far from beaten—and that despite the fact that its ranks had in the course of winter been ravaged by a terrible epidemic of sickness. Thus, no sooner had spring come than the Army of the Eastern Pyrenees resumed its offensive against Urrutia, whose forces were now drawn up behind the River Fluvià on either side of the village of Báscara. On this front at least, things went well for the Spaniards. Perignon's first two attempts to cross the river were repulsed with heavy casualties, and it was not until 14 July that the French, who were now commanded by General Scherer, returned to the charge. Once again, however, the Spaniards stood firm: not only were the attackers thrown back at every point, but the Spaniards actually crossed the river and drove back the French from its banks. Still worse, a mixed force of Spanish and Portuguese troops was also dispatched to retake the distant town of Puigcerdà. Commanded by Gregorio García de la Cuesta—the General Cuesta who figures with such infamy in British accounts of the Peninsular War—this force swept all before it, and on 25 July 1795 it stormed Puigcerdà and overcame its defenders in the midst of scenes of dreadful slaughter. Fighting spilled over into the streets of the town, and, according to French accounts at least, many of the defenders were massacred. But victory in the east was countered by defeat in the west. Eager to reinforce its position at Basel, the French government ordered the Army of the Western Pyrenees to resume its offensive of the previous year. Breaking through the Spanish lines at Irurzún on 6 July, this force stormed across Navarre and the Basque provinces and had within a few days reached the River Ebro at Miranda de Ebro and occupied Bilbao, the result being that the treaty that was finally signed at Basel on 22 July 1795 could not come soon enough for Carlos IV; hence the fact that Manuel de Godoy was rewarded with title "Prince of the Peace."[54]

Spain Triumphant: The Battle of Trouillas, 22 September 1793

In August 1793, as is well-known, the French unleashed the levée en masse on an unsuspecting world. Fired up by strength of numbers and revolutionary fervor alike, France's citizen-soldiers threw themselves upon the "mercenary" armies of the ancien régime and carried all before them. So at least runs the legend. Hardly had the genie been let out of the bottle, however, than the Spaniards proved that it could be bested. As we have seen, by the late summer of 1793 the Spanish invasion of Rousillon had run out of steam; the army of General Ricardos was outnumbered, short of supplies, and utterly exhausted, whilst its opponents had received many reinforcements as well as a new commander in the person of General Luc Dagobert. A vigorous general of the Bourbon army of noble descent, Dagobert, indeed, was now planning to take the offensive. On 22 September some 18,000 French troops duly appeared before the Spanish positions. On the right stood 5,000 infantry and 400 cavalry under Jacques Goguet; in the center, 6,000 infantry under Dagobert himself; and on the left, 7,000 infantry under D'Aoust, although nearly half this latter force was armed only with pikes, the French forces in the Pyrenees being very short of muskets. As for the Spaniards, who were perhaps 16,000 strong, they were deployed in the latest of several fortified camps that they had established in the course of their advance on Pamplona. Known as the Camp of Ponteilla, this base was protected by a line of entrenchments and abattis that ran in a semicircle along a range of low hills from Ponteilla on the extreme left to Nils on the extreme right.

The latter settlement standing on the banks of a substantial stream that joined the River Réat a little way to the east, the right flank of the position was particularly well protected. Not so, however, the left, which would have been wide open to attack had it not been for the fact that the village of Thuir, which stood some way to the west, was garrisoned as an outwork. Seeing this, Dagobert ordered Goguet to take Thuir and then hook behind the Spanish lines. In an attempt to distract Ricardos's attention from Thuir, D'Aoust was to seize a line of heights that ran southward from the River Réat and overlooked the main road to Spain, and demonstrate against the Spanish right. And finally Dagobert was to remain in reserve until the time was ripe for an advance on the Spanish center.

Thus far, thus good, but the day did not go as Dagobert expected. The garrison of Thuir, which still possessed its mediaeval walls and had been equipped with a number of field guns, repelled Goguet's first attacks, whereupon the French commander—who had been a medical student at the University of Montpellier in 1789 and had enlisted as a volunteer in 1792—allowed his troops to become bogged down in a useless *tiraillade* with the defenders. As a result Ricardos was given plenty of time to order up fresh troops from his reserve, and in no time all hope of Goguet getting round the Spanish left had evaporated. Nor did D'Aoust's forces prove of any assistance; having set off well behind schedule, they did not reach the heights they were supposed to take in time to draw off troops from the attack on Thuir, whilst, to make matters worse, when they did appear, a few long-range cannon shots sufficed to throw the whole force into a panic and send it flying to the rear.

Desperate to save the day, Dagobert now flung in his reserves. Deploying his men in three columns of attack, he sent one to storm Ponteilla and another to advance through a gap in the Spanish defenses just to the east of the village that was only blocked by an abatti. As for the third, it was to act as a reserve. His advance, however, was doomed. Directly above Ponteilla was a large battery mounting no fewer than twelve 24-pounder siege cannon, and the commander of this sector of the Spanish line—to be precise, the Duque de Osuna— ordered his infantry and artillery alike to hold their fire until the last possible moment. With the Spanish entrenchments only perhaps one hundred yards away, then, a terrible discharge rang out that cut down the front ranks of the column heading for the battery in swathes and stopped the advance in an instant. To the French left, however, matters were a little different. Here the attackers were more protected by virtue of the fact that they were advancing up a narrow valley that cut through the Spanish defenses. Reaching the abatti, they were therefore able to tear it down, and, egged on by Dagobert himself, get through to the other side. Fortunately for the Spaniards, Ricardos was well aware of the danger. Ordering the commander of his right wing, the Conde de la Unión, to attack the left flank of the enemy column with his horse, he himself rode into its other side with a mixed force of dragoons and guard cavalry. Caught between two fires, the French broke and fled back down the valley in great confusion. All that remained of Dagobert's array, then, was his third infantry column. This column had neither followed Dagobert across the abattis nor charged the battery on the ridge, but had rather halted in no-man's-land. Here it too met with disaster. Thus, the French commander now decided to lead the column across the Spanish front to reinforce Goguet. Seeing this, Ricardos brought up some fresh cavalry from his left. Splitting into two commands, one of them commanded by Diego de Godoy, the brother of the Spanish secretary of state and royal favorite, Manuel de Godoy, these assailed the French columns from left and right simultaneously. Cut off from their fellows, three French infantry battalions either laid down their arms or deserted to the Spaniards—according to one account, indeed, the Régiment de Vermandois crossed the lines en masse to shouts of "Vive l'Espagne!"—whilst Dagobert was left with no option but to retire from the field.

Had the Spaniards pursued the French commander with any vigor, he might have been in even worse trouble, but the troops sent to follow up the defenders' success were checked by a mixture of the difficult terrain and the continued fire of the French artillery, the result being that the Army of the Eastern Pyrenees was able to regroup in its original positions. Yet French casualties had been very heavy: the Régiment d'Infanterie de Champagne, for example, was almost wiped out, and, not counting the many men who absconded after the battle, total French losses may have amounted to as many as 6,000 men, including 1,500 prisoners. Along with the latter were taken ten cannon and several wagons of munitions, whilst Dagobert was in addition forced to burn much of his baggage train to prevent the Spaniards from getting their hands on still more of it. In terms of the campaign, it is true, all this made little difference; Dagobert's losses were soon made good, whilst Ricardos's could not be replaced, but the message was nonetheless clear enough. The onrushing columns of the republic were not invincible, but could be dealt with by a mixture of field fortification, the sophisticated use of firepower, and the presence of mobile reserves. Superior Spanish generalship certainly helped—Ricardos throughout both kept a clear head and displayed exemplary courage—as did the fact that the Spaniards were operating on interior lines, but, for all their revolutionary fervor, the forces of the republic could still be fought to a standstill on the battlefield. In the words of the Spanish official history, then, "The battle of Trouillas is a military action that is on every account worthy of being known and taken into account."[55]

Notes

1. Conde de Clonard, *Historia orgánica de las armas de infantería y caballería españolas desde la creación del ejército permanente hasta el dia* (Madrid, 1851–62), 6:43.
2. For the role played by the army in the Bourbon state, see J. L. Terrón Ponce, *Ejército y Política en la España de Carlos III* (Madrid: Ministerio de Defensa, 1997), 17–42.
3. For some useful contemporary accounts of these arrangements, see J. F. de Bourgoing, *A Modern State of Spain* (London, 1808), 1:176, 2:65; and A. Laborde, *A View of Spain* (London, 1809), 4:455–56, 496–97.
4. For all this complication, see C. J. Esdaile, *The Spanish Army in the Peninsular War* (Manchester: Manchester University Press, 1988), 3–4.
5. For a biography of the officer concerned, General Antonio Ricardos, see Estado Mayor Central del Ejército, *Campañas en los Pirineos a finales del siglo XVIII* (Madrid: Servicio Histórico Militar, 1949–59), 2:80–84.
6. Esdaile, *Spanish Army*, 4–5.
7. Ibid., 5. Details of the weapons used by the Spanish army may be found in M. Gómez Ruiz, *El Ejército de los Borbones* (Madrid: Servicio Histórico Militar, 1995), 4:582–89, whilst there are also some interesting remarks in W. Jacob, *Travels in the South of Spain* (London, 1811), 166.
8. *Ordenanzas de Su Majestad para el régimen, disciplina, subordinación y servicio de sus ejércitos* (Madrid, 1768), 5:iii–iv passim; "Memoria sobre la caballería presentada al Excmo. Sr. D. Jerónimo Caballero, por el Vizconde Dambly, commandante de escuadra que ha sido de caballería francesa," 26 February 1790, Real Academía de Historia (hereafter RAH) 2-MS135, no. 5.
9. *Ordenanzas*, 5:x, 1–59.
10. Entitled *La guerrilla, o tratado del servicio de las tropes ligeras en campaña*, a copy of this work may be found in the library of the Spanish army's Servicio de Historia y Cultura Militar.
11. J. Vigón, *Historia de la artillería española* (Madrid: Consejo Superior de Investigaciones Científicas, 1947), 2:304–23 passim.

12. Favorable comments may be found on the artillery in Bourgoing, *Modern State of Spain*, 1:71, and J. Townsend, *A Journey through Spain in the Years 1786 and 1787* (London, 1792), 2:278.

13. Clonard, *Historia orgánica*, 5:405.

14. J. R. Aymes, *La Guerra de España contra la Revolución Francesa, 1793–1795* (Alicante, Sp.: Instituto de Cultura Juan Gil-Albert, 1991), 310–42 passim.

15. C. Borreguero Beltrán, *El reclutamiento militar por quintas en la España del siglo XVIII: origenes del servicio militar obligatorio* (Valladolid: Universidad de Valladolid, 1989), 187.

16. For all these details, see J. Fàbregas Roig, *La Guerra Gran, 1793–1795: El protagonisme de Girona i la mobilització dels miquelets* (Lérida, Pagès 2000), 78–85.

17. For Saint Simon's Legión Real, see Clonard, *Historia orgánica*, 5:397.

18. Estado Mayor Central, *Campañas en los Pirineos*, 1:132. For detailed discussions of the officer corps, see Esdaile, *Spanish Army*, 14–24; Terrón, *Ejército y Política*, 43–80; and F. Andujar Castillo, *Los militares en la España del siglo XVIII: Un estudio social* (Granada: Universidad de Granada, 1991), 121–325.

19. J. Lynch, *Bourbon Spain, 1700–1808* (Oxford: Blackwell, 1989), 316.

20. Clonard, *Historia orgánica*, 5:291–309.

21. H. Swinburne, *Travels through Spain in the Years 1775 and 1776* (Dublin, 1779), 25.

22. Estado Mayor Central, *Campañas en los Pirineos*, 2:131–33.

23. Borreguero, *Reclutamiento militar*, 65–67.

24. Ibid., 373–74.

25. Swinburne, *Travels*, 26.

26. *Ordenanzas*, 2:i, 12–16.

27. Borreguero, *Reclutamiento militar*, 317–28.

28. Ibid., 329–35; Esdaile, *Spanish Army*, 13.

29. W. Dalrymple, *Travels through Spain and Portugal in 1774* (London, 1777), 65.

30. Laborde, *View of Spain*, 4:505.

31. The most up-to-date view on the recruitment of the Spanish army in the eighteenth century is contained in F. Puell de la Villa, *El soldado desconocido: de la leva a la "mili"* (Madrid: Biblióteca Nueva, 1996), 47–98; in justification of what has just been said, it is the belief of Puell that the principal source of recruits throughout the period was the leva.

32. There is a classic statement of the traditional view of popular feeling in R. Herr, *The Eighteenth-Century Revolution in Spain* (Princeton, N.J.: Princeton University Press, 1958), 297–315. What is particularly striking about the chapter concerned is that it is almost entirely founded on the official and semi-official "discourse" of the day rather than solid work in the Spanish archives.

33. Fàbregas, *Guerra Gran*, 94–105 passim.

34. P. Sahlins, *Boundaries: The Making of France and Spain in the Pyrenees* (Berkeley: University of California Press, 1989), 180.

35. Aymes, *Guerra de España*, 362–64.

36. Ibid., 103–104.

37. Estado Mayor Central, *Campañas en los Pirineos*, 2:131–32.

38. Ibid., III-ii, 3:369–75.

39. M. Blas Carbonell, *La aportación valenciana a la Guerra de 1793–1795* (Diputació de Valencia, Valencia, 1996), 20.

40. Ibid., 21.

41. Aymes, *Guerra de España*, 188–91.

42. Blas, *Aportación valenciana*, 20.

43. Esdaile, *Spanish Army*, 47–48.

44. M. de Godoy to Carlos IV, 26 February 1796, RAH 2-MS135, no. 7.

45. The phrase comes from the title Herr gives to the chapter of his *Eighteenth Century in Spain* that deals with the war of 1793–95.

46. Esdaile, *Spanish Army*, 39.

47. J. Cepeda Gómez, *El ejército en la política española, 1787–1843* (Madrid: Fundación Universitaria Española, 1990), 41.

48. M. de Godoy to Carlos IV, 26 February 1796, RAH. 2-MS135, no. 7.

49. Esdaile, *Spanish Army*, 38.

50. Ibid. After the war was over, the émigré units were amalgamated as the Borbón Light Infantry Regiment.

51. There is some confusion in the sources about the extent and timing of the sorteos decreed by the Spanish government in the course of the war of 1793–95. According to Borreguero, there was only one such measure in the form of a levy of 40,000 men in 1794 (Borreguero, *Reclutamiento militar*, 151). In this, however, she is in error; a little-known directory of all the decrees and regulations issued by the Spanish government in the first part of the reign of Carlos IV lists both the sorteos described. See S. Sánchez, ed., *Colección de todas las pragmáticas, cédulas, provisiones, autos acordados y otras providencias publicados en el actual reinado del Señor Don Carlos IV* (Madrid, 1794–1801), 1:307; 2:12–15, 102–104. Also interesting are the remarks contained in Bourgoing, *Modern State of Spain*, 3:243, 294.

52. For some details, see C. J. Esdaile, *Fighting Napoleon: Guerrillas, Bandits and Adventurers in Spain, 1808–1814* (New Haven, Conn.: Yale University Press, 2004), 61–89.

53. To assist the modern traveler, the author has made use of the Catalan form of the names that figure in the account of the campaign that follows. The Castilian forms are as follows: Sant Ferran—San Fernando; Figueres—Figueras; Sant Llorenç de la Muga—San Lorenzo de la Muga; Muntanya Negra—Montaña Negra; Girona—Gerona; Roses—Rozas.

54. The most detailed account of the war of 1793–95 is to be found in Estado Mayor Central, *Campañas en los Pirineos*, which is the Spanish army's official history of the campaign. This may be supplemented by Clonard, *Historia orgánica*, 5:337–421. Less detailed but more accessible is Aymes, *Guerra de España*, 41–90. For a Franco-centric account, see R. W. Phipps, *The Armies of the First French Republic and the Rise of the Marshals of Napoleon I* (Oxford: Clarendon Press, 1931), 3:216.

55. Estado Mayor Central, *Campañas en los Pirineos*, 2:499.

CHAPTER 7

THE ARMIES OF THE
GERMAN PRINCES

PETER H. WILSON

The armies of the German princes appear to epitomize every
weakness of old-regime military organization. They were
relatively small, poorly equipped, trained in the linear tactics of
eighteenth-century limited warfare, and, apparently, composed
of unenthusiastic mercenaries commanded by uneducated aristocratic adventurers. Above all, they lost and their defeat had profound consequences, spelling the end of the thousand-year-old
Holy Roman Empire to which the principalities belonged. Though
the empire survived until 1806, it suffered irrevocable damage in
the 1790s and was the only major European state not to be restored
in 1815. Military failure and political collapse have been generally
regarded as inevitable, because most historians assumed the empire
was in terminal decline since 1648. The princes were supposed
to contribute to the Imperial Army (Reichsarmee) that last mobilized during the Seven Years' War (1756–63) when it was routed
by Frederick the Great at Rossbach (1757). If it could not with-
stand Prussia's old-regime army, how could it defeat the French
citizens-in-arms?

The German Princes

This question already vexed contemporaries. Friedrich Christian
Laukhard (1758–1822) left one of the most influential personal cri-
tiques.[1] Originally a teacher, he served a decade with the Prussians
and later joined the Swabian contingent to the Imperial Army. He
went beyond compiling a list of material and technical deficiencies
to identity the root cause of the defeat: the absence of a true fatherland to defend. For Laukhard, the empire could neither organize

efficiently nor inspire loyalty, because it was divided into numerous comic opera states ruled by selfish, tyrannical princelings. These criticisms had been voiced already during the American Revolutionary War (1775–83) when six princes supplied 30,000 auxiliaries to the British and were accused of selling their subjects to fund lives of indolent luxury.[2] This largely liberal critique acquired more nationalist and reactionary overtones during the French revolutionary era and beyond as it became enmeshed in the political rivalry to decide Germany's future. Increasingly, the empire symbolized national disunity and shame that had to be erased if Germany was to be reborn as a dynamic, militarized great power.

The experiences of two twentieth-century world wars encouraged a reappraisal of the empire and with it, the princely armies. While many contemporaries indeed shared Laukhard's views, the majority regarded the empire as their fatherland and were convinced it would survive, despite its obvious faults.[3] In contrast to both Bourbon and revolutionary France, the empire was a decentralized political system where sovereignty was fragmented rather than concentrated in a national government. The empire was divided into territories, or "imperial estates" (Reichsstände), that handled their own internal affairs subject to varying degrees of supervision from imperial institutions. Contrary to the popular view, these territories were not independent, though they could make alliances with other countries provided these were not directed against the emperor or empire. There were 165 secular and 67 ecclesiastical principalities, as well as 51 imperial cities governed by magistrates elected on a narrow franchise. Power was in fact more concentrated than these numbers suggest, because many principalities had passed into the hands of a few dynasties. The Prussian Hohenzollerns controlled eighteen principalities, counties, and lordships of varying sizes, while the Wittelsbachs had twenty-one of which Bavaria and the Palatinate were the most important.[4] The Austrian Habsburgs had only five, but they were much larger, giving them nearly a third of the empire, compared to Prussia's 19 percent. Both powers held further land beyond the imperial frontiers, though it was not until the Second and Third Partitions of Poland (1793, 1795) that Prussia joined Austria in having more territory outside the empire than within it. Bavaria, the next largest, only held around a tenth of the empire, while Saxony and Hanover together held about the same. There were around fourteen medium-sized principalities of some importance,[5] while around a dozen others exercised some influence at regional level, as did six of the imperial cities.[6]

Around twenty territories possessed what might be called an army, though the hierarchy of formal political power did not match the actual distribution of military and fiscal resources. The four leading armed territories each had at least four times the number of men under arms in 1792 than the next group of six middling princes (see table). Another ten had between 1,000 and 2,000 apiece, including Hamburg and Nuremberg, the only two imperial cities with substantial forces. This group in turn had another substantial lead over the remaining 70 or so minor principalities, counties, and bishoprics, and the other 49 cities, most of which had 200 soldiers or less each. The combined total of around 120,000 men was fairly impressive, considering the French regular army mustered only 136,000 in 1792. By contrast, Prussia maintained 195,000, adding another 23,000 on mobilization in 1792, while the Habsburgs had 497,700 including light troops and support personnel. The disparity between the two German great powers and the other territories had grown more pronounced in the last third of the eighteenth century, contributing to the princes' declining political significance.

The Habsburgs had held the imperial title (with one break) since 1438, but could not dictate what the princes did. Decisions had to be agreed upon by the Imperial Diet (Reichstag) if they were to be binding on all territories. The constitution was intended to protect the weak against the strong by encouraging peaceful arbitration of disputes through the two imperial supreme courts. Both Austria and Prussia were effectively exempt from imperial jurisdiction, though they avoided gross transgressions of imperial law for fear of driving the princes into the arms of their rival. Those that did resort to force failed, as Hessen-Kassel discovered when it invaded tiny Schaumburg-Lippe in February 1787 and was forced by the courts to withdraw two months later.[7]

Legal protection extended deep into society through the web of imperial and territorial laws offering ordinary folk numerous opportunities to appeal against their lords. These rights were largely corporate, since a person's ability to invoke them depended on his or her membership in a legally recognized group, such as a craftsman belonging to a guild or a burgher of a particular town. They were thus liberties rather than abstract liberty in the French revolutionary sense, meaning they were neither uniform nor individual rights.

German military potential in order of army size, 1791/1792

Territory	Size (km2)	Population	Revenue (millions of fl)	Army
Saxony	26,812	1,452,000	11.25	26,773
Bavaria	57,563	2,007,858	7.0	19,696
Hanover	25,526	839,000	6.0	17,836
Hessen-Kassel	10,744	468,823	2.4	15,000
Hessen-Darmstadt	4,125	195,000	1.8	4,000
Würzburg	4,950	268,000	1.29	3,700
Württemberg	8,855	623,011	3.0	3,156
Mainz	7,095	343,500	2.2	3,082
Brunswick-Wolfenbüttel	3,828	168,000	1.838	3,060
Ansbach-Bayreuth	7,700	400,000	2.4	2,824
Baden	5,005	215,500	1.35	2,000
Münster	10,500	311,341	1.2	1,910
Hamburg (city)	413	150,000	1.7	1,770
Sachsen-Gotha	3,003	187,800	1.05	1,600
Mecklenburg-Schwerin	12,265	310,000	1.43	1,500
Trier	7,150	215,000	0.84	1,200
Cologne (electorate)	7,480	230,000	1.7	1,100
Salzburg	10,450	220,000	1.2	1,000
Liège	5,775	286,000	1.5	1,000
Nuremberg (city)	1,650	70,000	?	1,000
Bamberg	3,575	180,000	0.834	900
Frankfurt (city)	122	46,000	0.6	600
Bremen (city)	193	50,000	?	560
Hohenlohe	1,870	100,000	0.38	400
Ulm (city)	930	38,000	0.35	388
Cologne (city)	city only	54,000	?	258

German military potential in order of army size, 1791/1792 (*cont.*)

Territory	Size (km2)	Population	Revenue (millions of fl)	Army
Schwarzburg-Rudolstadt	990	50,000	?	250
Paderborn	2,970	124,000	0.597	200
Lippe-Detmold	1,209	71,000	0.203	135
Wied		440	23,000	?
Schaumburg-Lippe	340	20,000	0.113	83
Sachsen-Weimar	2,051	109,000	0.14	80
Worms (bishopric)	440	12,000	0.02	60
Mecklenburg-Strelitz	2,684	56,000	?	50
Schwäbisch-Hall (city)	330	14,750	0.09	46
Essen (convent)	155	1,900	?	20
Salm-Kyrburg	55	6,000	?	16

Note: The table shows the twenty largest armies and representative examples of the smaller forces.

Nonetheless, membership in a community gave Germans access to a wide range of basic rights, such as freedom from religious discrimination, protection from arbitrary arrest, and varying degrees of political and legal representation. These liberties were not universally respected, but they generally provided greater personal freedom than that elsewhere in Europe, including prerevolutionary France. Since they were local and particular, they reinforced a sense of place, whilst connecting individuals to the empire that guaranteed each community's autonomy. There were signs that this order was coming under increasing strain, not least from accelerating population growth that fuelled the numbers of underemployed paupers. However, most intellectuals remained convinced that the existing order offered the best means to solve these problems. There were popular protests, notably in the smaller territories, but while some of these adopted the language and symbols of revolutionary France, they remained primarily traditional and were intended to pressure governments into reducing taxes or remedying abuses, rather than overturning the established order. It was this conservative, decentralized socio-legal order that Germans fought to defend after 1792.[8]

The empire's defeat cannot be explained by drawing a false contrast with France since this implies that there was only one route to modernity and that the empire had chosen the wrong path. Certain institutions responded effectively after 1792, while individual armies fought well. Failure stemmed from a reluctance to resort to the kind of violent expedients used by the French, and because Austro-Prussian competition over German resources undermined the collective war effort.[9]

Structure

The decentralized character of imperial politics greatly complicates the discussion of German armies. Not only was there no single national army, but even those of the principalities rarely took the field as a single force since individual regiments were dispatched to fulfill different obligations. The primary duty was defense of the empire through the system of collective security established in the late fifteenth century that assigned each territory a fixed basic quota (*Simplum*). This could be provided either as soldiers or the cash equivalent of their monthly wage bill known as a Roman Month. Coordination was provided through the ten Imperial Circles (Kreise) into which the territories were grouped on a regional basis.[10] This structure was uneven, reflecting the geographical distribution of power across the empire. The Austrian and Burgundian (i.e., southern Netherlands) Kreise existed in name only since they were almost entirely composed of Habsburg territory. The Upper and Lower Saxon Kreise were dominated by Prussia, Saxony, and Hanover, but a more balanced mix of territories in the remaining six ensured these still functioned.

The larger territories sent entire regiments to fulfill their imperial obligations, but the smaller ones combined their contingents through the Kreis structure that regulated organization, pay, promotions, and supply. The official collective basic quota had been fixed in 1681 at 12,000 cavalry and 28,000 infantry, but territories were free to substitute one cavalryman for three infantry, or to provide part or all of their contingent in cash. Further complications arose through the practice of "moderation," which allowed some territories to reduce their quotas due to mitigating circumstances. Some of these reductions had not been sanctioned, creating uncertainty over the exact extent of current obligations.

The empire's devolved system allowed the Kreise to mobilize their members' contingents to meet particular threats, but offensive action required the Reichstag's approval. The Electoral Rhenish, Upper Rhenish, and Swabian Kreise had already mobilized some troops after December 1789 to secure the Rhine. The Kreise also coordinated military action to suppress discontent in a number of smaller Rhenish territories during 1789–91. Unrest was fanned by growing numbers of French émigrés who sought shelter, especially in Trier, and exaggerated the danger to frighten German governments into backing their calls for counterrevolution. Despite this, the authorities generally avoided violent repression, deploying troops mainly to overawe unruly peasants, students, and artisans, whilst attempting to address some grievances through modest reform. The largest action involved the deployment of around 5,000 Bavarian, Mainz, Trier, and Cologne troops against the Liège rebels in 1790–91.

The situation changed with the French declaration of war on 20 April 1792 against Austria and particularly after the failure of the combined Austro-Prussian counterinvasion of France that summer. Neither Austria nor Prussia was equipped to wage a protracted struggle unaided and both looked to the empire to provide assistance. The princes had relied on Austro-Prussian antagonism to preserve the empire's internal balance during the later eighteenth century but were unable to oppose their combined weight, especially as the Habsburgs could count on the support of the numerous minor Catholic ecclesiastical princes who traditionally looked to the emperor for protection. Some of these princes genuinely feared revolutionary France and advocated war to restore the Bourbons. A few secular princes objected to the French expropriation of their property in Alsace, which accompanied the Revolution's abolition of feudalism in August 1789. However, the majority favored negotiation, recognizing that Austria and Prussia would exploit any conflict to their own advantage. The French invasion of the Rhineland in October 1792 spread consternation, enabling Austria to rally a majority in the Reichstag to declare an official imperial war (*Reichskrieg*) on 23 March 1793.

The Reichstag authorized a triple quota (*Triplum*), raising this to a *Quintuplum* of 200,000 men on 13 October 1794, which remained nominally in force until the end of the War of the First Coalition in 1797. Another Quintuplum was authorized in September 1799 when the empire mobilized again in the War of the Second Coalition (1799–1802). Additional cash contributions were summoned to pay for the imperial general staff and fill the Imperial Operations Fund to cover campaign expenses. In all, 230 Roman Months' worth around 15 million florins (fl) were authorized in the first war, with a further 100 Roman Months in the second at a time when the minimum monthly food and pay bill of an infantryman was reckoned at 4 fl. Only 5 million fl were received in the first war, with little paid in the second. Troop numbers also fell short of official totals. Only 91,000 men were present in 1793, of whom 57,000 were Austrian or Prussia, while overall strength fell to 77,500 by the following December.

However, these totals are deceptive. It is necessary to deduct 36,000 men from the full 120,000 as the triple quota of the Habsburg monarchy that refused to integrate its forces with the Imperial Army. Prussia likewise kept its 12,000 men entirely separate. Overall numbers were further reduced by the practice of many territories contracting Austria or Prussia to provide their contingent instead. These payments, known as Relutions, were one of the primary attractions of the official mobilization to the two great powers, which used them to pay their own soldiers whom, in Austria's case at least, they would have sent anyway. Austria drew payments from 60 minor territories in lieu of 12,000 men, while Prussia received money for another 10,000 in 1793. Some relatively important territories resorted to this practice, including the electorate of Cologne, which paid 350,000 fl to Austria in place of 4,160 men. Sweden also paid Relutions on behalf of its German duchy of Pomerania. Further men were removed from the official Imperial Army by Austria's private agreements with several middling princes who provided their soldiers directly to the Habsburg army instead. Würzburg had already sent 2,477 infantry and dragoons to assist Austria against the Belgian rebels after 1790. As these remained in Austrian service until 1801, the emperor agreed in May 1793 to pay 264,000 fl into the Relutions fund in return for counting around half the auxiliaries as the bishopric's imperial contingent.[11]

Finally, another 6,700 men were removed by the loss of the territories west of the Rhine that were overrun before they could provide their contingents. The Electoral Rhenish Kreis was the worst affected, truncating the contribution of the three ecclesiastical electors in Mainz, Cologne, and Trier. Mainz had already signed a convention with Austria and Prussia on 14 August 1792 to provide 1,892 infantry, representing the bulk of its pre-war army. These were destroyed at the battle of Speyer on 30 September when the French overran the western part of the electorate. The army was partly reconstituted, numbering 1,900 men by July 1794, but now served largely as garrison troops.[12] The same fate befell Trier and Cologne, both of which lost extensive possessions west of the Rhine. Those units that survived were used to hold the fortresses along the river.

This shrinkage reduced the official contribution of the remaining princes to around 40,000 for 1793–95, rising to 66,000 with the Quintuplum thereafter. Though these numbers were not achieved, especially after 1796, mobilization was nonetheless impressive. The minor territories fielded disproportionately large numbers, belying the standard criticism that the empire's decentralized structure was incapable of effective action. With ninety-seven members, Swabia was the most fragmented region, but mobilized the largest contingent. It already deployed 4,400 men to secure its section of the Upper Rhine in 1792, increasing these to 6,800 with the official mobilization a year later. Another 11,700 were added in response to the Quintuplum in 1795. Only 11,330 were actually present that September, but they represented seven times the region's basic quota, or in excess of official requirements. The response was weaker in the second war due to altered political circumstances that included Baden's neutrality, which removed the second most potent contributor. Nonetheless, the other members fielded 5,052 men in May 1800, including 2,215 from the 29 ecclesiastical territories that together had only 18 percent of the Swabian population. In addition, Württemberg, the most powerful territory, dispatched 2,700 men to the Reichsarmee in March 1800, followed by the rest of its (then) 7,700-strong army a month later once it received British subsidies.[13]

Political factors impaired the contributions of the other Kreise, because the decision of one or more powerful members not to participate made a significant impact on numbers. The Franconian contingent was reduced by Prussia's acquisition of Ansbach-Bayreuth, the largest principality, on the abdication of its last native prince in January 1792. Bamberg and Würzburg, the next largest, provided their troops to Austria instead, while the two Hohenlohe princes sunk their personal fortunes in financing part of the Prince de

Condé's émigré legion.[14] Though the remaining 16 members possessed little over a quarter of the Franconian population, they still fielded a respectable 1,569 men in 1793–95. As in Swabia, their contribution is scarcely surprising since they had the most to lose if the empire was defeated.

The pattern was repeated in the Upper Rhine where the two rival Hessian landgraves wanted their involvement to bring additional land and status. Prior to 1796 they looked to Austria and Prussia to deliver these. While Wilhelm IX of Hessen-Kassel remained committed to the anti-French cause thereafter, his Darmstadt cousin Ludwig X took a more pragmatic line, especially after Austria abandoned him in 1799. Hessen-Kassel had already merged its Kreis regiment into the rest of its army in 1788 and had provided all its troops to the British after 1793. Hessen-Darmstadt had also disbanded its Kreis contingent in 1790, but did provide a brigade of 2,400 men in March 1793 in return for payments from the Relutions fund. These troops thus substituted for the contingents of other territories, rather than representing additional forces, reducing the Upper Rhine contribution to two weak infantry regiments from the other members that were destroyed at the siege of Mannheim in 1794.[15]

The Westphalian mobilization was disrupted by Prussia, which wanted the other members to pay it to field their contingents. Some, like the abbess of Essen, found it too expensive to raise their own forces and reluctantly agreed. The others met in Cologne in defiance of Prussia and voted to mobilize in May 1794. Only 2,434 of the full 9,920 men were sent, but the shortfall was largely due to Prussian and Bavarian noncooperation. Westphalian participation ended when the region was forced to leave the war following Prussia's declaration of neutrality across most of northern Germany in April 1795. Few Lower Saxons joined the Imperial Army, because the region's principal territories sent their soldiers elsewhere. Brunswick-Wolfenbüttel had sent its entire army into Dutch service in 1788 and paid Relutions from 1793 rather than raise additional troops. Both George III and his Hanoverian ministers strongly supported the imperial constitution and designated 3,066 men as the electorate's Kreis contingent in 1792, but then sent these along with the rest of its army into British pay from 1793. George's refusal to cooperate was in protest at Austria's attempts to subordinate all German units to its exclusive command.[16] Bavaria refused on the same grounds, sending only a token 2,500 men in 1793. Salzburg, the only other substantial member of the Bavarian Kreis, sent its regiment directly to the Austrian army from 1793 to 1801.

Prussia's refusal to cooperate also accounted for most of the missing Upper Saxons. The other principal member was electoral Saxony, which cooperated fully with the war effort, sending nearly 6,000 men in 1793. Though this number fell to 4,700 the following year, it rose to 9,700 in response to the Quintuplum in 1795. Having paid Relutions for the first two years, the other members now sent troops in response to the growing crisis after 1795. These included 1,745 infantry and dragoons from Gotha and Weimar in 1796, as well as another 7,943 electoral Saxons. Prussia made continual difficulties, insisting already in 1793 that the Saxons serve with its forces on the Lower Rhine rather than join the rest of the Imperial Army attached to the Austrians. The pressure increased once Prussia left the war and Saxony recalled its contingent in July 1796, formally joining the northern neutral zone that November.[17]

In addition to the Darmstadt brigade, Relutions were used to hire the émigré regiments. Brunswick and Paderborn seem to have contracted the Rohan corps directly to avoid being forced into similar arrangements with Prussia. Other payments came from the central Relutions fund as a form of Habsburg patronage of the émigrés. The 1,200-strong Dumouriez corps was hired in 1793, as were the Condé and Bourbon regiments, which together totaled 329 officers but only 1,125 other ranks! The Hohenlohe corps also never achieved its target strength, and all these units suffered high desertion due to their chaotic command and financial arrangements. The émigrés truly combined all the vices of old-regime armies with scarcely any of the virtues. It is not surprising that Laukhard took such a dim view of the German forces since he served briefly in an émigré regiment before joining the Swabians.

The second field of German participation was through the provision of troops for other armies. The Bourbons had twelve regiments in their army in 1789 commanded by German princes who provided some of the recruits. The princes resigned command by 1791 when the French released those soldiers who wanted to leave. Many enlisted in the émigré regiments or those of the princes who had previously been French colonels. Only Friedrich III of Salm-Kyrburg (1745–94) supported the Revolution, voting against the imperial declaration of war in 1793 and assuming command of a Parisian volunteer battalion, only to be executed by Robespierre. Few other

Germans accepted the French calls of fraternity. Just nine of the ninety officers in the Legion Germanique were actually Germans, while other attempts to recruit volunteers or even prisoners of war got a poor response.[18]

Rather more served the Dutch, who likewise had eight regiments in their army recruited and commanded by German princes. Nassau and Waldeck each provided three regiments that were absorbed into the army of the Batavian Republic after 1795. Other Germans served as auxiliaries in return for subsidies to their princes, covering at least some of the costs. Princes had long accepted foreign subsidies to reduce the expense of maintaining their armies, which represented their chief assets in international diplomacy. Mecklenburg-Schwerin, Ansbach-Bayreuth, Münster, and Brunswick had treaties from the 1780s that were activated when the republic entered the war in 1793, requiring the dispatch of 8,246 men. These mainly served in the defense of Maastricht until 1794, when most were recalled, though the 1,000 Mecklenburgers were retained by the Batavian Republic until 1796. The 2,000 Württemberg infantry supplied to the Dutch East India Company in 1786 were not so fortunate since they had been sent to South Africa and subsequently Sri Lanka, where they perished fighting the British by 1806.[19]

Britain was the principal partner since it had a long tradition of hiring German auxiliaries and was linked by kinship and alliance to several important dynasties. The majority came from Hanover, which sent 13,900 troops and support personnel in April 1793, followed by another 5,200 in 1794 at a cost of £1.39 million. Hessen-Kassel provided 12,000 in 1793, adding 535 artillery the following year, while Hessen-Darmstadt sent a mixed brigade of 3,000 and Baden provided 754 infantry from October 1793. Brunswick signed a series of agreements 1793–94 that remained unfulfilled while its army served the Dutch, finally supplying 1,874 men in November 1794 once its forces returned home earlier that year.[20] The soldiers entered British pay and command but remained under the authority of the princes who supplied them. Most treaties prohibited service overseas, though two Hanoverian infantry regiments were part of the British East India Company's forces from 1781 until 1792 when they returned home. Five battalions and the Carabinier Regiment from the Hessen-Kassel contingent were sent to Britain in 1793 for the planned Vendée landings, but returned when these were canceled the next year. The Darmstadt brigade marched to Trieste in 1796 to be shipped as reinforcements for Gibraltar, but like-wise returned home the following year. Otherwise, all went to the Austrian Netherlands, where they constituted a substantial part of the British army under the Duke of York. They escaped the Dutch collapse by retreating over the Ems early in 1795, but Prussia's with-drawal made further participation impossible because Hanover, Brunswick, and Hessen-Kassel were obliged to join its neutral zone. Britain subsidized around 26,000 Bavarian, Württemberg, and Mainz troops in 1800 as part of its assistance to Austria in the Second Coalition. The Mainz infantry and militia defended the Main val-ley, while the Bavarians and Württembergers cooperated with Kray's Austrians in the south.

Organization

The empire's political diversity was not reflected in German military organization, which followed the same basic pattern across the ter-ritories. Princes had long maintained personal bodyguards, but true permanent forces only emerged during the long struggles against Louis XIV's France after 1672. Though reduced in 1714, these forces were not disbanded as most of the previous ones had been after the Thirty Years' War. The practice of peacetime maintenance between 1714 and the next conflict in 1733 completed organization as terri-torial governments issued additional regulations covering billeting, discipline, discharge, pensions, and other administrative aspects.[21] Expanded again during the mid-eighteenth-century wars, most armies were reduced after 1763 when several territories also disman-tled their fortifications as they laid out new parks and avenues in their major towns. The new utilitarian spirit of the Enlightenment stimulated a lively discussion of military matters from the 1770s, but this concentrated on improving soldiers' status, morality, and welfare, rather than organization or tactics.[22]

Prussian influence was strong following its spectacular victories over France and Austria in the 1740s and 1750s, but emulation did not extend much beyond drill manuals and the style of uniforms. Austria remained influential, not least because it consistently main-tained the largest army. Those territories that provided men to the American Revolutionary War drew on that experience, especially for their light troops. France ceased to be a significant model after

1714, and only exerted influence again once the princes became Napoleon's allies. Imperial regulations followed Austrian practice and were important for the very small territories that maintained no troops beyond those required for their Kreis contingents.

The regiment remained the largest permanent formation, though the four principal armies had begun using brigades for administrative purposes. Regiments varied considerably in size, with strength dictated by economic and political rather than military reasons. There was a tendency throughout the eighteenth century to retain regiments as cadres rather than disband some and keep others at full strength at the end of each conflict. This was partly a question of prestige but also had a practical purpose since it was easier to find new recruits than experienced officers and NCOs. Criticism mounted during the long peace after 1763, because cadres often became superannuated. Princes assumed paternal responsibility for their personnel, improving pension arrangements introduced earlier in the century. However, the large debts left by the midcentury wars imposed tight budget constraints so that many officers simply remained in post rather than retiring and being replaced.

This situation tended to be more pronounced in the smaller armies, but the Bavarians also suffered badly through lack of funds and government neglect after 1777. An official investigation in 1788 revealed that the 2,840 cavalrymen had only 613 horses, while there were just another 13 to pull all the artillery and transport. A thoroughgoing reform was initiated, which, while more controversial, nonetheless typifies measures under way in other territories. These likewise exhibited a tension between those favoring ad hoc, practical measures to improve efficiency and enlightened reformers who believed that improving soldiers' welfare and status would spearhead wider social and moral regeneration. What made the Bavarian situation so controversial was the presence of Benjamin Thompson (1753–1814), a former Tory officer from Massachusetts who entered Bavarian service in 1784 and was ennobled as Count Rumford in 1792. Rumford usurped the reform agenda already proposed by others and steered it to further his own advancement, antagonizing many officers who resigned in protest. He represented the conservative, utilitarian strand of the Enlightenment, seeking to expand the army at no extra cost by obliging soldiers to grow their own food, work on civil construction projects, or accept extended unpaid leave. The furor over the new uniforms of 1792 exemplifies the wider issues. Rumford used his considerable scientific expertise to design a lightweight cotton summer uniform and a warmer, woolen winter one. His opponents criticized not only their plain appearance but the fact that they were poorly made by the inmates of the Munich workhouse. They lost no time in replacing the uniforms with new ones in the traditional light blue of the Bavarian army as soon as Rumford left the elector's service in 1798.[23]

The Saxon army had already undergone a series of thorough reforms after 1763 as part of a wider program to rebuild the shattered electorate after the Seven Years' War. The army also had the most recent experience of European conflict, having served alongside the Prussians against Austria in the War of the Bavarian Succession (1778–79), and was probably the most efficient of all the German armies on the eve of the French Revolutionary Wars.[24] Most of the Hessen-Kassel infantry had served in America, and the entire army was reorganized 1785–88 by consolidating into fewer but larger regiments. Henceforth, each Hessian infantry regiment had two battalions like their Bavarian and Saxon counterparts, but the Hanoverians continued with single battalion regiments like those of the smaller territories. Each battalion had four to ten companies, while cavalry regiments had anything from two to five squadrons, each generally of two companies.

The prewar organization largely disappeared after 1792 as all the larger and middling territories employed a depot system. Elderly and unfit personnel were discharged, but political and financial considerations made it impossible to expand the remaining cadres into the units required by imperial and treaty obligations. Field units had to be formed by drawing the best men from several prewar regiments that remained nominally as depots to train new recruits and guard the territory. For example, three Bavarian regiments had to be combined just to find the 787 infantry required as contribution to the Westphalian Kreis troops in 1794.[25] Saxony made the best use of this method, selecting different units on rotation each year 1793–96 so that most of the army gained campaign experience.

Most princes had personal bodyguard units, called Garde du Corps if mounted, or Garde or Leib Regiment if on foot. In the case of middling and smaller territories like Baden or Bamberg, the guard cavalry were dismounted in peacetime and expected to serve as the mounted element of the Kreis contingent if mobilized. The four largest armies all had one (or more) guard infantry regiment that received higher pay and that was counted as elite. Several territories also mustered at least a battalion of grenadiers, but often there was little to distinguish these from line infantry beyond their uniforms. Hanover and the smaller territories retained the older practice of maintaining a distinct grenadier company with each infantry regiment that could be combined in the field as elite battalions. Most also had separate units of riflemen (jäger) or light infantry (generally called fusiliers) trained to fight in extended order. This use of jägers and fusiliers was noticeable among the smaller territories that attempted to stress quality rather than quantity. Virtually all the Weimar infantry were organized as jägers after 1788, while the Trier jäger battalion was the electorate's primary field unit and served with distinction attached to the Prussians 1793–95.[26] Hessen-Kassel reorganized each of its infantry regiments into one grenadier and two musketeer battalions, each of four companies in 1795, adding a light company a year later. It also had a separate jäger battalion from 1787 and one of light infantry from 1788 that was expanded into two in 1799 and brigaded with the riflemen. Hanover formed a light infantry regiment in 1793 with two battalions, unlike its other regiments, which remained only one each.

Most of the cavalrymen were either dragoons or hussars in contrast to the heavier cuirassiers that had been prominent earlier in the century. Only Saxony retained four cuirassier regiments, Hessen-Kassel had three and Bavaria two, but Hanover's heavies lacked any body armor. Hanover, Saxony, and Bavaria each had two to four light dragoon or *cheveauleger* regiments, a troop type that formed the bulk of the cavalry in the smaller armies like Darmstadt's. Saxony and Hessen-Kassel each had a hussar regiment, while most minor territories had a hussar detachment as mounted police.

The four major armies had substantial field and garrison artillery, together with pioneers, pontoniers, and other specialists. They were grouped into companies for administrative purposes, but took the field in largely ad hoc batteries as required. The Württemberg army boasted a highly proficient artillery battalion, but most smaller forces possessed only regimental artillery with their infantry. Several experimented with horse artillery, but this remained underdeveloped due to the small size of German armies. German military practice was dictated by the nature of coalition warfare whereby soldiers served as contingents in other armies. As only the four largest armies had more than one cavalry brigade, there was little opportunity to develop horse artillery tactics. Instead, artillery was regarded as close support for the infantry, with whatever heavier pieces that were available being combined with those of coalition partners in position batteries. This scattered deployment also inhibited the dissemination of good practice between units in the same army, which could find themselves hundreds of miles apart. The strategy of cordon defense employed by Austria and Prussia exacerbated this difficulty by spreading troops in small detachments to hold a wide front. At least this strategy provided opportunities for outpost duty and German troops generally fought well in minor skirmishes.

Germany was a land of romantic castles rather than modern fortresses. Castles were still used to store equipment and house soldiers, but had little strategic value. The Duke of Württemberg was furious when the seventy-two-year old General Bilfinger surrendered the Hohentwiel castle perched on a mountain outcrop in May 1800, despite the fact that the garrison mustered only 108 men, most of whom were around the same age as their commander. Situated in an enclave miles from Württemberg, the castle served no real purpose, but had been counted as impregnable because it had withstood a long siege in the Thirty Years' War.[27] Of the six major fortresses, Ingolstadt protected the Danube route through Bavaria, while Mannheim guarded the Palatinate at the confluence of the Neckar with the Rhine. Ehrenbreitstein covered the Lower Rhine on the right bank opposite Koblenz, while Philippsburg and Kehl secured the Upper Rhine. Mainz occupied the central position on the left bank of the Middle Rhine protecting the entrance to the Main valley. Bavaria was responsible for Ingolstadt and Mannheim, while Ehrenbreitstein belonged to Trier. Kehl and Philippsburg were maintained by the Swabian and Franconian Kreise that abandoned them in the later eighteenth century in protest at the failure of other regions to share the cost. Both works were repaired after 1792 and were again garrisoned by Kreis troops. The Upper Rhinelanders helped the elector of Mainz maintain his fortress, and their troops formed part of the garrison when General von Gymnich surrendered without a fight on 21 October 1792. He had only half the 12,000 men considered necessary to man the works and claimed later that the Austrian and Prussian commanders acknowledged "the impossibility of repulsing an attack with a small number of troops of variable quality."[28] The loss of Mainz was a major psychological blow for the empire, while the city became the center of French efforts to foster German revolution. Very few joined the French, who were obliged to surrender the city after a three-month siege in 1793.[29]

Composition

Native subjects formed four-fifths to nine-tenths of each prince's army, with the remainder largely coming from neighboring territories. This was in stark contrast to the Prussian and Austrian armies that recruited around a third of their manpower from other German lands. Garrison units were often elderly men like that on the Hohentwiel, but most line privates were in their early twenties, with NCOs averaging in their late thirties and captains around forty-five.[30] Older men were preferred for their experience, and resistance to disease and because, after many years in the ranks, they were less likely to abscond than younger, new recruits who formed the bulk of deserters. Most men enlisted for three to six years, though Hessen-Kassel insisted on twelve.

Volunteers were generally unmarried younger sons unable to inherit the family farm or craftsmen in trades suffering underemployment. Conscription targeted similar groups, and there was often little to distinguish the two forms of recruitment, because conscripts frequently also received bounties like volunteers. The prominent place accorded the Prussian canton system of conscription in Anglophone historiography has obscured the fact that most territories used something similar.[31] The obligations to serve derived from feudal jurisdictions that had been reworked with the growth of the territorial state from the sixteenth century. This arrangement established a theoretical liability of universal service to defend the homeland expressed practically through a militia organization or, where this had been abolished, a conscription system using the same methods of each community recording the names of all eligible men on official lists (enrollment). In practice, most men were exempt on the grounds of age, disability, marital status, occupation, or wealth, though the latter were sometimes obliged to pay for a substitute. Exemptions reduced the available pool of recruits in Mainz to only 3,000 out of the 29,796 males aged fourteen to thirty enrolled on the lists.[32] Even then, the army would only take a selection (*Auswahl*) to fill vacancies. For example, the Württemberg government ordered the selection of 2,000 men in January 1794, followed by a further 1,600 in December to mobilize its Kreis contingent. Each community was assigned a quota, and the able-bodied men were summoned to appear on their marketplace or village green before local officials, an officer, and an army doctor. Volunteers were offered a bounty worth at least three years' pay, plus life exemption from state labor duties and a four-year contract. Only where insufficient volunteers came forward were the men required to roll dice or draw lots to see who had to serve.[33] These methods were identical to those used to embody militia regiments (*Landregimenter*) for home defense, such as that mobilized in Brunswick while the duchy's regular army served in the Netherlands between 1788 and 1794.

The imperial cities and larger territorial towns possessed their own civic guards (*Bürgerwehr*) in which all citizens were theoretically obliged to serve. These units were retained as expressions of civic autonomy, but were largely ceremonial. The imperial cities also maintained regulars (*Stadtsoldaten*) as police and to fulfill their obligations to the Kreise. They were recruited by voluntary enlistment like those of the principalities, though some cities with dependent villages could also conscript their rural subjects.

Outright impressment was a matter of last resort, except in Bavaria, which drafted criminals as an alternative punishment after 1769. This practice was widely condemned as deterring volunteers and contributing to soldiers' low social status. It was abolished in 1788 but was reintroduced five years later due to growing recruiting difficulties. Criminals formed a very small proportion of soldiers, but the controversy surrounding their presence is indicative of the wider debate on motivation, which grew more intense with the experience of fighting France. Desertion rates were relatively low and certainly no worse than those suffered by the French after 1792. The problem caused concern because of the difficulty of finding and paying replacements. Militiamen and conscripts were used because they were cheaper, but paid professionals on long-service contracts were considered militarily superior. German discussions of the citizen-in-arms remained conservative, with most intellectuals considering a citizen to be a subject with rights protected by imperial and territorial law. Patriotism meant loyalty to a prince and identification with a home community and the empire.

Such sentiments were not necessarily weaker than the more abstract concepts invoked by revolutionary France. Large numbers of

Germans responded to calls for arming the people (*Volksbewaffnung*) toward the end of 1793, which received Reichstag approval in January 1794. Some rulers expressed reservations about arming their subjects, but the popular mobilization was not an attempt to copy the French levée en masse. Instead, it applied some the new patriotic language to the existing militia and conscription systems. Folk memories of previous French invasions were reawakened by fresh atrocities like the firebombing of the unfortified town of Alt Breisach on 15 September 1793. The new militiamen were used, like those in earlier wars, to guard defensive lines in the Black Forest and Eifel mountains, as well as to harass the French, especially when they were retreating. Around 40,000 militiamen were mobilized in Swabia and the Austrian Breisgau to hold the Upper Rhine in 1794–97, while another 6,000 assembled in Trier to defend the Eifel. As with the original French levée en masse, it proved impossible to sustain the initial level of voluntary enthusiasm, and popular mobilization became a way of transforming limited conscription into universal service, as in Württemberg where the militia was replaced by a more extended draft for the regular army in December 1799. Mainz persisted with traditional methods, decreeing a *landsturm*, or total mobilization, in August 1799 that produced around 14,000 men who slowed the French advance up the Main valley.[34]

Popular enthusiasm extended to the home front, where people were far from indifferent to the war. The rapid expansion of print media in the last quarter of the eighteenth century meant that the population was better informed than in any previous conflict. Papers swiftly abandoned their neutral tone once the empire entered the war, and they began reporting the exploits of "their" soldiers. The inhabitants of garrison towns organized public subscriptions or held benefit concerts to raise money to supplement official welfare programs for soldiers' wives and dependents. Few Germans yet adopted the bourgeois rhetoric of nationalism, expressing their support in conventional terms of local patriotism or piety, such as the Saxon soldiers who wrote from the front that they would pray for those who had donated to the subscription fund.[35]

Ultimately, governments and their subjects were not prepared to embrace ideas of total war. Even those who felt that greater sacrifices would be necessary to defeat the French believed such extreme measures would destroy the ordered society they sought to defend. Germans struggled to preserve normalcy in abnormal times. Mainz infantryman Georg Biethan was granted discharge in March 1793 despite having three years to serve, because there was no one to farm his land. Musketeers Reichard, Kaufmann and Reise were also discharged prematurely to work for their parents.[36]

Command

Administration was handled by a war council in each territory, which reported either directly to the prince or through his civil cabinet or privy council. Most of these institutions were very small, with that in Württemberg numbering only ten staff, though there were a few other junior officials overseeing the barracks, while the church consistory appointed army chaplains.[37] Military administration was becoming more professional in line with its civil counterpart as rulers renounced the prerogative to hire and fire at will and introduced more formal appointment procedures, career paths, and pension arrangements. The Bavarian Court War Council was reorganized in May 1792 along functional lines with departments for personnel, finance, procurement, and auditing, while its staff already wore distinctive uniforms from 1788. Such councils were transformed into war ministries around 1806 as the surviving principalities expanded their governments to integrate the lands they annexed after 1803.

Operational matters and strategic planning were handled by separate general staffs that assumed a more institutionalized character during the later eighteenth century. Princes no longer commanded their troops in person, though their sons or relatives frequently still held senior ranks. Most armies were top-heavy, with Bavaria having 59 generals for less than 20,000 men in 1786.[38] Such inflated numbers were a consequence of delaying retirement, and the actual active staffs were much smaller. Most armies were assisted by a separate general quartermaster staff to plan supply arrangements, accommodation, and march routes. Their personnel were generally employed in peacetime to map the territory and often attained a high degree of technical expertise and practical experience. The same was true of the engineers who often oversaw civil construction projects. Mobilization revealed numerous shortcomings, especially a lack of transport, tents, and other material. Like the other problems, these difficulties stemmed from prewar budget constraints.

Rivalry between Austria and Prussia exacerbated the difficulties after 1792 by arousing the princes' suspicions that any resources they contributed would be misappropriated. The Habsburgs sought to monopolize the imperial high command, and seven of the eight active generals named by the emperor on 8 April 1793 already held Habsburg rank, with the eighth being a Prussian. Friedrich Josias von Sachsen-Coburg (1737–1815) commanded in 1793, being replaced the following year by Albert von Sachsen-Teschen (1738–1822), the former governor of the Austrian Netherlands. Another Austrian general, Karl Joseph von Clerfayt (1733–98), commanded in 1795, before the emperor simply placed the Imperial Army under his own field marshal, the Archduke Charles (1771–1847), on 21 February 1796, who remained its commander until 1801. Attempts to control the Swabian contingent led the Austrians to threaten to arrest its general in March 1795, while their refusal to allow the Reichstag to audit the accounts of the Imperial Operations Fund further contributed to the growing disillusionment with the war effort.[39]

Performance

The Germans' main task was the defense of the Rhine, with the Netherlands as a subsidiary front. Operations began on the Rhine as Hessen-Kassel contributed 5,500 men to the abortive Austro-Prussian invasion of France in the summer of 1792. Mainz and Trier mobilized as Mainz and Frankfurt fell that October, but a Hessian and Prussian counterattack recovered the latter on 2 December. Saxony, Bavaria, Hessen-Kassel, and Darmstadt together contributed a third of the troops involved in the recapture of Mainz on 22 July 1793. The Saxons accompanied the Prussians advancing into Alsace, contributing to the victory at Kaiserslautern in November, where several units fought with distinction.

The fighting shifted northwestward to the Netherlands where the Hanoverian, Hessian, and other auxiliaries with the Anglo-Dutch crumbled before the French invasion. Resistance collapsed after Fleurus in June 1794, enabling the French to push into the Lower Rhine as well as the Dutch Republic. The Trier regulars and militia made a fighting withdrawal as the French overran the western part of the electorate left of the river. The situation grew critical after Prussia made peace at Basel in April 1795, neutralizing northern Germany. The Westphalian and Lower Saxon territories were obliged to leave the war. Hanover provided 11,500 men to Prussia's Army of Observation until 1801, while Brunswick supplied another 3,000 until 1798. Hessen-Kassel joined the neutral zone in August 1795, removing another of the more potent armies, while a general armistice suspended operations along the Rhine between January and May 1796.

The Imperial Army meanwhile mobilized to hold the Upper Rhine, which remained relatively quiet until 1796. Several French probes were repulsed, notably by the Swabians at Kehl, which came under periodic, but intense bombardment from the French on the opposite bank at Strasbourg. The situation changed dramatically with a coordinated attack by two French armies under Jourdan and Moreau in June 1796. Napoleon's successes in Italy had obliged the Austrians to redirect 25,000 of their men from the Rhine. Having failed to stem the invasion, Archduke Charles made a strategic withdrawal, abandoning most of southern Germany. The princes now faced a stark choice of futile resistance, joining Prussia's neutrality, or cutting their own deal with France. The Saxons reluctantly chose the second option, taking most of their minor neighbors with them. Prussia meanwhile adjusted its zone in agreement with France that August, abandoning the region immediately east of the Rhine south of the Ruhr, as well as the western half of the Main valley. This measure secured the rest of north Germany until 1806, but exposed the Lower and Middle Rhine to French attack.

Once Württemberg and Baden made their own conventions with France in July 1796, Austria feared the rest of Swabia would follow. Eight thousand Austrians surprised the remaining 3,000 Swabian troops in their camp at Biberach and disarmed them on 29 July. This humiliation was regarded as further evidence that Austria could not be trusted.[40] Suspicions grew as details emerged on Austria's own Treaty of Campo Formio with France in October 1797 whereby the emperor accepted the loss of the left bank in return for French agreement that he could take Salzburg and part of Bavaria. The public furor deterred Austria from implementing these annexations, but it was clear that the mediatisation, or incorporation of all the ecclesiastical and minor territories by their larger neighbors, was on the agenda. More territories began to defect, such as Darmstadt, which signed its own treaty of neutrality with France in March 1798.

Worse, Austria agreed to withdraw all its troops behind the Inn in December 1797, leaving the minor armies holding the entire Rhine front. Officially, operations were suspended while a congress met at Rastatt to work out a definitive peace. In practice, the French maintained constant pressure, hoping the remaining princes would abandon Austria. The Austrians had already evacuated Mainz on 10 December, taking most of the artillery with them and leaving only 3,000 Nassau, Westphalian, Cologne, and Mainz troops behind. The elector sanctioned surrender, and the French stayed sixteen years. The Trier and Cologne defenders of Ehrenbreitstein were made of sterner stuff, enduring a blockade from April 1797 until January 1799 when they finally marched out.

The Defense of Mannheim, 24–25 January 1798

The eviction of the imperial garrison in Mannheim exemplifies the predicament of the minor armies during the Revolutionary Wars. The Austrians withdrew on 31 December 1797, allowing the French to seize the outer perimeter between Waldsee and Frankenthal contrary to the truce. Command devolved to Bavarian colonel von Bartels, who had 2,824 Bavarian, Franconian, Upper Rhenish, and Westphalian Kreis troops. The Austrians had removed most of the heavy artillery and other equipment, but Bartels still held the Rheinschanze outworks left of the Rhine, together with Mannheim on the right bank. The French attacked on 24 January, seizing the weakly defended villages of Neuhofen and Edigheim to the west of the defenders' main positions. Bartels rejected a summons to surrender the next day and sent Lieutenant Colonel von Karg with a Palatine battalion to reinforce the Rheinschanze. This battalion came under heavy attack that evening, but Karg managed to escape across the Rhine and pull up the bridge, foiling pursuit. The French high command refused to acknowledge any breach of the truce, but did suspend operations. The Bavarian elector decided to demilitarize Mannheim altogether to prevent further attacks on the city. The garrison withdrew to Philippsburg in November, and the fortifications were dismantled a month later.[41]

The loss of key positions along the Rhine, as well as the neutrality of the entire north, left the south exposed by the start of the War of the Second Coalition in 1799. Though Archduke Charles's

Austrians repulsed the French attack on the Upper Rhine, the Russians' defeat in Switzerland meant the French outflanked his positions by the next campaign in 1800. Baden remained neutral, but Württemberg rejoined the war and the other Swabians mobilized. Mainz fought on in the Main valley, while a few other units served as garrison troops. Individual units continued to fight bravely, like the Fürstenberg Kreis contingent, which lost 203 of its 411 men at Engen on 3 May. However, Bavaria was the only large territory still involved, and its army accompanied the Austrians at their major defeats at Meßkirch and Hohenlinden.[42]

The empire accepted the loss of the left bank at the Peace of Lunéville in February 1801, initiating the process of internal reorganization that destroyed much of its traditional structure. While many still hoped the venerable constitution could be saved, Austria's defeat in 1805 left sixteen princes no choice but to join France in the Confederation of the Rhine. As the secretary of Austria's delegation to the Reichstag correctly predicted, the empire's demise exposed Germans to the full force of aggressive centralized government the French had endured since 1793.[43]

Notes

1. F. C. Laukhard, *Schilderung der jetzigen Reichsarmee, nach ihrer wahren Gestalt* (Cologne, 1796).

2. H. Dippel, *Germany and the American Revolution, 1770–1800* (Chapel Hill: Published for the Institute of Early American History and Culture by the University of North Carolina Press, 1977); P. H. Wilson, "The German "Soldier Trade" of the Seventeenth and Eighteenth Centuries: A Reassessment," *International History Review* 18 (1996): 757–92.

3. Older, but still useful, discussions of the reform debate include K. Epstein, *The Genesis of German Conservatism* (Princeton, N.J.: Princeton University Press, 1966); and J. G. Gagliardo, *Reich and nation. The Holy Roman Empire as Idea and Reality, 1763–1806* (Bloomington: Indiana University Press, 1980). The revised view is presented by W. Burgdorf, *Reichskonstitution und Nation* (Mainz: P. von Zabern, 1998); K. Härter, *Reichstag und Revolution: 1789–1806* (Göttingen: Vandenhoeck and Ruprecht, 1992); and K. O., Frhr. von Aretin, *Das alte Reich, 1648–1806*, 3 vols. (Stuttgart: Klett Cotta, 1993–97), vol. 3. For the military structure, see P. H. Wilson, *German Armies: War and German Politics, 1648–1806* (London: University College London Press, 1998).

4. The Palatine branch inherited Bavaria in 1777 when its ruling line died out. Officially called Pfalz-Bayern, it will be referred to as Bavaria here. It passed to the junior Zweibrücken line in 1798.

5. Six principalities were governed by hereditary secular rulers: Württemberg, Baden, Mecklenburg-Schwerin, Brunswick-Wolfenbüttel,

Hessen-Kassel, and Hessen-Darmstadt. The other eight were ruled by ecclesiastical princes elected by the local cathedral chapter: Mainz, Cologne, Trier, Salzburg, Würzburg, Bamberg, Münster, and Paderborn. For a full breakdown of the territories and their populations, see P. H. Wilson, *From Reich to Revolution: German History, 1558–1806* (Basingstoke, UK: Palgrave Macmillan, 2004), 364–77.

6. Frankfurt, Nuremberg, Augsburg, Hamburg, Bremen, and Cologne.

7. T. Hartwig, *Der Überfall der Grafschaft Schaumburg-Lippe durch Landgraf Wilhelm IX. Von Hessen-Kassel* (Hanover: Geibel, 1911).

8. M. Rowe, *From Reich to State. The Rhineland in the Revolutionary Age, 1780–1830* (Cambridge: Cambridge University Press, 2003); G. Schmidt, "Die 'deutsche Freiheit' und der westfälische Friede," in *Frieden und Krieg in der frühen Neuzeit*, ed. R. G. Asch and Wulf Eckart Voß (Munich: Fink, 2001), 323–47.

9. For policy of the major belligerents toward the empire, see K. A. Roider, *Baron Thugut and Austria's Response to the French Revolution* (Princeton, N.J.: Princeton University Press, 1987); M. C. Dean, *Austrian Policy during the French Revolutionary Wars, 1796–1799* (Vienna: Austrian Army Historical Museum, Military Historical Institute, 1993); L. Kittstein, *Politik im Zeitalter der Revolution: Untersuchungen zur Preußischen Staatlichkeit, 1792–1807* (Stuttgart: Steiner, 2003); S. S. Biro, *The German Policy of Revolutionary France: A Study in French Diplomacy during the War of the First Coalition, 1792–1797*, 2 vols. (Cambridge, Mass.: Harvard University Press, 1957).

10. W. Dotzauer, *Die deutschen Reichskreise (1383–1806)* (Stuttgart: Steiner, 1998). Some dynasties ruled territories in more than one Kreis, notably the Prussian Hohenzollerns, who had land in Upper and Lower Saxony, as well as Westphalia, and the Wittelsbachs, whose main electorate lay in the Bavarian Kreis, but who also held land in the Electoral Rhenish and Westphalian Kreise, as well as two enclaves in Swabia. For a brief summary of the imperial constitution, see P. H. Wilson, *The Holy Roman Empire, 1495–1806*, 2nd ed. (Basingstoke, UK: Macmillan, 2011).

11. E. Hagen, "Die fürstlich würzburgische Hausinfanterie vom Jahre 1757 bis zur Einverleibung des Fürstbistums in Bayern 1803," *Darstellungen aus Bayerischen Kriegs- und Heeresgeschichte* 20 (1911): 51–109; H. Helmes, *Aus der Geschichte der Würzburger Truppen (1628–1802)* (Würzburg: Stürtz, 1909), 84–96. Bamberg entered into a similar arrangement.

12. Haus-, Hof- und Staatsarchiv Vienna [hereafter HHStA], Mainzer Erzkanzler Akten [hereafter MEA], Militaria 121, esp. 10 July 1794. See also A. Störkel, "Das Kurmainzer Militär beim Ausbruch der französischen Revolution," *Mainzer Zeitschrift* 84/85 (1989/90): 143–66.

13. H. G. Borck, *Der Schwäbische Reichskreis im Zeitalter der französischen Revolutionskriege (1792–1806)* (Stuttgart: Kohlhammer, 1970); Württemberg General Quarter Master Staff, "Quellenstudien über die Kriegsgeschichte der württembergischen Truppen von 1792 an," *Württembergisches Jahrbuch* (1845): 211–35. The mobilization of the

Swabian, Franconian, Bavarian, Westphalian, and Electoral Rhenish Kreise is detailed in two volumes of printed decisions contained in HHStA, MEA, Militaria 121.

14. F. K. Erbprinz zu Hohenlohe-Waldenburg, "Über hohenlohischen Militäwesen," *Württembergisch Franken* 50 (1966): 212–41.

15. Darmstadt's treaty with the empire was renewed on 19 May 1796; see Staatsarchiv Darmstadt [hereafter StAD], A6 Nr.1441. See also L. Pelizaeus, *Der Aufstieg Württembergs und Hessens zur Kurwürde, 1692–1806* (Frankfurt am Main: Lang, 2000); J. R. Dieterich, "Die Politik Landgraf Ludwigs X. von Hessen-Darmstadt von 1790-1806," *Archiv für Hessische Geschichte und Altertumskunde* NF 7 (1910), 417–53.

16. T. Riotte, *Hannover in der britischen Politik (1792–1815)* (Münster: LIT, 2005). Hanover was linked to Britain by personal union, 1714–1837.

17. O. Schuster and F. A. Francke, *Geschichte der Sächsischen Armee*, 3 vols. (Leipzig: Duncker and Humblot, 1885), 2:190–224. Anhalt-Zerbst provided a free corps of 449 horse and foot to Austria 1792–97, which passed fully into Austrian service after 1798. For another contingent, see Lutz Unbehaun and Jens Henkel, *Das Schwarzburger Militär* (Rudolstadt: Thüringer Landesmuseum, 1994).

18. R. Dufraisse, "Les populations de la rive gauche du Rhin et le service militair à la fin de l'Ancien Régime et à l'Epoque Révolutionaire," *Revue Historique* 231 (1964): 103–40, esp. 113, 123.

19. J. Prinz, *Das württembergische Kapregiment, 1786–1808* (Stuttgart: Strecker and Schröder, 1932). For the others in Dutch service, see Wilson, *German Armies* (311) and the sources cited there.

20. The Darmstadt treaty of 5 October 1793 was renewed for six years on 10 June 1796, but was terminated in 1797: StAD, A6 Nr.1226–28. Wolfenbüttel had contracted for 2,200 men, but sent only 1,874. See O. Elster, *Geschichte der stehenden Truppen im Herzogtum Braunschweig-Wolfenbüttel*, 2 vols. (Leipzig: Heinsius, 1899–1901), 2:469–72.

21. Good examples in R. Pröve, *Stehendes Heer und städtische Gesellschaft im 18. Jahrhundert* (Munich: Oldenbourg, 1995).

22. D. Hohrath and K. Gerteis, eds., *Die Kriegskunst im Lichte der Vernunft: Militär und Aufklärung im 18. Jahrhundert*, 2 vols. (Hamburg: Meiner, 1999–2000).

23. B. Pohlmann, "Graf Rumford in bayerischen Diensten (1784–1790)," *Zeitschrift für bayerische Landesgeschichte* 54 (1991): 369–433; S. C. Brown, *Benjamin Thompson, Count Rumford* (Cambridge, Mass.: MIT Press, 1979). Useful documents are found in S. C. Brown, ed., *Collected Works of Count Rumford*, 5 vols. (Cambridge, Mass.: Belknap Press of Harvard University Press, 1968-70), vol. 5.

24. J. Hofmann, *Die Kursächsische Armee 1769 bis zum Beginn der Bayerischen Erbfolgekrieges* (Leipzig: Hirzel, 1914); R. Mielsch, "Die Kursächsische Armee im Bayerischen Erbfolgekriege 1778/79," *Neues Archiv für sächsische Geschichte* 53 (1932): 73–103; 54 (1933): 46–74;

R. Müller and W. Rother, *Die Kurfürstlich-Sächsische Armee um 1791* (Berlin: Militärverlag der Deutschen Demokratischen Republik, 1990). The latter work includes a superb set of contemporary paintings illustrating the entire Saxon army in 1791.

25. F. Münich, *Geschichte der Entwicklung der Bayerischen Armee seit zwei Jahrhunderten* (Munich, 1866), 163–64.

26. (Lt. Col.) Möllmann, "Zur Geschichte des Kurtrierischen Militärs," supplement, *Trierisches Archiv* 1 (1901): 60–87.

27. K. von Martens, *Geschichte von Hohentwiel* (Stuttgart, 1857).

28. HHStA, MEA Militaria 121, Gymnich to Elector von Erthal, 18 June 1793. The file contains other papers relating to the capitulation and subsequent inquiry. The garrison consisted of 1,121 Mainz, 704 Upper Rhenish, and 854 Austrian regulars, 300–400 Mainz militia, 100 students, and 3,000 armed citizens with 193 cannon. See also A. Börckel, *Geschichte von Mainz als Festung und Garnison von der Römerzeit bis zur Gegenwart* (Mainz: J. Diemer, 1913), 99–102.

29. For the wider context, see T. C. W. Blanning, *Reform and Revolution in Mainz, 1743–1803* (Cambridge: Cambridge University Press, 1974); and B. Blisch, *Friedrich Carl Joseph von Erthal (1774–1802)* (Frankfurt am Main: Lang,, 2005).

30. B. Sicken, "Die Streitkräfte des Hochstifts Würzburg gegen Ende des Ancien Régime," *Zeitschrift für bayerischen Landegeschichte* 47 (1984): 691–744.

31. P. H. Wilson, "Social Militarisation in Eighteenth-Century Germany," *German History* 18 (2000): 1–39.

32. R. Harms, "Landmiliz und stehendes Heer in Kurmainz," *Archiv für hessische Geschichte und Altertumskunde* NF 6 (1909): 380–84.

33. A. Pfister, *Der Milizgedanke in Württemberg und die Versuche zu seiner Verwirklichung* (Stuttgart, 1883).

34. HHStA, MEA Militaria for suggestions for Mainz volunteer units in 1794.

35. S. Kroll, *Soldaten im 18. Jahrhundert zwischen Friedensaltag und Kriegserfahrung: Lebenswelten und Kultur in der Kursächsischen Armee, 1728–1796* (Paderborn: Schöningh, 2006), 365–79, 572–73, 584.

36. HHStA, MEA Militaria 121, 12 and 24 March 1793. The file contains many other examples, most of whom provided replacement recruits.

37. Hauptstaatsarchiv Stuttgart, A30a Bü.11, A202 Bü.2212, containing the official structure and personnel appointments for the Württemberg military administration in this period.

38. Münich, *Entwicklung*, 150–51.

39. H. Neuhaus, "Das Problem der militärischen Exekutive in der Spätphase des alten Reiches," in *Staatsverfassung und Heeresverfassung*, ed. J. Kunisch and B. Stollberg-Rillinger (Berlin: Duncker and Humblot, 1986), 297–346; A. von Schempp, "Kompetenzstreit zwischen dem Schwäbischen Kreis und dem Reichs-General-Feldmarschall Herzog Albrecht von Sachsen-Teschen . . . im Jahre 1795," *Beiheft zum Militärwochenblatt* 9 (1908): 371–96.

40. A. von Schempp, "Die Entwaffnung und Auflösung des Schwäbischen Kreiskorps am 29 Juli. 1796," *Besondere Beilage des Staatsanzeiges für Württemberg* 14 (1911): 209–15; H. Zirkel, "Der Letzte Feldzug der Schwäbischen Kreisarmee 1793–1796," *Zeitschrift für bayerische Landesgeschichte* 35 (1972): 840–70.

41. O. Bezzel, *Geschichte des Kurpfalzbayerischen Heeres, 1778–1803* (Munich: Verlag Bayerisches Kriegsarchiv, 1930), 443–55; C. Frhr. von Bönninghausen, *Die kriegerische Tätigkeit der münsterschen Truppen, 1651–1800* (Coesfeld: privately printed, 1978), 189–92.

42. F. Dollinger, "Baar, Schwarzwald und Oberrhein im zweiten Koalitionskrieg (1799/1801)," *Zeitschrift für die Geschichte des Oberrheins* 93 (1941): 333–402; H. Bücheler, W. Fischer, and R. Kessinger, *Die Schlacht bei Messkirch 5ter Mai 1800* (Meßkirch: Gmeiner, 2000).

43. HHStA, Titel und Wappen, Kart.3, memorandum of Joseph Haas, May 1806. See also H. C. Kraus, *Das Ende des alten Deutschland: Krise und Auflösung des Heiligen Römischen Reiches Deutscher Nation 1806* (Berlin: Duncker and Humblot, 2006).

CHAPTER 8

THE ARMIES OF THE ITALIAN STATES

CIRO PAOLETTI

The main difficulty when exploring the military dimensions of Italy during the French Revolution is the lack of political unity in the peninsula. This disunity resulted in a fragmented military landscape due to the differing requirements of the respective Italian states. The diversity of the Italian states was clearly reflected in equally diverse military organizations. At the end of the eighteenth century, Italy was divided into sixteen states: the Kingdom of Sardinia, which included the island of Sardinia, the Principality of Piedmont, the Duchy of Aosta, the Duchy of Savoy, and the County of Nice; the Kingdom of Naples, which comprised the entire Italian peninsula south of Rome and whose king also ruled Sicily and was the feudal master of the island of Malta and of the Stato dei Presidi on the Tuscan coast; the Papal States, including the large part of central Italy from the Adriatic coast south of Venice to the Tyrrhenian coast south of Tuscany and north of Naples; the Principalities of Monaco—an independent enclave in the County of Nice—and Piombino, on the Tuscan coast; the Grand Duchy of Tuscany; the Duchies of Milan and Mantua, grouped in what was usually called Austrian Lombardy; the Duchy of Parma and Piacenza; the Duchy of Modena; the Duchy of Massa and Carrara; the Republics of Genoa, Lucca, San Marino, and Venice; and the whole Dalmatian coast of the Adriatic Sea and the Ionian Islands, including Corfu. The sixteenth and last state was the Order of the Knights Hospitallers of Saint John of Jerusalem, which was a feudatory possession of the Kingdom of Sicily, because it retained the island of Malta, thus being commonly known as the Order of Malta.

Tuscany, Milan, Mantua, and Modena were directly linked to the Holy Roman Empire. Milan and Mantua were personally retained by Emperor Joseph II, while his younger brother Peter Leopold—later

Emperor Leopold II—was the grand duke of Tuscany. Modena too, was tied to the Habsburgs, and its ruling family changed from Este to Austria-Este by the time of the French Revolution.

The Bourbon presence was as significant as that of the Habsburgs in Italy. Naples and Sicily were ruled by the young king Ferdinand IV. His father, Charles VII, ruled from 1733 until 1759, and later the Spanish throne as Charles III, so Sicily and Naples passed to Ferdinand. The new king of Spain, Charles IV, was Ferdinand's eldest brother, and the duke of Parma was his cousin. Bourbon-ruled states—Parma and Naples—did not need substantial military institutions because they were sure that, in case of war, support from Bourbon-ruled Spain and France was forthcoming. Modena and Tuscany, on the other hand, were deeply involved in the Habsburg military system, with its strong presence in Lombardy. Their military organizations were not terribly large or effective.

Since the eve of the seventeenth century, Genoa had been a banking house for the Spanish empire; its role and its preferred neutrality did not change, but favored the Bourbons ruling Spain. Venice continued to look to the sea. Its maritime traffic needed to be secured against the Northern African piracy, and this is why Venice had a large fleet and its infantry regiments were trained to serve both on ship and on land. The Papal States had fought on land for the last time in 1708, preferring neutrality in European conflicts since the end of the War for the Spanish Succession. Piedmont possessed a solid military organization until 1756, due to the fear of being caught between a Franco-Austrian conflict.

The French-Austrian alliance prior to the Seven Years' War substantially neutralized Italy. The newly established Bourbon-Habsburg friendship in the middle of the eighteenth century meant that Italy could no longer be considered a battlefield; therefore, Italian princes had no reason after 1755 to maintain large standing armies. The states normally possessed what they considered necessary to feel safe, and, in the event they had maritime interests, they focused more on the navy than the army. Under these conditions, it is clear that no Italian state needed a highly effective military organization prior to 1792.

Naples

The Neapolitan army was reorganized in 1765 and again in the 1780s, when Minister John Francis Edward Acton reformed the institution. According to his plan, issued on 14 January 1788, the infantry was divided into twenty regiments, composing ten brigades. Cavalry had eight regiments. The army was supposed to have 57,857 men in peacetime, to be increased to 64,543 in case of war, but this remained an impossibility until 1798. The army's effectiveness was poor; this was expected from an army whose last bullet had been shot in 1746. The navy was a good second-rank one. It had forty-four men-of-war, including many good vessels.

Venice

The Venetian army was reduced to simple garrison duties in 1720. It was divided into *oltremarini*—meaning "overseas"—and Italian regiments, both of infantry and cavalry. The Infantry had twenty-eight regiments: ten oltremarini—each composed of eight companies—and eighteen Italians, whose strength was no more than 480 men each. The total strength in 1782 was 11,705 men, and the number increased to 15,620 in 1794. At this time the cavalry never had more than 1,220 men, while the artillery did not pass 800.

The total military strength of the Venetian Republic was 60,000 men, including 40,000 members of the *Cernide*—the Venetian militia—and possessed 102 men-of-war, including 35 ships still under construction in the Arsenal, the Venetian shipyard.

Other Italian Armies

All remaining Italian states possessed armed forces typical of ancien régime institutions, simply composed of regiments and not organized into larger units, such as brigades or divisions. The Order of the Knights of Malta had 2,400 soldiers, 1,200 seamen, and some as fifteen men-of-war. The Grand Duchy of Tuscany in 1765 had 5,420 men—4,200 in three infantry regiments, 205 composing the artillery corps, and a 234-dragoon regiment, with the remaining being in the coastal towers, in the navy, and in the veteran units—but grand duke Peter Leopold considered them so costly that he decided to reduce the army and the fleet. In 1776, the army was cut to roughly 3,400 men, and later the grand duke completely disbanded it, leaving only a militia composed of urban or rural companies. He sold his three frigate navy to the Kingdom of Naples.

Lucca had 700 men—500 in the city and 200 in the towns of Viareggio and Montignoso—along with 70 Swiss Guards; but the militia was considered the core of the military as it consisted of 2,800 members in the city and 25,000 more in the little republic. Massa and Carrara had practically nothing, and their castles were garrisoned by the Austrians. Parma had 1,500 infantrymen, a mounted company of guards of merely 54 men, and roughly 12,000 members of the City and Country Militia (Milizia Urbana and Milizia Forese).

Modena had a large army, at least for its size and by contemporary Italian standards; over 150,000 inhabitants, the duchy had a militia, called the "Legion" composed of 10,061 infantrymen, 464 cavalrymen, and 360 artillerists, normally drilled in peacetime and called in case of war. The Republic of Genoa had normally 4,000 soldiers, of which 2,500 were infantrymen and the remaining were comprised of cavalrymen and artillerymen. The republic had also a 12,000-member militia and a small fleet composed of no more than six galleys. The Papal army's strength amounted to only 5,000 men. They were considered the best paid, but least effective, army in Italy. The navy comprised six galleys.

Piedmont

The Piedmontese army, or the Royal Sardinian Troops, as it was called at that time, was the largest and most effective in the peninsula. It proved to be one of the best armies of the wars of the first half of the eighteenth century. It was—in modern terms—a good example of a middling state's army for hire. It was highly flexible and possessed solid sustainability and a capability to project itself beyond its frontiers. During the reign of King Victor Amadeus III, (r. 1773–96) the old eighteenth-century organization was revised. In 1786, Victor Amadeus divided his regiments into two lines, or wings. Each line was divided in two departments. Each department was composed of two divisions, and a division consisted of two brigades, respectively comprising two regiments. Two battalions formed a regiment, and a battalion had two centuries. The century consisted of two companies of two platoons each. Platoons were divided into two dormitories, which divided in two maniples. A company had sixty men in wartime and forty in peace. This resulted in weak regiments and proved unsatisfactory in war, but the idea was good, if it came too soon. In peacetime, the infantry was supposed to have 24,000 men and the whole army was to have no more than 35,000, while wartime strength was foreseen in 45,000 men.

The Piedmontese army's artillery was also rather advanced for such a minor power. Savoy's troops had used breach-loading cannons since at least 1703, and shortly before the War for the Austrian Succession (1740–48), they possessed mountain guns that could be disassembled into three pieces. The Piedmontese also had leather cannons that could be used only once. Piedmontese studies concerning artillery were quite advanced due to the late grand master of artillery Papacino d'Antoni.

The limitations of Piedmont's population did not allow the king to field a large army. No more than 60,000 men could be maintained, if one wanted to have crops harvested annually to feed the state and the army. Considering that France could easily organize armies three times as large, the strategy of the House of Savoy since 1560 consisted of resisting any attempt cross the Alps through the construction and defense of alpine fortresses. In case the French were able overwhelm this resistance, the next step consisted of a defensive ring of fortified cities with the fortified capital, the city of Turin, at the center. In case of war, all the territories comprising the kingdom had to mobilize the provincial regiments to augment the military strength of the crown. Since 1560 a militia had been established both in Piedmont and in the Duchy of Savoy, as well as in the Kingdom of Sardinia, which had its own. According to the law issued in second half of the sixteenth century by Duke Emmanuel Philibert I, each man between eighteen and fifty was liable for the provincial levy.

Italian Fleets and Navies

Italian navies had contended with Muslim piracy since the fall of the Roman Empire. Italian fleets consisted mainly of galleys, as in the Roman and medieval period. Only Venice and Naples had effective sailing ships, not considering the two frigates comprising the entire Piedmontese blue-water navy. The Venetian fleet had previously experienced problems during the 1684–99 First Morea War, when developing the operational cooperation between galleys and sailing ships, made difficult by the difference in speed and maneuverability; but galleys remained on duty with Venetian fleet until the end of the republic in 1797, while the Piedmontese fleet used them after the 1814 Restoration.

Venetian and Neapolitan fleets acted promptly against the Barbary pirates. The Neapolitan fleet conducted numerous raids and participated in the joint Spanish-Portuguese-Neapolitan-Maltese expedition against Algiers in the summer of 1784. Venice directed several operations against pirates from Tripoli and Tunis. Italian raids against Tunis in 1784, 1785, and 1786 employed floating mortars, batteries regularly used by Italian navies.

Global Force in Italy

On the eve of the French Revolution, Italy had a global force of approximately 100,000, which could be augmented by an additional 150,000 from the various militias and provincial regiments. The respective navies totaled 180 warships, ranging in size from two-decker vessels to galleys. It was an impressive force for a single state, yet not so impressive when considering it derived from eleven independent states, including Austria. This total is irrespective of the smallest states of Monaco, San Marino, Massa, and Piombino. Overall, Italian armed forces were largely ineffective and rather poorly prepared for war due to the lack of training, and as a consequence of the long peace following the Treaty of Aix-la-Chapelle in 1748. Only the navies could be considered good; unfortunately, the French came by land instead of by sea.

Reactions to the Revolution

The Italian princes were not very interested in the Revolution. Some of them, such as Peter Leopold, Ferdinand of Naples, and Victor Amadeus of Sardinia, were personally involved because their relatives belonged to the French royal family—Queen Marie Antoinette was Peter Leopold's sister and Ferdinand's sister-in-law; and both the brothers of Louis XVI had married Victor Amadeus's daughters—but their intimate relationship did not demand a war against France.

War came only when French troops invaded Savoy and Nice in 1792. But in this case too the war was not perceived as an Italian problem: it was Piedmont's problem and nothing more. No help came from other Italian states until the following year in 1793, when the Papal States, Naples, and Tuscany joined Piedmont and the First Coalition. Indeed, most Italian states remained neutral, because this was their policy in previous conflicts. Moreover, according to their way of thinking, nothing new was happening because it was the fifth time in one hundred years and the fourth in the eighteenth century that the French fought against the Habsburgs in Italy. Neutrality had sufficed in the past, and neutrality was seen as a prudent policy in 1793, or so the princes believed.

The Eve of the War

On 22 September 1792, French troops entered the Duchy of Savoy and the County of Nice. The Piedmontese army was divided into two corps. Lieutenant General De Courten commanded the Corps of Nice, which contained 8,500 infantrymen, 600 cavalrymen, and eight guns.[1] Lieutenant General Lazzari commanded the Corps of Savoy, consisting of 10,329 infantrymen, 1,200 cavalrymen, and sixteen guns.[2] Lazzari's force was concentrated near Lake Geneva and the city of Montmélian. Lazzari however, was a poor commander, and he could not avoid the French invasion, although the Piedmontese monarch did not favor a direct engagement.

The French National Convention declared the Alps and the Rhine the natural frontiers of France in early 1793, thereby making war in Italy a necessity to achieve its strategic objectives. The First Coalition against France was formed in London. Naples joined, committing its full strength. In late 1792, when Admiral Latouche-Tréville presented the French ultimatum, Naples had only 206 cannons. During winter it added 179 more artillery pieces, 23 mortars, and 4 howitzers. There were 15,000 troops available in 1792 supported by twelve provincial regiments, while 150 artillery barges and 60 armed boats were added to the fleet. In the early days of 1793, the Neapolitans fielded 36,000 men, while the navy had 102 warships and 8,600 sailors.

Pope Pius VI acted promptly—and poorly—too. On 30 May 1792, a general mobilization was declared in the Papal States. It was costly, and in April 1793 papal ministers advised a reduction, but the pope refused and ordered a corps to garrison the Romagna. Drawing troops from Ferrara, Forte Urbano, Bologna, and the Castel Sant'Angelo garrisons, the corps deployed between Faenza and Imola. Its meager size included 752 infantrymen, 150 dragoons, many Customs Guards (Guardia di Finanza), and 40 artillerists with six guns. In November 1792, a second corps composed of 528 infantrymen, 120 cavalrymen, 77 gunners, and nineteen guns took place on the Tyrrhenian coast from Terracina to Lago di Caprolace, while the coastal garrisons were increased and the navy prepared its ships, (five galleys, two light coast-guards ships, and thirteen variously armed boats).

The Piedmontese Army Composition

The structure and organization of the Royal Sardinian Troops changed in wartime according to the mobilization requirements and available forces. The army increased its strength with the calling of the militias and organization of Free Corps. In the spring of 1793, the Piedmontese army boasted 35,000 infantrymen, 3,000 artillerists, and 3,200 cavalrymen and dragoons in Piedmont, supported by 5,000 chasseurs (light infantry) and Alpine militiamen. Austria dispatched an auxiliary corps of 4,400 infantrymen, 800 dragoons, and 800 Grenzers. The majority of the allied cavalry—roughly 3,400 to 4,000—remained in reserve between Saluzzo and Pinerolo. Two-thirds of the gunners and 12,000 infantrymen were employed in garrisons. The remaining 34,000 men of the field army were divided into four corps and deployed along the Alpine passes.

According the 1786 *Regolamento*, in case of war grenadier and chasseur companies representing the elite troops had to be grouped into converged regiments. The army thus organized five grenadier regiments totaling twelve battalions, including the two belonging to the Royal Grenadiers Regiment (Reggimento Granatieri Reali) (see appendix 1). Of the twenty chasseur companies, sixteen were grouped into two battalions: the I in Breglio and the II in Susa. On 20 March 1796, these two battalions were combined to form a regiment composed of eighteen companies. The number of chasseur

companies increased between the years 1793–96. An additional sixteen companies were formed, including four companies of chasseurs and twelve autonomous—and mostly volunteer—companies
(Free Corps).[3]

Following Sardinia's actions in previous wars, on 10 October
1792, King Victor Amadeus III declared a "general armament" of the
militia, which included volunteers aged sixteen to sixty. Companies
numbered thirty-six to forty-eight men, with three or four officers.
Two companies formed a century, and three centuries composed a
battalion commanded by a major. In December 1792, the militia had
391 centuries and 35,602 men. Unfortunately, the state lacked the
requisite weapons and equipment to arm the newly raised troops.
In response, companies were called to active duty according to local
necessity. Indeed, the only militia employed were those raised in the
mountains: no more than 10,000 men. The others did not fight and
were employed in garrisons, relieving the regulars for campaigning
with the army.

On 6 January 1794, an official report revealed that the militia was neither well trained nor led. This resulted in its immediate reorganization into 429 town-companies—the equivalent of the
number of regular army companies. Fusiliers composed 339 companies, of no more than 100 men each, for a total of 32,628 fusiliers.
The other companies had 5,418 chasseurs, while the 512 gunners
composed sixteen gunner platoons (32 gunners and four light cannons each) assigned to sixteen militia regiments. The ninety Alpine
chausser companies from Chisone and Luserna valleys, including
respectively 1,240 and 2,340 men, were enhanced with 2,520 men
from Oneglia and 558 from Loano. These companies were much
smaller, boasting no more than sixty men each. Militia gunners
served in mountain batteries. They proved so good that the Supreme
Command increased their number to eighteen and later twenty-one
companies, each composed of sixty-one men.[4] The gunners had the
option to either accept or refuse the hard mountain service, but they
hated the French to such an extent that they generally accepted this
difficult service.

In December 1793, the king permitted the establishment of a
Free Corps (volunteers) composed of 2,133 soldiers divided into thirteen companies, which was sometimes referred to as the "Foreign
Legion." Three more Free Corps were established in 1794: a company
composed of 150 chasseurs enrolled by Captain Michele Antonio

Piano, a 120-man carabinier company commanded by Count Luigi Martin Montù Beccaria, and another carabinier company organized by Giuseppe Pandini. Shortly thereafter, the first two companies doubled and increased to centuries.[5]

The Regie Truppe Sarde included the Legione Reale delle Truppe Leggiere (Royal Legion of Light Troops), commanded by General Dellera. Originally, the unit was deployed as customs guards. It had four battalions, each composed of six companies, grenadiers and chasseurs included. On 7 April 1795, in Mondovì, Dellera reorganized the legion into two regiments, each composed of 1,389 men, divided into fourteen companies: ten fusilier, two grenadier, and two chasseur companies.

In January 1793, the regional governments in Vesubia and Roia valleys—County of Nice—organized volunteer bands too, which fought bravely and effectively against the French. When the Upper Nice was lost in late Spring 1794, the bands were concentrated into eight companies of Cacciatori scelti del Nizzardo—County of Nice Elite Chasseurs[6]—which fought until the end of the war in 1796.

Warfare

It is critical to understand that the French received very little support from the population of the Kingdom of Piedmont-Sardinia. City bourgeoisie more or less accepted the French because of the political advantages they could provide, sharing local political power. The common people, peasants and artisans, rejected the French and their revolution. Some scholars suppose that this was the traditional reaction of defending one's own home and goods, and some consider it a reaction against the bourgeoisie, who oppressed the people and were closely allied to the French. It is hard to say, and one should consider that the answer differed from one town to another. What is clear is that there was a strong reaction to French occupation. For example, in Levanzo, where French general André Masséna was born, the French garrison was massacred, and resistance began at the initiative of Count della Rocca, second lieutenant in the Nizza Infantry Provincial Regiment. No less than four of Masséna's relatives fought against the Revolution and against Masséna himself: Pietro, a captain of the militia, who was wounded many times; Onorato, an ensign from Oneglia, who was appointed second lieutenant in

October 1795 "in award of his bravery"; Maurizio, a sergeant in the Piemonte Infantry Regiment, who received the Golden Medal for Bravery having been the first to enter the fort of Spinarda on 22 June 1795; another Maurizio, a sergeant too—and, like Masséna, a former soldier from the French Royal Italien Regiment—who took French general Barthélemy Joubert prisoner in Bagnasco on 8 April 1796.[7]

A revealing story concerning anti-French sentiment relates to the Moriana Regiment. It enrolled soldiers from the Moriana valley in Savoy. When Savoy was occupied in 1792, the former commander and most of the officers joined the French, but, at the end of the short 1792 campaign, the soldiers met in Susa to fight the new campaign with the Piedmontese.

The king appointed Colonel Roero, Marquis di San Severino as the new commander of the Moriana Regiment. Enrico Costa, Marquis de Beauregard wrote:

> Few among us hoped the soldiers to keep their word after four months under republican rule. Anyway, the colonel reached Susa on the said day. He traced in the snow the camp, disposing the fires, preparing the barracks. When all was done, not caring of the very cold weather, he was seen walking here and there around Susa's main square, as a maître d' waiting in the hall for the guests invited to lunchtime. He did not need to wait too long: at ten o'clock in the morning the first soldier came. His name was Grillet, he was from Lanslevillard, one of the closest village to the Moncenisio. That good young man left home the day before and arrived through some narrow and harsh paths. Then appeared two corporals from Epicrrc, who had turned their coats not to allow the people to see their uniform. Then, three by three, or four by four, through terribly narrow and uncomfortable paths all the others came. And as the joining of creeks makes the river, so it was wonderful to see over time the companies increase until complete. Within five days the regiment came back to two thirds of its strength. . . .
>
> When the colonel of the Moriana Regiment passed in review for the first time, some of the soldiers paraded with old rusty muskets, with sheathe less swords and empty cartridge-boxes. They wore strange uniforms: some had the wool cap, red or black, on their heads; some had fox or goat fur berets. These men looked grotesque, but it was tear-jerking too because of such bravery.
>
> The colonel took out of his breast-pocket the flag's tassel he had saved and tied it up on the point of his sword and raised it up shouting, "Viva il Re!" from all along the lines a loud shout "Viva il Re!" answered him.[8]

This passage provides a clear idea of the spirit of the common people in 1793 and thereafter. It is no wonder that the four infantry and two cavalry regiments from French-speaking Savoy fought very well throughout the whole war, enrolling some 1,000 volunteers during the short period when Savoy was liberated from the French. Indeed, popular reaction led to the rapid expansion of militia and free units. But the mutual hate rendered the war terrible and bloody. For instance, the volunteer bands from Vesubia and Roia valleys fought wearing regular uniforms, but the French shot them when captured because the county had been occupied and annexed to France, and the French considered them traitors and subsequently pillaged and destroyed the villages and towns supporting them. This obviously increased the existing hatred against the French. A report from the French Varo Army Corps stated: "Inhabitants in mountain villages are so exasperated that they swore to exterminate all the soldiers. Every day some soldier is killed, in the city itself: these 'barbets' are to be feared more than enemy troops."[9] And the French *Courier Universel* recorded on 30 May 1793, "Barbets wait for us behind a stone or a bush and shoot us, whilst we do not realize from where shooting comes. These damned peasants do more damages than line soldiers, they know the country and they escape from a canyon to another continuously shooting and let us not reach them."[10]

More than 2,000 partisans came from Upper Nice, which was inhabited by 150,000 persons, two-thirds of them living in the occupied zone. Moreover, these 2,000 were what remained in the county after many men had been conscripted and were serving in the Piemonte and the Nizza Infantry Regiments of the Piedmontese army. One must consider the anti-French insurgency as a clear demonstration of popular will. On the other side of the front, Piedmontese general Sant'Andrea wrote, "These active and restless volunteers, brave till foolhardiness, restlessly attacked the enemy, they watched the encampments and made reconnaissance for regular troops. They took everything attacking convoys and isolated garrisons. They easily passed over the mountain obstacles, penetrated deep in enemy lines, taking prisoners, who were transferred to encampments before they could realize what did it happen."[11]

Daily Life

The soldier's daily life was hard. When the Royal Grenadiers Regiment went to the Little Saint Bernard Pass, Marquis de Beauregard wrote to his wife in February 1793:

> We must leave the barracks just when the soldiers would need another week resting. Tomorrow we shall go to the mountains; the snow falls deep and we shall live like Tartars. . . . Imagine the cold's harshness, when the storm whistles in the encampments, wrenching the tents out of the iced ground and the whirling snow chokes the fires, whose woods blacken and smoke without flame.
>
> Imagine the depth of the piled snow, with the wolves following the column step by step, the black swarm of the gloomily croaking crows. Oh, the terrible nights in the outposts! The cold breaks the oaks' bark; the soldiers eat iced bread broken using the gunstock, and quenches himself with melted snow; there is the sentinel, a few steps from his resting comrades; he swoons because of the hunger, he trembles because of the cold, ice crystals hang from his moustaches, the hand leaves skin shreds on the iced rifle barrel.
>
> . . . For lack of space, we, thirteen officers, sleep, eat, whistle, sing and work all in the same room; what do I say: room? A barrack plunged in the snow, from which we come out only during duty hours, because during each guard-duty one can lose the skin of the face.[12]

More or less other parts of the front experienced the same situation. In the southern Alps, at Authion Hill, where the Royal Grenadiers arrived on 15 January 1794, Beauregard continued:

> We reached the Authion under a heavy rainfall and we have found that nothing lacks here, a part for the wood to warm us, the shelter to stay covered and in general what is needed to drink and eat; in fact, the detachments we are relieving look like a legion of ghosts. . . .
>
> As the major I received the best lodging: I must enter on my hands and knees; but it makes envious all my most never satisfied comrades, because they have as a lodging no more that holes covered by the snow. . . .
>
> There is a door, a window and a good chimney in my hovel; and it is big enough to have the camp bed inside.[13]

Leadership and Performance

Leadership in the Piedmontese army was as good as it could be after a forty-year peace: ineffective because of the lack of training and exercise. By eighteenth-century standards, the Piedmontese army could be considered good; unfortunately, eighteenth-century standards had been turned upside down by the French. Piedmontese headquarters was far from brilliant and, above all, was far from what was required to win. From what can be deduced by contemporary accounts and documents, it appears that low-ranking officers from ensigns to lieutenant colonels clearly understood the new warfare and quickly and effectively adopted it. Unfortunately, senior officers, including regimental commanders—colonels—and all the generals did not understand well what was happening. They considered the old style a good one because by definition it was the traditional means of war, and their troops had to be better than the revolutionaries. Moreover, international agreements between Turin and Vienna gave the Austrians—represented by General De Vins—the supreme command and this substantially stopped any kind of initiative. De Vins was repeatedly asked to attack, but his task consisted of defending Austria in Piedmont instead of attacking France, and he did not move. This caused a paralysis of the allied supreme command and stopped any kind of offensive operation. No opportunity was exploited—for example, the Upper Faucigny or the Lyon insurgencies—because he did not permit local initiatives, or any initiatives at all. The rebellion at Toulon (1793) was a British affair and not seen as an opportunity by the Austrians.

In spite of poor leadership at the highest levels, performance on the field was quite good whenever possible. The Piedmontese, concomitant with most eighteenth-century armies, were not terribly fast in maneuvering. They were, however, quite good in exploiting terrain. Moreover, they had a very good artillery tradition, and their volley fire was effective because of the training and because most of the conscripts came from the countryside and had good practice as hunters. Therefore, when they could fight the French by exploiting their own positions and using their fire, the Piedmontese normally prevailed; but if the French were able to maneuver in open field, the French usually prevailed thanks to their scattered battle order and their speed, which weakened and deprived the Piedmontese fire of its effect.

On the eve of the war and until the end of the 1793 campaign, the Piedmontese and, above all, Austrian headquarters did not realize that small enemy movements could be pieces of a bigger strategic puzzle, which, when achieved, forced them to retreat—for example, the retreat from the Roche-Cevins after a six-week skirmish against the French—because they simply did not see moving masses. Lastly, Piedmont had a long tradition of guerrilla warfare made by local militias. The militia organization had existed since 1560, and it had worked quite well during the Nine Years' War (1688–97) and the Spanish and the Austrian Succession Wars (respectively 1701–14 and 1740–48).

War, 1793–1795

In 1793, the French launched an offensive into Italy. The Piedmontese army—32,000 men divided into four separate corps—fought all along the Alps.[14] They defeated the French at Authion Hill on 12 June 1793, but their plans for recapturing Savoy and Nice failed because the corps commanded by the Duke of Aosta was unable to executed the complex operation dictated by the plan.

The coalition took advantage of the civil war in France, and sent an expeditionary force to the rebellious city of Toulon. Britain organized a multinational force to attack and destroy the French Mediterranean fleet at port. The British, Spanish, 8,000 Neapolitan, and 2,500 Piedmontese troops entered the city to support the French rebels. Moreover, Ferdinand IV of Naples agreed to send eleven ships—three ships of the line, four frigates, and four smaller ships— to join the British Mediterranean fleet.

The next campaign saw an increased Piedmontese army but few differences in the military situation. The Royal Sardinian Troops increased to 40,000 men—31,000 infantrymen, 2,600 cavalrymen, 1,200 artillerists with 113 guns, and 1,600 men in the Free Corps— but battalion strength decreased to 350 or 325 men, and companies and squadrons were no more than 80 men each.[15]

Throughout 1794, the Piedmontese repelled all French attempts to force the Alpine passes into northern Italy. French units commanded by General Masséna attacked the Testa della Nava on 25 April and Saccarello on 27 April. Masséna forced the Piedmontese to retreat to Briga. Then, after ten more days of clashes, on 10 May they were forced to withdraw to Borgo San Dalmazzo. But Masséna did not achieve a strategic victory, and the campaign ended with substantial Piedmontese defensive success.

Military victories created diplomatic benefit, as Emperor Leopold II—the former Grand Duke of Tuscany—agreed to formal military support. According to the treaty signed at Valenciennes, however, Piedmont was responsible for active defense while Austrian forces would be deployed as a strategic reserve in the Padana Plain. At the same time, Austria assumed the supreme coalition command in Italy and assigned it to General De Vins. The agreement did not provide financial subsidies for Piedmont, making the burden of Italian defense very expensive. It was clear that Austrians did not want not to fight in Italy. They only looked for good results with the least possible effort. Germany and the Austrian Netherlands remained their primary focus. Piedmont thus had to fight, and Austria expected advantages. Victor Amadeus III did not like this situation but had little choice (see appendix 2). Piedmontese soldiers sang, "When the enemy is strong, De Vins says it's impossible to assail him; when the enemy is weak De Vins says he is not to be feared. Let God be praised and Let De Vins be thanked."[16]

In early June 1795, the coalition had more than 78,000 men: 58,200 infantrymen, 5,600 cavalrymen, and 1,800 artillerymen serving 140 field guns, supported by 13,000 militiamen divided between 7,000 along the Western Alps and 6,000 in the Maritime Alps. The 1795 Alpine campaign was simple. The Piedmontese thwarted two French offensives in June. On the heels of these victories, De Vins was asked by the Piedmontese commander General Colli Marchini to commit his forces to a counteroffensive. He did not oblige his allies, and the respite permitted the French to reorganize their army. In November, Masséna defeated the Austrians in Loano and opened the route to Lombardy by occupying Liguria—that is to say the Republic of Genoa—which was compelled to accept the French presence to avoid further domestic interference. On 26 November, the Piedmontese attacked Masséna at Spinarda Hill and achieved a significant strategic result. The French army withdrew to winter quarters to recuperate.

At the conclusion of 1795 then, the Italian front remained beyond the grasp of French armies, although they had achieved significant results in Spain and Germany. This was largely due to the nature of the terrain. The Alps hampered operations. Contemporary accounts depict a situation closer to World War I instead of traditional eighteenth- or nineteenth-century battlefields. Troops on both sides spent long periods guarding trenches and field fortifications. They lived in small and smoky bunkers, which they could enter only on their knees. Cold, rain, snow, and mud were considered normal weather. Patrols as well as artillery duels were commonplace. On occasion, raids were conducted. The mountain battlefield prevented the French from fully utilizing their new tactics.

The French minister of war Lazare Carnot had organized a new army. He decreed that it had to *"agir toujours en masse"*[17]—to act ever in mass—because winning needed only "fire, steel and patriotism."[18] Inspired by this new doctrine and supported by the new, light, and easy-to-repair Gribeauval cannon and by general conscription established on 23 August 1793, the French army overwhelmed coalition armies. Outnumbered by the French and disoriented by their speed and by their echeloned battle order, coalition troops had been defeated everywhere, except in the Alps. All of this changed in 1796, when Napoleon Bonaparte was appointed commander in chief of the French Army of Italy.

1796

As it is well known, in 1795 the French Directory sought to settle affairs abroad in order to calm the domestic front. It successfully pursued negotiations with Prussia and Spain. The former kingdom was far more concerned about Russian designs on the rump of Poland and wanted the freedom to focus its efforts in the east. Spain suffered terribly from French invasion and wanted to withdraw from the coalition before the French marched on Madrid. All of this was settled at the Peace of Basel in 1795, concluding war with Prussia and later Spain. Austria and Britain remained France's enemies. As war with Britain meant war at sea, the continental effort was now concentrated fully against Austria in Germany—that is to say the Holy Roman Empire—and Italy.

Lazare Carnot remained in charge of military affairs and presented a clear plan for French operations in 1796. It was simple and resembled French strategy during the War of Spanish Succession. Two armies advanced through southern Germany and northern Italy to meet in Tyrol and then attack Vienna. Accordingly, Victor

Amadeus III had to be forced from the coalition. This would facilitate the movement of a French army through northern Italy without worrying about its lines of communications across the Alps. Coincidentally, at this time Piedmont was experiencing significant financial and strategic difficulties. War expenses increased substantially, and Austrian support was poor. Alliance conditions were hard to maintain in the face of increasing French pressure, and it was clear that no more help could be expected from the other members of the coalition. Piedmont wanted to reach a separate and not dishonorable peace. The situation was rather complex and would require entire volumes to adequately address it.[19]

Contacts existed between Barras and the French royal family in exile. The Bourbons persuaded Victor Amadeus III, their father-in-law, to reach an agreement with France. This can be deduced by what happened later. Piedmont would accept peace in exchange for Lombardy. France would have thus secured its army's communications and improved its position in its war against Austria. Piedmont would have lost Savoy and Nice, but Lombardy was sufficient compensation. French troops would have reached Trent and, through Brenner Pass, Innsbruck, and later Vienna. Austria would have been defeated and victory achieved. All of this is speculation, but what we know for sure is that the Bourbon ambassador in Turin acted according to these plans.[20]

The British ambassador in Turin, Mr. Trevor, divined the imminent armistice between France and Piedmont. He wrote to his colleague in Vienna, warning him that France had offered Lombardy to Piedmont in December 1795.[21] The Austrian ambassador in Turin, Marquis Gherardini, warned his government too. In January 1796, he wrote about French offers to Piedmont and on 13 February that the king of France—the exiled Louis XVIII—proposed that his father-in-law accept the peace and an alliance with France.[22] On 6 February 1796, Trevor warned London and Vienna that if no Austrian help came, Piedmont would accept a separate peace and neutralize Italy.

What did this mean in regard to Napoleon? It meant that when Napoleon was appointed commander of the Army of Italy, the game was over. Everything had been decided. Piedmont needed only a comedy instead of a war. Turin lost Savoy and Nice to gain Lombardy, two poor territories in change of the richest part of Italy. Napoleon was only a puppet who had to play the role that Barras and the others wrote for him. Nobody could then divine what sort of military genius he was. He himself did not know. He simply knew that all was ready to finish the war. In fact, some twenty years later, when on Saint Helena, he pronounced these revealing words: "Vendemiaire and Montenotte too did not lead me to believe that I was a superior man. Only after Lodi I realized I could, in conclusion, be an important feature on the political scene. Then the first spark set off my great ambition."[23]

On 6 March 1796, Napoleon received very detailed operational instructions prepared by Carnot. He had to pass rapidly through Piedmont, not caring to take Turin or destroying Piedmont. He had to seize Mantua and Trento and invade Austria as soon as possible. The 1796 campaign is so well known that is unnecessary to describe here. Piedmontese troops fought well, but they could not change something previously decided at the top levels, and, within a few weeks, the campaign was over (see appendix 3). On 26 April 1796, Victor Amadeus III signed an armistice. Now Napoleon could concentrate on the Austrian army, supported by a Neapolitan cavalry brigade.

The Social Composition of Italian Armies

A discussion of the social composition of Italian armies is both relatively simple and yet incredibly complex. Officers came from aristocracy and, in a very few cases and only in technical corps (and not in all the states), from the middle class. Noncommissioned officers came from the lower classes and began as privates. Privates were from the lower class. Of course, there were exceptions; in some cases in Piedmont a noncommissioned officer became an officer and attained the rank of captain. The Venetian navy could have ship commanders who did not belong to the aristocracy, but there was a difference between nobles from the city of Venice (*patrizi*) and nobles from the territories (*nobili di Terraferma*), not to mention those noblemen from Dalmatia and from the relics of the Greek domains of Venice. This was not the case in Genoa, and the situation was decidedly different in Rome.

Case Study of Battle: Authion Hill, 8–12 June 1793

In Nice's Maritime Alps, Marquis de Beauregard wrote, "The Authion is a sort of narrow valley from Saorgio to the Raus Hill. Along the valley a creek flows. Our positions are on the left bank, on the steep slope of the mountain, which is cultivated in terraces, made of flat strips of earth supported by dry-stone walls, all arranged in steps. In the biggest steps there are some ghastly holes and a chapel. . . . From the top of these mountains one sees the whole chain of the Alps and in the end one sees the sea."[24]

Piedmontese troops commanded by Benedetto Maria Maurizio of Savoy, Duke of Chiablese, the king's brother, were disposed along a west-east oriented line, facing south, on the heights from Authion Hill to Mount Capelet, or Cappelletto. The Piedmontese left wing had 8,000 men and seven guns (see appendix 4) on the Brouis Hill; the right had 4,000 men and some twelve guns on Authion (see appendix 5).

The French Armée du Var—commanded by General Brunet and drawn from Kellerman's Armée des Alpes—was in the valley. Brunet's army had 20,000 men with 7,000 in Peiracava and San Colombano, General Dumerbion had 10,000 at Sospello, and General Sérurier led the remaining 3,000 men in Roccabigliera. Their task consisted of breaking the Piedmontese line to cross the mountains in order to enter the Padana Plain from the southwest.

At dawn on 8 June 1793, Brunet began the attack against Authion. He sent three columns commanded by General d'Ortoman against the outposts at Mantegas, Camp Argent, and Tueis. Piedmontese militia garrisoning the outpost were ordered to withdraw, but they were too late. The French central column engaged them in front, while the two remaining columns flanked them. General Dellera ordered the IX Grenadiers Battalion to advance from Authion to support the militia, allowing it to withdraw. The grenadiers, however, were engaged by the French and were forced to retreat to their original position.

On the left, things went badly for the Piedmontese. The French brigade under General Miakowski crossed a stream and attacked Roches de Goeta, destroying the I Battalion of the Vercelli Infantry Provincial Regiment. The Piedmontese I/Chasseurs Battalion counterattacked, but Miakowski repelled it, defeating three Piedmontese battalions—II/Vercelli, II/Nizza, and II/Saluzzo—ejecting them from the Col Freddo redoubt. Miakowski mastered the Linieras Heights and menaced Perus Hill at the conclusion of this engagement. After a failed second counterattack by the Austrian 2nd Garrison Regiment, Colonel Policarpo d'Osasco, with all his grenadiers, was forced to retreat. He crossed the Roia River at the bottom of the valley and concentrated in Breglio with troopers belonging to six separate battalions.

Dumerbion and Miakowski moved against Brouis Hill's second position on Béolet-Albarea, while a bit north French general Gardanne attacked Molinetto, garrisoned by volunteer bands. Dumerbion had been repeatedly repulsed, but Gardanne gained the Molinetto, in spite of the counterattack by I/Casale Infantry Regiment from Milleforche Hill. Masséna and d'Ortoman exploited the opportunity presented. Masséna marched against Mangiabò Hill while d'Ortoman encircled and attacked the rear of the Piedmontese at Béolet. General Sant'Andrea was forced to abandon Brouis Hill. He then ordered a general withdrawal across the Maglia Creek and concentrated his troops on Mangiabò, placing the I and IV/Grenadiers Battalions on the slope.

As the Piedmontese left was forced to retreat, Sérurier failed to gain the key position at Authion. General Micas led his advanced guard into the Piedmontese cross fire until reaching the foot of Raus Hill. The terrain in front of the Testa di Ruggero proved to be impassable, especially under the fire of Captain Auda's militia and the Acqui infantrymen and the I/Legione Reale Truppe Leggere shooting from the Cappeletto Height. Sérurier personally led a second attempt. His column was savaged by two guns and infantry volleys. He was attacked in flank by the Swiss Regiment Christ and was compelled to withdraw to the shouts of the Piedmontese, *"Viva il Re! Viva l'Artiglieria!"*—"Long live the King! Long live the Artillery!"

Brunet attacked Milleforche Hill, in the center of Piedmontese line, but the Lombardia Infantry Regiment threw him back. Moreover, at 2 P.M. Colli and Dellera personally led a sortie and forced the French to the other side of the Bevera Creek. The first day was over. French casualties probably totaled 1,200 men, while the Piedmontese and Austrians suffered 500. The French stood and reorganized on the slope of Mount Ciarmetta.

That same evening a skirmish between patrols occurred. The Piedmontese lost fourteen men—one dead, four wounded, nine prisoners—but realized the new French disposition and accordingly reorganized their front. They called three more battalions—I and V/Royal Grenadiers and the I/Austrian Belgioioso Infantry Regiment—and moved their guns from Cappelletto to the Testa di Toro (Bull's Head).

On 10 June, General Micas was informed of this and attacked with 1,500 men. He took the Terra Rossa and Cappelletto redoubts, but the Piedmontese put two more mountain guns on the heights, and their canister critically aided a counterattack on 11 June at dawn. Subsequently, Brunet modified his plans according to the new Piedmontese dispositions. He put his right on the newly conquered heights and decided to move the following day, 12 June. Unfortunately for him, his new position was good for defense and bad for attacking; in fact, French troops now had to descend the valley, cross a creek (there were three different creeks dividing the different French sectors from the Piedmontese positions) under enemy fire, and climb the opposite slope, one by one, under enemy fire. Not caring about this, Brunet directed his men in repeated assaults against Authion and Milleforche, what they had already done on 8 June, when they surrounded the enemy and forced them to retreat. Sérurier had to make a diversion against Cappelletto and Terra Rossa, but in fact he had to move against Milleforche on the right. Miakowski had to attack it on the left supported by General Lecointre. D'Ortoman was in charge of attacking Authion and Raus Hills, whilst a fourth column made a diversion against the Bull's Head.

It was foolhardy, and Brunet disliked this idea, but the French *représentant en mission* forced him. They wanted another attack and Brunet preferred to risk the life of his men instead of losing his own head by being charged as an "enemy of the people." Thus, on 12 June 1793 at 7 A.M., after a two-day rain, Brunet ordered the attack. Miakowski moved then halted because of the mud in front of the Piedmontese outposts. Colli realized the situation. He left a few forces in front of Miakowski and concentrated all he had on Milleforche and Authion. Piedmontese batteries quickly stopped the French attempt against Raus Hill. Their volleys wounded Lecointre and stopped the attack against Molinetto too. Miakowski and Sérurier, however, succeeded in joining their forces before Authion. Sérurier then attacked three times. Well-directed artillery fire by Captain Vaira supported the I/Grenadiers, commanded by the Marquis Dichat, forcing the French back. Then, French *tirail-leurs* (light infantry, sharpshooters) reached one of the two batteries through a narrow goat path and massacred the gunners. Captain Vaira, who was with the other battery, turned his remaining guns and annihilated the enemy with a quick succession of shots.

The surviving French retreated, whilst at the same moment Sérurier's third and final attack was repelled. Piedmontese grenadiers came out of their positions and pursued the enemy with their bayonets. The French collapsed and fled. They infected Lecointre's men with panic, and the entire force was routed eighteen miles to Scarena, down the valley, shouting everywhere that the Piedmontese were marching on Nice.

Seeing the opportunity, Dellera sortied with all his battalions. The Lombardia Regiment pushed Miakowski's troops to the Parsella wood. But Miakowski reorganized his men and attacked Milleforche once more; Austrians of the Belgioioso Regiment resisted, supported by the Casale and Sardegna infantry regiments, but Miakowski realized his men were surrounded by the I/Grenadiers and the Free Corps. The French grenadiers now faced a bayonet charge by I, V, and IX/Grenadiers and the Royal Grenadiers. The hand-to-hand fighting was bloody, and no quarter was given. Grenadiers on both the sides fell down the mountain grasping each other.

D'Ortoman was now alone on the field. Brunet recalled him, determining the battle was over. The Piedmontese had won, but victory did not mask serious problems. First, some of the colonels, especially the commander of the Vercelli Infantry Provincial Regiment, was court-martialed. Second, the Piedmontese had not fought well during the first day, the 8th, when the French could exploit their echeloned order and their ability to move fast. Things changed when the second French attempt was made against that position on the 12th, but only after a political order. Brunet was too experienced a soldier to try such a gamble. He was pretty sure it was going to fail because of the terrain. Therefore, the victory was due largely to the poor conditions faced by the attacking force. French troops performed very well; but the Piedmontese demonstrated their own ability to win thanks to the terrain, and in spite of the inferior quality of their training. Nevertheless, the artillery and grenadiers acquitted themselves well.

Casualties were high on both sides. The Piedmontese admitted slightly fewer than 2,400 men—roughly 20 percent of their total force—killed, wounded, imprisoned, and missing in action. Brunet admitted only to 280 dead and 1,252 wounded and imprisoned. This figure was probably too low. In fact, a few months later, Brunet was sent to the guillotine for lying to the représentant en mission by reducing his claim of casualties at Authion. According to Jomini, who later studied the battle, French casualties should have been, all included, 1,200 men on 8 June and 2,000 on 12 June—that is to say, 16 percent of total French forces.

The French situation was bad. Paris directed Kellerman to Nice to save it. He modified the French dispositions and waited for the enemy's offensive, but the allies were unable to exploit their tactical success and turn it into a strategic victory. This was a further demonstration of the poor quality of their supreme command.

Appendices

Appendix 1

The army had one Royal Grenadiers Regiments composed of two battalions. Then the army, according to the rules foreseen for war, created ten other Grenadiers Battalions. These ten battalions had been composed using the Grenadiers Companies belonging to each Infantry Regiment.

Eight out of ten Grenadiers Battalions were grouped into four regiments, and each regiment was named after its commander; the remaining two battalions out of the ten remained independent, and have been called "isolated"; so, there were twelve Grenadiers Battalions (two composing the Royal Grenadiers Regiment, eight composing the four Grenadiers Regiments organized for the war duties, and two independent Grenadiers Battalions). The following table shows, by battalion, which Grenadiers companies coming from which Infantry Regiment composed each Grenadiers Battalion. It reports only the ten battalions composed by the companies coming from each Infantry Regiment, because the two battalions composing the Royal Grenadiers Regiments already existed in that regiment.

I Battalion	isolated	2 companies from Guardie, Asti, and Casale regiments
II Battalion	(Regt. Bertone)	2 cos. from Savoia, La Marina, and Torino
III Battalion	isolated	2 cos. from Monferrato, Piemonte, and Rockmondet (the last was Swiss)
IV Battalion	(Regt. Osasco)	2 cos. from Saluzzo, Vercelli, and Tortona
V Battalion	(Regt. Osasco)	2 cos. from Aosta, Mondovì, and De Courten (the last was Swiss)
VI Battalion	(Regt. Saluggia)	2 cos. from Chiablese, Genevese, and Reale Alemanno (the last was German-speaking)
VII Battalion	(Regt. Saluggia)	2 cos. from Moriana, Ivrea, and Pinerolo
VIII Battalion	(Regt. Solaro)	2 cos. from Nizza, Sardegna, and Della Regina
IX Battalion	(Regt. Solaro)	2 cos. from Acqui, Lombardia, and Christ (the last was Swiss)
X Battalion	(Regt. Bertone)	2 cos. from Novara and Susa

Appendix 2

Allied Order of Battle in 1795

A) The "Armata di Lombardia" (commanded by Austrian general Wallis), consisting of 20,700 Austrian infantrymen in 23 battalions and 1,750 Sardinians in 5 bns.; 2,788 cavalrymen; and 772 gunners with 38 guns, was divided into:
   1) Austrian Division Winckheim
      avant-garde: 900 Croats—Regiment Gyulaj and 400 Uhlans—Regiment Metzaros;
      Rukawina Brigade (Bukawina): 5 bns., totaling 4,500 infantrymen between the Bormida and Ellero Rivers;

Terniczy Brigade: 4 bns. of 3,600 infantrymen;
Pittony Brigade: 5 bns. of 4,500 infantrymen;
Liptay Brigade: 6 bns. of 5,400 infantrymen.

2) Mixed Division Turckheim:

Austrian-Sardinian Brigade Cantù: 3 Austrian bns. of
2,700 men and 5 Sardinian bns. of 1,750 men;

Austrian Brigade Fischer: 6 dragoons squadrons of 1,200
men in Alessandria;

Neapolitan Dragoons Brigade of the Prince di Cutò: 12
sqns. of 1,200 men at Mortara.

B) The "Armata Austro-sarda" (commanded by General Michelan-
gelo Alessandro count Colli Marchini), consisting of 30 Sardinian
bns. of 9,000 men and 5 Austrian bns. with 4,500 men, supported
by 32 guns, was divided into:

1) Argenteau Division: 2 Austrian bns. of 1,800 uomini and 14
Sardinian bns. of 4,200 men in Ceva;

2) Provera Brigade: 3 Austrian bns. of 2,700 men in Morozzo,
Millesimo, and Mombarcaro;

3) Colli Division: 16 Sardinian bns. of 4,800 Piedmontese and
Swiss soldiers in Mondovì.

C) The Duke of Aosta's Army Corps, consisting of 21 Sardinian bns.
of 8,200 men and 1 Austrian bn. with 800 men; 2,580 cavalrymen,
and 43 guns; and 1,600 men of the Free Corps, was divided into:

1) The Division of Cuneo, Gesso e Stura: 8 bns. of 2,800
Sardinians; the Austrian bn. with 800 men; and Free Corps with
1,600 men;

2) Maira and Varaita Valleys Brigade: 9 bns. and 4 companies of
3,550 infantrymen and 16 guns;

3) Luserna Valley Brigade: 2 bns. and 5 cos. of 1,850 infantrymen, 480 cavalrymen, and 27 guns;

4) Cavalry Division: 1,600 Sardinian and 500 Austrian cavalrymen in Borgo San Dalmazzo.

D) The Duke of Monferrato's Army Corps, consisting of 31
Sardinian bns. of 10,675 infantrymen, 320 cavalrymen, and 38
guns, was divided into:

1) Val Susa Division: 16 bns. and 2 cos. of 5,450 infantrymen
and 12 guns;

2) Val d'Aosta Division: 14 bns. and 2 cos. of 5,225 infantrymen, 320 cavalrymen, and 26 guns.

Appendix 3

Battle Order of the Allied Army in March 1796

Commander: Lt. Gen. Baron Colli Marchini; strength: 30,767 men (including 737 officers)

Saluzzo Division, commanded by Maj. Gen. Count de Sonnaz, with 5,001 men divided as follows:

in Verzuolo: 486 men composing 4 squadrons of the Piemonte Reale Regiment and 2 battalions including 1,199 Pioneers;

in Busca: 1,125 men composing 2 bns. of the Asti Infantry Regiment;

in Saluzzo: 1,320 men composing 2 bns. of the Austrian Belgioioso Infantry Regiment;

in Sampeyre: 1 century—130 free chasseurs of Sardinia;

in Varaita Valley: 3 Renaud, Orage, and Arnaud companies including 320 militiamen;

in Maira Valley: 4 Ponza, Cocchio, and Tarditi cos. including 388 militiamen.

Borgo San Dalmazzo Division, commanded by Maj. Gen. Count Christ (Swiss in Sardinian service), with 7,239 men divided as follows:

in the Forts of Demonte and Vinay: 1,255 men composing 3 bns. of the Swiss Infantry Regiment Streng in Sardinian service;

in Stura Valley: 900 militiamen belonging to the 9 cos. Argentera, Bersezio, Preynard, Ferrieres, Pont-Bernard, Pietraporzio, Sambuco, Pianche, Poal, Vinadio, and Demonte;

in Valdieri: Free chausseurs Bovarino co., 126 men;

in Entraque Valley: 144 militiamen belonging to Cerruti and Dalmazzo cos.;

in Limonetto: Antignano Legion (1 bn.) including 334 men;

in Limone: Nice's chasseurs cos. Conte and Galla of 155 men and Piano Free Company of 101 men;

in Vallone San Giovanni: 57 volunteers commanded by Gastaldi, and 15 gunners;

in Borgo San Dalmazzo: 252 Artillery and Train soldiers;

in Dronero: Piemonte Infantry Regiment (2 bns.) of 998 men and Gandolfo and Re Militia cos. of 194 men;

at the Certosa di Pesio: 1,027 men composing the Christ Swiss Infantry Regiment in Sardinian service (2 bns.) and 2 De Caroli volunteer cos. of 106 men;

Cuneo garrison: 531 men composing the I Battalion of the Sardegna Infantry Regiment, 851 soldiers of the Peyer-im-Hoff Swiss Infantry Regiment in Sardinian Service (3 bns.), and 1 century—143 men—of the Reale Marina (Royal Navy) Corps.

Ceva Corps
1st Division of the Left, in Mulazzano, commanded by (Swiss) Col. Brempt in Sardinian Service, including 3,942 men;
    in Mulazzano: Headquarter and Real Alemanno (German-speaking soldiers) Infantry Regiment (2 bns.) with 510 men;
    in Marsaglia and Mulazzano: Genevese Infantry Regiment (2 bns.) with 1,018 men;
    in Niella and Briaglio: Chiablese Infantry Regiment (2 bns.) with 742 men and the I Battalion of the Savoia Infantry Regiment with 500 men;
    in Mombarcaro and Morango: Vercelli Infantry Regiment (2 bns.) with 1,172 men.

2nd Division of the Left in Ceva, commanded by Gen. Montafia, deputy commander: Brigadier Vitale, including 5,316 men:
    in Ceva: Comando, 3 bns.: 386 men of the Infantry Regiment Savoia II Battalion and 983 men of the Infantry Regiment Stettler II and III Battalions;
    in the Fort of Ceva: 491 men composing the Infantry Regiment Stettler I Battalion;
    in Oggo: 406 men belonging to Tortona militia cos. and 113 free chasseurs of the Martin Company.

Avant-garde on the Bormida River, in Montezemolo, commanded by Col. Count di Millesimo:
    in Priero: 6 cos. (478 men) of the 2nd Chasseurs Battalion Colli Ricci;
    in Montezemolo: Headquarter and 2 cos. of 2nd Colli Ricci;
    in Cengio: 1 co. (150 Croats and Barré free chasseurs);
    in Millesimo: La Rocque Nice's chasseur co. (76 men);
    in Cairo: 3 cos.: 135 Croats, 73 Oneglia militiamen, 115 Acqui chasseurs;
    in Sale: Acqui Infantry Regiment's I Battalion of 537 men;
    in Cortemilia: Acqui Infantry Regiment's II Battalion of 530 men.

Avant-garde on the Tanaro River, in Bagnasco, commanded by Maj. Ferrero:

in Bagnasco: Headquarter and 4 cos.: Free chasseurs Buriasco and Arancini with 155 men and Nice's chasseurs Crestini and Falque with 130 men;

in Perla: 1 mixed co. composed of Geletti's 87 Nice's chasseurs and Pandini's 26 Free chasseurs;

in Morreres: I Saluggia Chasseurs Battalion of 420 men;

Malpotremo: 25 Croats.

3rd Division of the Right, in San Michele, commanded by Col. Marquis Dichat, including 3,253 men:

in Lesegno: Oneglia Infantry Regiment's I Battalion of 714 men;

in San Michele: Headquarter, the 2nd Grenadiers Battalion and Oneglia Chasseurs Battalion's 3 cos. of 417 men;

in Pamparato and Serra: the Reale Legione Leggera's 6 cos. of 345 men;

in Tagliante: D'Agliano Free chasseurs co. of 167 men;

in Frabosa: Torino Infantry Regiment of 225 men; 378 militia-men and volunteers from Casotto and Mongia Valleys.

Avant-garde in the Mongia and Casotto Valleys:

in Viola: 2 cos. (102 Nice's chasseurs commanded by Domerego and 149 chasseurs commanded by Cauvin);

in Mombasiglio: 320 men composing 1 bn. of the Legione Balegno;

in Mombasiglio and Battifolle: 1 co. (69 Croats from Gyulaj Free Corps);

in Terre and Montaldo: 367 men composing 1 bn. of the Legione Bellegarde.

4th Reserve Division in Mondovì, commanded by Col. Marquis de Bellegarde, including some 6,000 men:

in Madonna di Vico: VIII Grenadiers Battalion (441 men) of the Dichat Grenadiers Regiment;

in Mondovì and Cittadella: Headquarter, IX Grenadiers Battalion (441 men) of the Dichat Grenadiers Regiment, and 2 bns. composing the Royal Grenadiers Regiment (844 men);

in Breo: Varax Grenadiers Regiment (2 bns., 953 men);

in Carassone: 2 Grenadiers bns.: one commanded by Lt.

Col. Chiusana with 522 grenadiers, one commanded by Lt. Col. Andermatt with 228 men;

    in Villanuova: Tour Grenadiers bn.: 530 men;

    in Benevagienna and Carrù: Esery Grenadiers Regiment: 2 bns. of 1,102 men;

    in La Margarita and Morozzo: 2 bns. and 1 co. from the Mondovì Infantry Regiment.

"Divisione di Riserva" (Austro-Sardinian Reserve Division), commanded by Maj. Gen. Giovanni Provera, including 5,038 men:

    Austrian Brigade:

        On 13 April, 1,712 men between Bric Pattaria and Cosseria: 2 Grenadier cos. from Strassoldo Regiment and Headquarter Dragoon patrols;

        in Bric Pattaria: 2 Belgioioso fusiliers bns.;

        Around and inside Cosseria Castle: 550 Croats from the Gyulaj Free Corps;

        Sardinian Brigade commanded by Col. Count di Mussano:

        in and around Cherasco: the Guards Regiment (2 bns.), Torino Infantry Regiment (2 bns.), and Casale Infantry Regiment (2 bns.)

  Other Sardinian troops

        Attached to Austrian Army and provisionally under the orders of Bukawina Brigade (Argenteau Division): Brigadier Avogadro di Valdengo with Monferrato Regiment (2 bns.) and La Marina Infantry Regiment (2 bns.): 1,500 men; in Cuneo: 8 cavalry sqns. composing Savoia Cavalry Regiment, Aosta Cavalry Regiment, and Cavalleggeri di S. M. (His Majesty's Light Cavalrymen Regiment), and 12 dragoons sqns. composing Dragoni di Sua Maestà (His Majesty's Dragoons Regiment), Dragoni di Piemonte, Dragoni della Regina (Queen's Dragoons), and Dragoni del Chiablese;

    On Cozie and Graie Alps and in garrisons: 34 bns. as follows:

        9 belonging to Infantry National Ordinary Regiments Saluzzo (2 bns.), Aosta (2 bns.), La Regina (2 bns.), Lombardia (2 bns.), and Oneglia (1 bn.);

        2 Grenadiers Battalions;

           1. belonging to Infantry Provincial Regiments Nizza (2 bns.), Moriana, (2 bns.) Susa (2 bns.), Pinerolo (2 bns.), Ivrea (2 bns.), Novara (2 bns.), and Tortona (1 bn.);

6 belonging to Swiss Infantry Ordinary Regiments
   Schmidt, Bachmann, and Zimmermann (2 bns. each);
4 composing 2 Garrison Regiments (1 Sardinian and 1
   Austrian).

Appendix 4

Battle Order of the Left Wing: Headquarter in Breglio, commanded by Gen. Count di Sant'Andrea

in Roches de Goeta—also called Haute Liniéras: Col. cavalier d'Osasco with the I Battalion of the Vercelli Infantry Provincial Regiment and 2 light guns;

on the Liniéras Heights: 2 companies of the II Battalion of the Vercelli Infantry Provincial Regiment, supported by militiamen and volunteers in different outposts;

in the Grangia di Fontanin (the Little Fountain Farm): 2 cos. of the II Battalion of the Vercelli Infantry Provincial Regiment as sector reserve;

at Col Froid (Cold Hill)—also called Basses Liniéras: a reduct garrisoned by the II Battalion of the Nizza Infantry Regiment and the II Battalion of the Saluzzo Infantry Regiment;

at Monte Béolet and Albarea: the I Chasseurs Battalion, except for one of its cos.;

on Colle del Perus: the I Battalion of the 4th Grenadiers Regiment, supported by 2 cos. of the Austrian 2nd Garrison Regiment with 2 small and 3 medium-caliber guns;

along the Niega Creek: cavalier Radicati's militiamen and volunteers;

in front of the Bevera Creek: one co. of Canale Carabineers-Chasseurs and a volunteer band from Nice;

in the Molinetto (Little Mill) and in the couple of Bevera left outposts: one co. of Canale Carabineers-Chasseurs and Cauvin volunteer band;

at Grangia di Sambuco: Del Carretto Free Corps and La Motte Guards-Chasseurs co.;

on Col del Brouis: the I Battalion of the La Regina Infantry Regiment, I and II Battalion of the Tortona Infantry Regiment, I Battalion of the Oneglia Infantry Regiment, I Battalion of the Saluzzo Infantry Regiment, I Battalion of the Nizza Infantry

Regiment, I Battalion of the Sardinia Infantry Regiment, I and VIII Grenadiers Battalions, and remaining 2 cos. of the Austrian 2nd Garrison Regiment.

Appendix 5

Battle order of the Right Wing: Headquarter in Fromagine, then at Authion, commanded by Gens. Colli Marchini and Dellera

in Terra Rossa (Red Lands) Count della Rocca with a company composed of Levenzo and Berra volunteer bands and other volunteers;

at Testa di Ruggero (Roger's Head): a co. composed of Nice's volunteer bands commanded by Cap. Auda;

on the Cima del Cappelletto (Little-Cap Height): a century from Acqui;

on Col di Raus: Brig. Costa di Montafia commanding I and the II Battalion of the Acqui Infantry Regiment, supported by 2 guns, garrisoning a dry-earth trench;

in the Baissa di Saint-Véran, Orthighea, and Grangia di Paret (Paret Farm): the I Light Battalion of Antignano supported by 2 guns;

on Cima Tueis, Camp Argent, and Mantegas: Lieutenant Roccaforte militiamen supported by 150 more volunteers;

on Milleforche (One Thousand Forks) Height: the I and II Battalion of the Casale Infantry Regiment, I and II Battalion of the Lombardia Infantry Regiment, I Battalion of the Christ Swiss Infantry Regiment in Sardinian service, and IX Grenadiers Battalion;

on the Testa (Head) of the Authion: artillerymen serving 2 howitzers and a half dozen guns garrisoning the line under construction.

Notes

1. Infantry Regiments: La Regina, Lombardia, Nizza, and Mondovì; the I Piemonte, II Saluzzo, I (Swiss) de Courten, I (Swiss) Christ, two infantry companies composing the IV Battalion of the Legione degli Accampamenti (Encampement Legion), the Equipaggi (crews) Battalion, and the Granatieri delle Fregate (Frigate Grenadiers) Battalion; a squadron of the Dragoni di Piemonte (Dragoons of Piedmont) Regiment and two squadrons (II and III) of the Aosta Cavalleria Regiment; two Artillery companies and auxiliary gunners, and a company of "invalidi."

2. The Savoy Army Corps was composed of the Aosta, Genevese, La Marina, Monferrato, Moriana, Sardegna, Susa, and Rokmondet (Swiss from Bern) infantry regiments, the I Guardie, II Savoia, II Casale, and I and III Legione dei Campamenti battalions; the Cavalleggeri di Sua Maestà (His Majesty's Lightcavalrymen) Regiment; the I and III squadrons of the Dragoni della Regina (Queen's Dragoons) Regiment; the 5th Company of the Legione Reale Truppe Leggere (Royal Light Troops Legion), and an Artillery company.

3. These included two companies from Oneglia, three from Asti, one from Mondovì, two from Savoy, one from Aosta, one from Novara, one from Verceli, and the last from a mixed reserve company.

4. Eight companies were organized just grouping the existing sixteen gunner platoons. The remaining ten came after transforming and training ten chasseur companies.

5. In winter 1793–94, because of the casualties of the last campaign, the corps was reorganized into eleven companies, each composed of 160 men (1st d'Isone, 2nd Saissi, 3rd di Buriasco, 4th Patono, 5th de Bonneaud, 6th Reserve, 7th Piano First, 8th Piano Second, 9th Pandini, 10th d'Agliano, and 11th Quincinetto). On 17 February 1795, companies were one more time reorganized into 1st Pandini, 2nd Buriasco, 3rd Saissi, 4th Francini, 5th Martin, 6th Bovarino, 7th Rivarona, 8th Patono, 9th Piano, 10th De Bonneaud, and 11th Reserve.

6. Named, as usual, after their respective commanders, they were 1st Company Larocque, 2nd Cristini, 3rd Tordo, 4th Giletta, 5th Cauvin, 6th Domerego, 7th Comes, and 8th Galea.

7. *Enciclopedia Militare*, 6 vols. (Milano: Il Popolo d'Italia, 1921–30), 4:902, s.v. "Masséna, Maurizio"; for the other three, see Alberico Lo Faso di Serradifalco, *La difesa di un Regno* (Udine: Gaspari, 2009) 421; Virgilio Ilari, Piero Crociani, and Ciro Paoletti, *La guerra delle Alpi: 1792–1796* (Rome: USSME, 2000), 39, 209, 215, and 263.

8. Enrico Costa de Beaurcgard, *Un uomo d'altri tempi* (Turin: Tipografia e libreria San Giuseppe degli artigianelli, 1897), 113–14.

9. Quoted in Ilari, Crociani, and Paoletti, *Guerra delle Alpi*, 55.

10. Quoted in ibid.

11. Ibid.

12. Costa de Beauregard, *Uomo d'altri tempi*, 120–21.

13. Ibid., 161.

14. Val d'Aosta Army Corps, including 9,500 infantrymen, 400 cavalrymen, and fourteen guns; Val di Susa Army Corp with 800 grenadiers, 200 cavalrymen, and nine guns; Army Corps of the Po valleys, with 7,000 infantrymen and eight guns; Army Corps of the County of Nice, with 14,000 infantrymen and twenty-four guns.

15. The infantry had 87 battalions, 9 autonomous companies, and 6 Free Corps centuries as follows: 20 National Ordinary Battalions (80 companies); 13 foreign battalions (52 companies); 28 provincial battalions (112 companies); 1 garrison battalion (10 companies); 11 regimental grenadiers battalions (66 companies); 4 special, elite provincial battalions (8 Royal Grenadiers companies and 8 Pioneers Companies);

4 light battalions (16 companies); 4 Regimental chasseurs battalions (16 companies); autonomous chasseurs companies; 2 Nice's Volunteer Chasseurs battalions (8 companies); and 6 Free Corps centuries.

The cavalry had 32 squadrons, including dragoons, and the artillery had 30 companies. The militia had 321 fusiliers companies, 90 Alpine chasseurs companies, and 18 gunners companies. Heavy artillery (with 8- and 16-pound cannons and howitzers) had 16 gunner companies; field and mountain artillery consisted of 56 teams (16 men and 2 guns each): 52 teams had 3- or 4-pound light guns supporting fusiliers and grenadiers battalions; the remaining 4 teams had 8-pound medium guns supporting 8 Regimental Grenadiers battalions.

16. Costa de Beauregard, *Uomo d'altri tempi*, 123.

17. Lazare Carnot, quoted in Michael Howard, *War in European History* (Oxford: Oxford University Press, 1976), 151.

18. Ibid.

19. There are only two books in Italian literature about this. The first is Guglielmo Ferrero, *Avventura: Bonaparte in Italia (1796–1797)*, published by Il Corbaccio. Its first edition appeared in 1936; the second, in 1996. The second, and more detailed, book is Ilari, Crociani, and Paoletti, *Guerra delle Alpi.*

20. For specific sources supporting this argument, see Ilari, Crociani, and Paoletti, *Guerra delle Alpi*, 261 passim; Costa de Beauregard, *Uomo d'altri tempi*; and Ferrero, *Avventura*. Ilari, Crociani, and Paoletti, *Guerra delle Alpi*; Virgilio Ilari, Piero Crociani, and Ciro Paoletti, *Storia militare dell'Italia giacobina (1796–1802)* (Rome: USSME, 2001); Virgilio Ilari, "La Guerra delle Alpi: le ragioni di una rimozione storica," in *Le truppe leggere nella Guerra delle Alpi*, ed. Valentina Barberis, Dario Del Monte, and Roberto Sconfienza (Turin: Gioventura Piemonteisa, 2006); Emanuel de Las Cases, *Memoriale di Sant'Elena* (Rome: Casini, 1969); Ciro Paoletti, *Gli Italiani in armi—cinque secoli di storia militare nazionale, 1494–2000* (Rome: USSME, 2001); Ciro Paoletti, *A Military History of Italy* (Westport, Conn.: Praeger, 2007); and Arturo Segre, *Vittorio Emanuele I: 1759–1824* (Turin: Paravia, 1935).

21. All these documents were quoted for the first time by Ferrero. They are in Public Record Office, F.O. 67, 20, and 21.

22. Ferrero, *Avventura*, 24.

23. Quoted in Las Cases, *Memoriale di Sant'Elena*, 79.

24. Costa de Beauregard, *Un uomo d'altri tempi*, 161.

CHAPTER 9

THE OTTOMAN ARMY

VIRGINIA H. AKSAN

On 21 October 1798, the city of Cairo exploded as the city's population confronted the French troops under Bonaparte, stationed there since July, following the defeat of the Ottoman Mamluk chieftains Murad and Ibrahim Beys at the Battle of the Pyramids.[1] Ostensibly, the riots were instigated by the merchants of the city, who were resistant to the oppressive taxes and forced requisitioning imposed by the ill-financed expeditionary force, crippled by the British destruction of its fleet at the Battle of the Nile (also known as the Battle of Aboukir) the previous August. Just as significant was the anger of the general population at the disrespect of French engineers, who knocked down local buildings and walls, sacred or otherwise, in carrying out their orders to secure the city defenses and modernize neighborhoods, especially around the mosque and tenth-century university complex of al-Azhar. The absence of coherent leadership among the rebels allowed the French to organize their superior artillery and mow down the mutinous population, perhaps as many as 3,000, with at least another three hundred executions in the days that followed. French losses in the street fighting may have been as great as three hundred.[2]

Bonaparte had decided to celebrate year VII of the First Republic (22 September 1792) in Cairo by erecting an obelisk (also called a pyramid) that celebrated that date on one side and the defeat of the Mamluks in year VI on the other, with the equivalent translated in Arabic on the other two faces. Two entrances to the colonnade sported a triumphal arch and a portico with the Muslim professions of faith: There is no God but Allah and Muhammad is his Prophet. As one historian has noted, "Bonaparte was still attempting to associate republican virtue with an Islam coated in a sort of deism."[3] As reported by his chief ideologue, Constantine Volney, writing in *Le Moniteur*, Bonaparte achieved the creation of an Arab nation by his reforms and aimed at "the resurrection of former Arab glory, the destruction of the Ottomans, and the purification of Islam."[4] Bonaparte's Egyptian observers are said to have viewed the obelisk as "the stake on which they had been impaled and the symbol of the conquest of their country"[5]

That same September 1798, in the face of public pressure to defend the sacred cities of Mecca and Medina, Sultan Selim III (1789–1807) declared war on the putative ancient friend of the Ottomans. To understand how the Ottomans confronted the French invasion in 1798 requires a brief look at Sultan Selim III's predicament in regard to European diplomacy and his reform agenda; a survey of Ottoman military preparedness in the 1790s; and, finally, a description of the Anglo-Ottoman campaign in 1800–1801 that forced the removal of the last of the French army from the Nile Delta. Militarily insignificant, the final Anglo-Ottoman coalition campaign has received less attention, largely because of the absence of the Bonapartes and the Sidney Smiths. Nevertheless, a closer examination of the sources documenting the mobilization and deployment of Ottoman resources for a major campaign in Egypt is long overdue. Such an emphasis reveals clearly the difficulties facing the Ottoman sultan and the military reformers at the end of the eighteenth century. This brief confrontation of three imperial world views left a lasting imprint on the course of later world history.

The state of the Ottoman military prevented an immediate campaign against the French invasion, but diplomatic negotiations, first with Russia to prevent Bonaparte's securing of the Ionian Islands, and then with Great Britain, led to the signing of both Russian and Anglo-Ottoman alliances in January 1799, with mutual guarantees for their respective territories. What Ottomans call the War of the Triple Alliance brought together the Ottoman, British, and Russian fleets in the eastern Mediterranean, the latter for the first time via the Bosphorus and the Dardanelles.[6]

The Russo-Ottoman alliance against Napoleon Bonaparte, 1799 to 1806, arose out of an Ottoman concern for the stability of the Adriatic frontier with the arrival of the French in northern Italy and Venetia. A joint Russo-Ottoman fleet succeeded in occupying the Ionian Islands after a four-month siege of Corfu and expelled the French from the territory, an exceptional collaboration that resulted in the formation of the Septinsular, or Ionian, Republic (1800–1807) under Russo-Ottoman protection. The political status of the new Ionian Republic was determined as much by the Ottoman policy of establishing buffer states as it was by the new international climate emerging at the end of the eighteenth century. Ottoman archival evidence reveals considerable wrangling over the protocol and financial obligations of the republic, which was considered independent by Russia but was understood to be a tributary state by the sultan. While the events in the Adriatic are beyond the scope of this chapter, they nonetheless presage many of the difficulties facing the Ottomans with respect to the new maritime powers in the Mediterranean. There are two striking aspects of this Ottoman-Russian collaboration: first, under cover of the alliance the Russians dispatched 10,000 troops to Corfu by 1802, and second, they continued to expect the Ottomans to pay for the provisioning of their Mediterranean fleet even when relations between the two empires deteriorated after 1805. The short-lived Ionian Republic protected the Ottoman Adriatic frontier until the Franco-Russian rapprochement in the Treaty of Tilsit in 1807 broke the back of Selim III's Francophilia and contributed to the fall of his regime. Russian-Ottoman negotiations were more often influenced by concerns over local Christian-Muslim populations and events in Serbia and the principalities than by Bonaparte's military adventures.[7] In 1805, the Ottomans had signed a renewal of the alliance with Russia only, but refused to allow troops into the principalities. Then Selim III, encouraged by Bonaparte's victories, recognized the emperor in early 1806. By the end of the year, with Selim III firmly back in the French camp, the Russians had occupied the principalities, an act of aggression that inaugurated almost a century of conflict between the two powers.

In mid-1798, the British were already concerned about the potential threat of the French invasion on trade with India. Even though Admiral Horatio Nelson crippled Bonaparte's fleet and source of provisions at Aboukir Bay in August 1798, concerns about Russian southern expansionism and the protection of the routes to India continued to drive much of the debate on the Eastern Question in London. By October 1798, Commodore Sir Sidney Smith was ordered to join his brother Spencer Smith in Istanbul to negotiate an alliance. In November, a military mission was organized under General George Koehler, an artillery expert, to support the Ottomans in their confrontation with Bonaparte, while the British squadron also guarded the eastern Mediterranean from further French threats. Koehler was instructed "to offer every assistance to the Turks in their military operations . . . whilst trying to ensure that there was not 'even the possibility of General Bonaparte's using any part of his force to the annoyance of the British dominions in India.'"[8] The Anglo-Ottoman alliance was also signed in January of 1799.

In February 1799, Bonaparte marched in Syria and captured Arish. In spite of immense difficulties and great suffering from heat, hunger, and disease, the French defeated the garrison stationed at Jaffa rather easily, and then executed some 2,500 Turkish prisoners of war, which became Bonaparte's black legend in later accounts.[9] He continued his march north to Acre, where, after an extended siege defended by the combined Anglo-Ottoman naval and land forces, he was compelled to withdraw at the end of May with heavy losses.

By August 1799, Bonaparte slipped from Egypt to France, leaving General Jean Baptiste Kléber in command to extract the remaining French forces from the cul-de-sac they found for themselves in Cairo. General Kléber was eager to do so, and hence Sidney Smith facilitated the signing of Convention of Arish of 1800, the conditions of which proved unacceptable to the British government, prolonging the conflict. In early 1800, a more significant British mission collaborated with the Ottoman land forces to remove the remnants of the French army from Egypt. The last of Bonaparte's troops were carried back to France on British warships in September 1801, leaving behind one-third of their original 35,000 fellows, who had succumbed more to disease, climate, and hunger than to actual wounds.

Thus ended the grand adventure of Bonaparte, styled the Grand Sultan (Sultan Kebir) and Conqueror of Egypt, and even "The Muhammad of the West" by Victor Hugo.[10] These events are invariably described as the beginning of the modern or secular age in the Middle East, a "litmus test of empire" awakening the somnolent Orient, or, inaugurating Middle East colonialism, with the French pioneering "a form of imperialism that deployed liberal rhetoric and institutions for the extraction of resources and geopolitical advantage."[11] The confrontation certainly inaugurated the age of ideology, which the French and Ottomans deployed with considerable effectiveness. Imbued with the zeal of the Revolution, which championed liberty and tolerance, Bonaparte professed friendship and brotherhood with the Muslims of Egypt and declared his wish to continue his good relationship with Ottoman Sultan Selim III and his desire to eliminate the tyranny of the Mamluks.

While Egyptian chronicler al-Jabarti likened the French invasion to a jihad, Selim III actually declared one, noting that the invasion was a violation of international law at the same time that he ordered subversive activities in a general call to arms against the French. At first, Selim III hesitated to condemn the Revolution in France, out of respect for an old friendship, he argued, but those the Revolution brought to power had subverted

> under an illusive idea of liberty . . . every established government, . . . the abolishment of all religions, the destruction of every country, the plunder of property, and the dissolution of all human society— to occupy themselves in nothing but in misleading and imposing upon the ignorant amongst the people . . . and render the govern- ment permanent in their hands. . . . The French planned to divide Arabia into various Republics; to attack the whole Mahometan sect, in its religion and country; and by a gradual progression, to extirpate all Mussulmans from the face of the Earth.

Egyptians were warned that once the Frenchmen were in con- trol, they would "spread hatred and excite the people to revolt; ultimately to destroy the Holy Places and all the Muslims."[12] The language likely helped to stir up the streets of Cairo in October 1798.

State of Ottoman Affairs in the 1790s

The Ottomans were at a particularly vulnerable moment in their history in 1798. They did not participate in the continental wars that permanently altered the international balance of power between Britain and France in the mid-eighteenth century. Nor were they privy to the military reform incubator of the eastern European bat- tlefields of the Seven Years' War (1756–63), where Russian mili- tary leaders learned valuable lessons that they would apply to the later campaigns on the Ottoman Danube. Participation in the Austro-Prussian engagements was pivotal to the military transfor- mation of Catherine II's era and produced generals such as Pyotr A. Rumyantsev and Aleksandr Suvorov, who were to provide such decisive leadership in the two Ottoman-Russian wars at the end of the century. Confrontations with Prussia also compelled Russia and Austria to conduct a considerable reorganization of their mili- tary systems.[13]

As a result of the preoccupations of the major powers in eastern Europe, the period prior to 1768 was largely peaceful in Ottoman territories. With the exception of the Iranian frontier, which erupted in warfare and rebellion after the breakup of the Safavid order in the 1720s, the Ottoman Empire had enjoyed peace on its western frontier for close to forty years. Several astute grand viziers, such as Koca Ragıb Pasha, grand vizier 1757–63, convinced more than one sultan of the virtue of peace and multilateral negotiations, especially in an age of contraction and financial instability. As a result, the empire achieved two decades of tranquility and economic recovery, benefiting as well from an expanding world economy.[14]

After 1763, the European powers became obsessed with the future of Poland, which had increasingly been drawn into the Russian sphere of influence. The French urged the Ottomans to go to war with Russia repeatedly as part of Louis XV's so-called secret diplomacy, but the Ottomans steadfastly maintained their neutrality. In early 1768, however, the Bar Confederation of anti-Russian Poles appealed to the sultan for protection and was chased into Ottoman territory by Russian troops. Ottoman ultimatums for the withdrawal of Russian troops from Poland were ignored. When the Ottomans declared war in September 1768, the Russians had no recourse but to respond. Catherine II's aggressive southern policy in the Ukraine caused the Ottomans equal concern about the status of the Crimea. The Tatars of Bahçesaray served the sultan, historically called upon to inaugurate hostilities with advance raids into Poland and other parts of Europe. By the end of the eighteenth century, however, they were a much spent and divided force, a weakness exploited by Russian commanders in the Crimea and poorly understood in Istanbul.

The period of peace led to an almost complete collapse of any system of discipline and recruitment in the Ottoman army. The traditional infantry army, the Janissaries, had been badly neglected and dispersed across the Ottoman territories. Most Janissaries melted into countryside activities as tradesmen and farmers; joined regional armies of local governors or other officials, as armed militia; or became laws-unto-themselves in some of the major cities of the empire. Even the Janissary regiments responsible for manning the border fortresses, who could count on periodic if erratic wages, had to be newly reconstituted for the campaigns that began in 1768.

The bedrock of the traditional provincial military organization was the timariot, or *sipahi*, a cavalryman (sometime infantry) who in theory supported himself on a fief known as a timar, a system

overseen by the central appointment of provincial governors, experienced soldiers, who regularly rotated across the empire, often on
their way to the ultimate post as grand vizier. The system, never
applied uniformly across the empire, was already in steep decline by
1768. The traditional land grants proved unable to support either the
peasants or the soldier-landlord. When timariot troops mobilized,
they tended to show up to maintain their status but otherwise lacked
military training, and equipment, which they were required to supply themselves. Desertion became endemic; huge numbers of the
absent were routinely stricken from the rolls at each major muster
on the battlefront. Indeed, the Ottomans created different mobilization strategies for large-scale campaigns, which had the unintended
consequence of empowering local power brokers and redistributing
state wealth into provincial hands.[15]

The financial consequences of the return to war were dire. The
tenuous economic recovery was devastated by two decades of warfare on which the Ottomans now embarked, impeding any effort at
serious military and fiscal reform until the peace of Jassy in 1792.
Between 1760 and 1800, prices trebled, deficit budgets became the
norm, and the state occasionally resorted to forced loans from its
officers and countrywide gentry or confiscation of their estates in
order to continue to finance warfare.[16] This caused a regionaliza-
tion of violence and led to the emergence of important provincial
families who demanded a share of the sultan's power in return for
defending his borders.[17]

The Ottomans, by neglect and then necessity, evolved from
maintaining a standing army to raising a volunteer, militia-based
confederative force, paid for by a combination of agricultural taxes,
increasingly exorbitant exactions, and demands for provisions and
services in kind. This was combined with direct support from the
sultan's private treasury when necessary. The eighteenth century
consequently saw the explosion in the number of tax farms and their
conversion into lifetime holdings because of the financial needs of
the government, a process that has led to this period being called
the age of the *ayan*, "elite gentry" or "warlord," for want of a better translation.

Ottoman regional warlords contributed enormously to the success or failure of the Ottoman war effort. War profiteering became a
constant stimulus for temporary, if mistrustful and reluctant, loyalties, and generated regional foci of power, manipulated by colorful and

controversial figures, such as Tepedelenli Ali Pasha, of Iannina, who both challenged and cooperated with the late-eighteenth-century, early-nineteenth-century Ottoman state. Muhammad Ali of Egypt, who opposed Sultan Mahmud II (1808–39) from the 1820s onward, emerged from precisely this context in the confusion following the Bonaparte episode. The conflict between the last of the traditional orders, the Janissaries, increasingly irrelevant centrally appointed governors, and these new local military elites is one of the constant motifs of the late Ottoman chronicles.

By the time of Bonaparte's invasion, the sultan relied on local coalitions of officials whose legitimacy was conferred by local Muslim judges and whose empowerment was facilitated by the decentralization of tax collection and by the concentration of both mobilization and supply in their hands.[18] Those who prevailed amassed regional armies when called on to mobilize for large campaigns and maintained their private forces in between. Local courts recorded the orders and transactions of the Istanbul-provincial networks as the state was forced to appoint provincial governors from among these prevailing power elites. They assumed responsibility for campaign preparations: mobilizing troops, requisitioning grain and biscuit (*peksimed*), supplying draught animals and wagons, and provisioning the bivouacs along the route of the army's passage. Blanket condemnation of the corrupt and abusive state of affairs predominates in much of the historiography, but there are glimpses of honesty in the reports of concerned bureaucrats or military men that dot the account books of the war periods, allowing us to take the measure of the realities of Ottoman warfare. Still, one of the most obvious consequences of shrinking territories was that the tax burden was redistributed to smaller, often dislocated populations, which is evident in local court records. While we are not yet in a position to talk about the burden of taxation for the whole period, there is clearly emerging evidence of severe pressures on local resources after 1760.[19]

The fighting forces for these latter-day Ottoman armies came from the peripheries and semiautonomous territories of the empire: Albania and the Caucasus. Albanians, Kurds, and Circassians were certainly part of the traditional Janissary organization, and Circassian slaves were part of the Ottoman court early on, but the new military formations were tribal, itinerant, and for-hire, mobilized and financed by local commanders. The most common term for such troops in the 1801 campaign was *delis* (meaning "mad" or "crazy"), but they were called many other things in the Ottoman documents: *sekban*, *levend*, or *başıbozuk* and utilized as auxiliary forces. *Başıbozuk* ("crazy"; literally "broken-headed") became the notorious term for the atrocities committed by such auxiliaries in the Balkans of the 1870s. It is these troops who by mid-1750 proved to be the most difficult to organize and discipline, who were generally the first to demand payment and provisions, and who were the first to turn and leave when Ottoman commanders were slow to respond to their demands.

The two Turkish wars of Catherine II, as they are known, 1768–74 and 1787–92, exposed the Ottoman military weakness to all of Europe. The territorial losses were profound; wholesale slaughter of garrison towns along the Danube by the Russians was the order of the day, and the specter of Russia in Istanbul was very real, especially for those living in Bulgaria, Thrace, and in the city itself. Equally important, it was the moment when the population at large, which in earlier times stood to benefit from an organized, well-paid, and hungry army on its territories, suffered tremendously from the lack of order and destructive rapaciousness of undisciplined troops and lack of leadership. The Ottomans made a last-ditch effort, fighting on their own territory and among unreliable, angry populations.

The clamor for reform began on the battlefields of Kartal (Kagul) north of the Danube in 1770, when Rumyantsev observed what he called the last of the Janissaries fall to Russian massed artillery and men while defending the grand vizier's tent.[20] The voices for military and fiscal reform grew louder with each loss until 1792, when peace allowed the sultan to turn to the problems facing his empire.

The World of Selim III

It is hard not to sympathize with Selim III, who, coming to the throne in the midst of a disastrous war, was prey to the vicissitudes of internal and international politics. In the midst of military collapse, he called together a consultative assembly, already an extraordinary gesture for a new sultan, and asked for its advice. This inaugurated what is generally called the *Nizam-ı Cedid*, or new order, which refers both to the full range of Selim III's reforms as well as to the new regiments of troops, which introduced European formations, uniforms, discipline, and drill to the Ottoman context in the first serious way. One of the very first acts that resulted was the order to rebuild the artillery corps. Ottoman historian Ahmed Cevdet described the sultan's first encounter with the full extent of the corruption represented by inaccurate military records. Selim intended that each battalion (*orta*) of the Janissaries be equipped with ten experienced artillerymen, to be paid from the vacancies in the rolls. Looking at a recent register of active artillerymen, in order to estimate the financing available for the new recruits, the sultan found that, of 1,059 troops listed, 33 were wounded and 90 were assigned to the foundry, 90 to the rapid infantry corps, 76 to the fire brigade, and 770 handicapped, old, or retired to guard duty, all on the sultan's payroll. Selim's advisors warned him that it would take decades to settle the claims and rectify the registers in order to accumulate salaries for new recruits. The sultan responded angrily:

> My God! What kind of situation is this? Two of the barbers who shave me say they are members of the artillery corps! If we call for soldiers, we are told, 'What can we do? There are no salaried soldiers to go on campaign.' Let others be enrolled, we say, and we are told, 'There is no money in the treasury.' If we say there must be a remedy, we are told, 'Now is not the time to interfere with the regiments.' We are not saying remove them all; rather enroll them [new recruits] as others perish.[21]

The sultan's frustration was intentionally made obvious by Cevdet, an admirer of Selim III, most likely to emphasize the new sultan's innocence regarding the extent of the corruption.

Most observers agree that the sultan could count on approximately 40,000 so-called Janissaries across the empire as his fighting force, 10 percent perhaps of the reputed 400,000 registered. Of those, 10,000–15,000 were responsible for the safety of sultan and city in Istanbul. Small wonder, then, that as many as 80,000–100,000 auxiliaries were mobilized from the more militant, local populations on a regular basis for major campaigns.[22] They were the source of considerable trouble when demobilized, ready manpower for the regional armies that emerged, and resistant to the kind of disciplined and well-trained forces required by the new enemies on the Danube and the seasoned troops of Bonaparte.

Selim III's reign is most often characterized as the period when the first serious attempts at military reform failed, but the condemnation is simply too categorical. The years after 1792 were a prelude to the complete overhaul of the Ottoman system of governance, not just the military. Selim III's reforms left nothing untouched, including renewal of the treasury by revoking tax farms, reclaiming alienated properties from charitable status, reorganizing the grain delivery system to a perpetually hungry Istanbul, and rebuilding the gunpowder works and cannon foundries. It is the new troops, however, who are important to this discussion because their first real performance was at Acre in 1799. Selim III's advisors had recommended the creation of regiments from new, raw recruits from the countryside; that they be organized in small companies of crack infantry, drilled constantly, and that foreign officers be consulted and their military manuals be used during the reorganization. Selim III followed much of the advice; he built new barracks, created parade grounds, and ordered daily drills, but initially chose to recruit from within the existing Janissary regiments. When that practice proved unpopular and unsustainable, new soldiers were drawn from the streets of Istanbul and the provinces, isolated in separate barracks, and organized entirely along European lines into regiments of twelve companies of one hundred infantrymen each, with gunners attached to the regiments. The commander of the regiment was the equivalent of a colonel, later a major (*binbaşı*). In 1798, there were approximately 6,000 such soldiers in Levend Çiftliği, one of the new barracks. Some of these troops supported Sir Sydney Smith and Ahmed Cezzar at Acre (see below). By 1806, the records indicated the army had grown to over 22,000, with close to 1,600 officers.[23]

Selim III was desperate for accurate intelligence throughout the 1798–1807 period. His reign is notable for his singular achievement regarding multilateral diplomacy. He struggled to maintain the integrity of the Ottoman Empire as territories bordering the empire succumbed to the colonial powers of France, Britain, and Russia. His inclination was to maintain ties with France, even as the Directory and Bonaparte betrayed that trust repeatedly. Under the sultan's aegis, resident Ottoman representatives were sent to the capitals of Europe for the first time, and London was signaled out as the first recipient of the new diplomats as the French Revolution made it more difficult to choose Paris. Selim III's diplomatic initiative annoyed Catherine II and angered the French, the latter long considered the oldest friends of the Ottomans.[24]

Selim III had corresponded with the French court before becoming sultan, and stubbornly remained a Francophile. French military missions were a sporadic feature of the Ottoman landscape from the 1770s until the death of French foreign minister Vergennes, former ambassador to Istanbul, in 1787.[25] With the withdrawal of the French mission in 1788, Great Britain appeared to have the opportunity to step into the void, but in the 1790s this was by no means official policy. British officials were more engaged with India and Europe than with the Middle East, and Britain's Levant Company was close to dissolution. The British ambassador in Istanbul never heard more than ten times a year from his government in London. By contrast, French Ambassador Choiseul-Gouffier (1784–92) received special dispatches from Izmir (Smyrna) on a regular basis, and was a particular source of information on international affairs for Selim III.[26] The French dominated eastern Mediterranean trade between Marseilles and the Ottoman ports, particularly Izmir. Selim III consistently maneuvered to reestablish the French connection even after the Revolution forced a breach in relations. What appeared inexplicable to many foreign observers around him, and is usually elided as Selim III's Francophilia, should be understood as the sultan's attempt to gather more accurate intelligence in the bid for Ottoman autonomy.

Ambassador Raymond Verinac (1795–97), the first fully accredited French republican representative in Istanbul, persuaded Selim III to appoint Seyyid (Moralı) Ali Efendi as a permanent ambassador to Paris in 1797. Ali Efendi was received in Paris in the style of Molière's "Bourgeois Gentilhomme" to judge by one account.[27] He was accompanied by one of the more notorious of Ottoman dragomans, Pangiotis Codrika, who served Talleyrand in keeping his Ottoman employer ignorant of French intentions in Alexandria. Although Seyyid Ali was ill-equipped to serve as ambassador (his sultan noted on one document, "What an ass!"), the whole enterprise represents a significant shift in Ottoman diplomatic practices, which had until then relied on the hothouse of Istanbul foreign representatives and the occasional extraordinary ambassador to select countries.[28]

Undeterred by British and Russian opposition to his relations with France, Selim III continued to appoint ambassadors to Paris: Mehmed Said Halet Efendi (1803–1806), and Muhib Efendi (1806–11). In spite of their presence in Paris, Selim III was compelled, on at least three occasions to appoint special plenipotentiaries to resolve delicate negotiations, such as that of Mehmed Said Galib Efendi, dispatched to sign the Treaty of Paris on 25 June 1802, which reestablished Ottoman-French relations with Napoleon's government.

Selim III had great ambitions, but worked against almost insurmountable odds, notably entrenched beneficiaries of the old system, conservative resistance to his innovations, and an empty treasury. His initiatives raised the ire of critics in his own court, which was deeply divided into pro-French and pro-war camps, so when pressed to respond to French aggression in Egypt, Selim III abandoned his reform project and allies altogether. Bonaparte's public representations of the sultan as permitting the French invasion had inflamed the street in Istanbul. So too did the alliance with Russia. Pierre Ruffin, French *chargé d'affaires*, was charged with the unenviable task of convincing the Ottomans that Bonparte's invasion was not intended as aggression against the sultan. In early August 1798, Grand Vizier İzzet Mehmed Pasha warned Ruffin that French residents in the empire would be subject to house arrest, but by the end of that month, the grand vizier himself was dismissed and arrested along with the rest of the pro-French government officials. Pierre Ruffin and his staff followed the former grand vizier into prison along with all French merchants and their property across the empire. Selim III appointed Yusuf Ziya Pasha (1798–1805), known conservative and head of the pro-war party, as grand vizier. Yusuf Ziya was ordered to cooperate with the British mission, which arrived the same year, commanded by General George Koehler and seventy-six military engineers and artillery experts. The new grand vizier informed Egyptian officials by mid-September 1798 that an army was on its way from Damascus.[29]

But it was not quite that simple. It was not until April 1799 that the combined British-Ottoman fleets sailed through the Dardanelles on the way to Alexandria. In June, the grand vizier left Istanbul, just as Bonaparte was forced to lift the siege at Acre, which had been ably defended by Governor Ahmed Cezzar Pasha, with the aid of Mamluk cavalry from Egypt; delis, who were largely Albanians; Bedouin Arabs (called *Urbani*); and Druze[30] from Mount Lebanon. The British lent support from the sea under the command of Sir Sidney Smith and his squadron. Ahmed Cezzar Pasha was already a legend in Syria by the time of the siege. He had appealed to his sultan to be appointed commander in chief of Egypt and given the funds to lead the fight against the French, but he was instead appointed commander in chief of Acre and the region up to Jaffa, and promised support of two Ottoman armies of 50,000 troops each, part of the full-scale mobilization under Grand Admiral Küçük Hüseyin and Grand Vizier Yusuf Ziya. A regiment of the Nizam-i Cedid army was sent to support him as he had already deployed his own troops in Jaffa and Arish.[31] The rest of the help promised from Istanbul was slow to make its appearance in Acre. In mid-April, advance Ottoman troops from Damascus and Aleppo engaged with French General Kléber at Mount Tabor and were defeated when reinforcements relieved him. More than two months into the siege, some 480 Janissaries who had been dispatched from Izmir arrived, and on the fifty-first day, a fleet of Ottoman corvettes and transports, carrying 3,000 guards and sailors sent from Rhodes, dropped anchor in the Acre port. Sidney Smith wrote of the deployment of the new arrivals: "I had to combat the pasha's [Ahmed Cezzar] repugnance to admitting any troops, but his Albanians, into the garden of his seraglio. . . . There were not above two hundred of the original thousand Albanians left. This was no time for debate and I overruled his objections, by introducing the Chifflick [Nizam] regiment of thousand men, armed with bayonets and disciplined after the European method."[32]

Ahmed Cezzar's determined and heroic defense of the ancient crusader castle, combined with tactical and artillery support from both British and Ottoman ships in the harbor, led to Bonaparte's lifting of the siege at the end of May. Returned to Cairo and professing his great victory at Acre, Bonaparte and his army next confronted some 10,000 Ottoman soldiers under command of Köse Mustafa Pasha as they were unloaded from ships under cover of the combined British and Ottoman fleet in Aboukir Bay, in July 1799. Bonaparte decimated the Ottoman troops by 25 July, but suffered equally large casualties on the French side. He left Egypt thereafter, having realized, as most observers did, that it would be an impossible campaign to sustain. General Kléber was instructed to bring the conflict to a close.

Ottoman grand vizier Yusuf Ziya arrived in Damascus slightly over two weeks after Bonaparte left for France in August 1799. In theory, he then had access to a combined force of 65,000 men. The distance of the march from Istanbul to Egypt meant that the original army of 15,000 Janissaries that left Istanbul in June anticipated adding troops and provisions as it traveled to the battlefront.

When provisions were distributed in Damascus in September, they were given to an army then numbering 24,420 individuals: 12,885 Janissaries, 2,980 officials (of the divan), 5,083 other soldiers, 1,000 with the Şerif Pasha (governor of Mecca), 410 with the Muhzır Agha (commander of grand vizier's guards), 657 artillerymen, and 1,405 armorymen.[33]

Final estimates of the size report additionally 20,000 local soldiers (presumably delis and other militias) and 20,000 Arabs from the Syrian tribes in the area. In addition, the army in Egypt amounted to 10,000 Bedouins, 20,000 Mamluks, and 5,000 Janissaries. Many Mamluks fleeing Egypt also joined up with the Ottoman army. Eventually, both Mamluk chieftains, Murad and Ibrahim Beys, joined the Ottoman army.[34]

The mobilization happened neither quickly nor in an orderly fashion, which meant that the grand vizier waited in Haifa and could only move to Gaza when he had assembled a sufficient force. Negotiations with General Kléber began as the Ottomans crossed the desert from Gaza to Arish, because the large army was in need of the provisions and water available in Arish and the Nile Delta. On 17 December 1799, the Ottomans surrounded and recaptured Arish, enough to accelerate the French signing of the Convention of Arish on 24 January 1800, which allowed their unfettered exit from Alexandria on Ottoman ships. The conditions proved odious to London, a situation that then involved months of European wrangling, futile meetings between Ambassador Ali Efendi and Talleyrand, and the apparent abandonment of the remaining French army in Egypt.

On the ground, preparations for the evacuation had continued. The Ottomans assembled the forty-five ships promised for the transport of the French while Kléber ordered the remaining troops to assemble at Alexandria via Damietta and Rosetta. In March, just as Kléber was about to surrender Cairo to Yusuf Ziya Pasha, he received word of the British disavowal of the terms of the convention. Demanding the grand vizier's immediate withdrawal from the Upper Nile region, he proceeded to attack the Ottoman army when it failed to do so. Assuming the campaign over, the Ottomans were disorganized, lacking coordinated leadership and experiencing significant desertion. The Ottoman Mamluk allies, home again, proved disruptive coalition partners. The Ottomans were badly beaten by the discipline of the French soldiers (some 20,000) and the expert

French artillery fire at Heliopolis on 22 March 1800. The Ottoman army withdrew, plundered by their tribal allies as they went, first to Bilbeis, where the grand vizier tried vainly to reassemble his forces, then to Arish, and finally to Jaffa, where the grand vizier would spend another ten months reorganizing the army for another assault on Egypt. The Mamluks divided their loyalties; Ibrahim Bey retreated with the Ottomans, while Murad Bey, who had not been much more than a spectator at Heliopolis, came to an agreement with Kléber in exchange for the governorship of Said. The French captured all the Ottoman supply ships assembled at Alexandria for their withdrawal and were in charge of Egypt once again, where they would remain for another seventeen months, although without the leadership of Kléber, who was assassinated in July and replaced by the less able and much-disliked general Abdullah Menou.[35]

The Final Confrontation, 1801

Assuming that the Ottomans were not going to be able to forcibly remove the French by themselves, the British dispatched a much larger force of ships and two divisions of troops to the eastern Mediterranean in October 1800 under the command of Sir Ralph Abercromby.[36] By March 1801, the British landed the new arrivals in Aboukir, shortly before Ottoman contingents under Grand Admiral Küçük Hüseyin Pasha also arrived by ship.[37] The first of 6,000 sepoys from British India left Bombay in December and arrived in Qusayr on the Red Sea in May.[38] The combined army amassed in Aboukir under the British and Ottoman was estimated at 15,000 British soldiers under Abercromby—and upon his death, General Hely Hutchinson—and 6,000 Ottomans under Grand Admiral Küçük Hüseyin. In addition, Grand Vizier Yusuf Ziya's army of 15,000—which grew to 25,000 by the time of its arrival in Egypt—left Gaza in mid-March to cross the Sinai Desert again, arriving on the eastern side of the Nile delta in mid-April. By early April, the combined Ottoman and British force had begun to press its attack on the French from three directions: Aboukir, Rosetta, and Rahmaniye, while the grand vizier confronted the French on the same terrain as the previous year. The campaign was effectively over by mid-1801. The Convention for the Evacuation of Egypt was signed on 27 June; the main difference now being that the British would transport the remainder of the Army of the Orient back to France. A triumphant procession, led by Ottoman commanders Küçük Hüseyin and Yusuf Ziya and British general Hutchinson, entered Cairo on 12 July. The final troops of Bonaparte's army embarked from Alexandria in September. At the time of the French surrender, there were 8,223 French troops left in Cairo, and 4,000 British under the command of Hutchinson, numbers that do not include any of the Mamluks or Ottomans who might at that time have numbered over 30,000.[39]

Grand Vizier Yusuf Ziya had spent the ten months in Jaffa trying to rebuild his army but would never mobilize the supposed 50,000 that were expected to make up his forces. After the defeat at Heliopolis, most of the previous year's assembled forces had fled, not just to Damascus and Aleppo, but across the Taurus Mountains into Anatolia, or by sea to Cyprus.[40] So part of the explanation for the long delay in forcing the French evacuation was simply the lack of Ottoman manpower. In July 1800, General Koehler and other members of the British mission had joined the grand vizier in Jaffa, among them William Wittman, a surgeon. Wittman's keen observations on the Ottoman military camp in this period are perhaps the most illuminating account of this era. First, the state of the camp obsessed him. The Turkish troops were "encamped in the most confused and irregular manner. . . . The only regulation that seemed to border somewhat on system was, that each Pacha, or military governor, was surrounded by his own men." Cook tents and retail tents for coffee and tobacco were run by the Janissaries. The tents themselves were pitched among the abodes of the dead; and the bodies of those who had been interred were very superficially covered. The carcasses of dead animals, such as camels, horses, and asses were scattered in among the tents.[41] The military mission officials themselves were camped with the grand vizier in a garden filled with fruit trees of all varieties. They were given good provisions, including lamb and rice, and guarded by a detachment of Janissaries. There was a *hamam* (bath) tent available to them.[42]

Wittman noted the inability of the grand vizier to impose his authority on most of his troops. On 7 August, two hundred Janissaries arrived from Istanbul, inspected by the vizier and observed by members of the mission:

> The infantry and artillery were drawn up into three bodies, that is, a main body and two wings, nearly in a line, with the guns

in front. While the whole advanced slowly, a firing was kept up exclusively by the artillery; and the movement having been continued for the space of six or seven hundred yards, the troops faced to the right about, when, the guns again being brought to their front, they returned to their former ground in the same manner as when they advanced. . . . During the whole time, the infantry remained with the arms shouldered, the Albanians shouting.[43]

By 17 August, 1,600 Mamluks were in the camp under Ibrahim Bey, but within a month more than half had died of plague or left. The grand vizier lost thirty-six members of his own family and entourage before the plague dissipated.

Wittman continued: 1,500 cavalrymen arrived from Konya at the end of August, while a corps of Albanians, consisting of about 1,000, left for Arish on 31 August. Their departure from the camps was accompanied by a general discharge of bullets. Ottoman soldiers furnished their own ammunition except on the day of the battle. In October, the Albanians mutinied when the grand vizier tried to muster them. Half of them deserted, and, although the grand vizier sent 1,000 delis after them, they escaped.[44]

The problems with manpower worsened as the question of provisions and pay mounted. Soldiers came and went in search of better pay: Ahmed Cezzar's army at Acre was paying more; on the other hand, it was his habit to chop off the noses of deserters, one way those in Jaffa knew where their Albanians had been. The Ottoman soldier was allowed five to ten aspers, a penny to twopence English, per day, for everything beyond rice, bread, biscuit, and barley for the horses and pack animals. By mid-November, the Janissaries revolted over back pay, but the treasury arrived by sea just in time to prevent a massive mutiny. Camp livestock was consuming fifteen tons of fodder daily by the end of November. Surrounding towns were beginning to resist exactions of money and supplies. By January 1801, Yusuf Ziya had an effective force of 10,000 at Jaffa, 2,000 at Gaza, and 4,000 at Arish under Tahir Pasha. In February, the Janissaries rioted over the lack of fodder. Ahmed Cezzar of Acre sent detachments of five hundred Albanians from time to time. Wittman witnessed much fighting and rivalry between Albanians and Janissaries over supplies and privileges.[45]

Finally, on 12 March 1801, the grand vizier himself began the march across the desert to Gaza and from there to Arish, where, after a strenuous crossing, his force was met with ships of supplies on 20 March. His men had at that point 50,000 animals with them and continued to be short of everything, especially barley, causing riots in the camp. What is particularly noteworthy is the way in which water was delivered to troops by a small corps of Janissaries, mounted on horses with bells and leather sacks filled with forty gallons of water. One of the reasons the French were suffering was that they did not have a similar system. Even in the apparent chaos, some remnants of order were to be found.[46]

The grand vizier ordered the army train stripped down to the bare essentials; the camels were designated to carry water, barley, biscuit, and tents only.[47] Many of the Arab (Bedouin) drovers slipped out of camp with their camels. The lean version of the army managed eighteen miles in one day and arrived in Salahieh, which had been recaptured by Tahir Pasha, in the last week of April 1801. As the grand vizier neared Cairo, he detached Commander Ibrahim Pasha (of Aleppo) to secure Damietta, and then confronted the French at El Hanka on 11 May 1801 with his remaining army. The combined cavalry and infantry force, now augmented by Mamluks and Arabs, withstood the French for close to ten hours before the French capitulated, the only real battle in which the grand vizier participated. On 24 May, British general Hutchinson's army joined the grand vizier in Ben el Hazer, and the coordination of the French evacuation began in earnest.[48]

Franco-Ottoman hostilities officially ceased with the Treaty of Paris in June 1802, which renewed all French capitulations and established their diplomatic predominance in Istanbul much to the chagrin of the British, who would shortly resume their fight against Napoleon Bonaparte. Selim III preferred neutrality to breaking the treaty with France and insisted that the British evacuate Egypt. The last of the British troops left Egypt in March 1803 in order to restore good relations. In 1806, Selim III elected to recognize Napoleon as emperor of the French and closed the Dardanelles to Russian warships. In February 1807, the British sailed into Istanbul with warships in support of Russia, but found the French fortifying and enabling the resistance of the population to the British. The British fleet was forced to withdraw in early March but made a brief landing at Alexandria in support of their allies, the Mamluks, who were the target for elimination following the restoration of Egypt to Ottoman control. The British failed to make a landing when confronted by the Albanian troops of the Ottoman governor at Rosetta and sailed away from what has been described as a "phoney war."[49] The tumult generated by the events in Istanbul and Cairo, however, stimulated an enormous revolt in Istanbul in May 1807, which brought down the government of Selim III.

On the surface, the Ottoman Empire escaped with little damage, or no more than the usual damage inflicted on local populations by warfare and local oppressors. Selim III's preference for the French connection, as well as Anglo-Russian vulnerability to Napoleonic ambitions elsewhere, restored Ottoman sovereignty to Egypt, however tenuously. Selim was grateful for the assistance of the British military mission. Yusuf Ziya had the honorific "gazi" (Conqueror of Egypt) attached to his name by the sultan, who also established a medal, called the Order of the Crescent, which he bestowed on the British officers "to perpetuate the signal services rendered."[50]

Some Final Considerations

The first colonial thrust into the Middle East was over in a few short years, but the consequences reverberated for another hundred. New narratives of the Bonaparte adventure appear in every generation of historians, as each new invasion of the Middle East unfolds. The confrontation between the highly disciplined French infantry formations and the largely voluntary and immensely proud Mamluk cavalry is a visual image repeatedly invoked by nineteenth-century romantics. Walsh's observation of the Mamluks is typical in its effusion for their "grand and splendid" appearance.

> Osman Bey Tambourgi [successor to Murad Bey] arrived with his Mamalukes. They appeared to be about 1,200 in number: every individual superbly mounted, richly dressed, and attended by a servant on foot, carrying a long stick in his hand. But the magnificence of the beys or chiefs, was beyond any thing that can be conceived. They were lodged in spacious tents, divided into several apartments, the insides lined with rich stuffs, and the bottom covered with beautiful Turkey carpets. . . . Indeed, a Mamaluke may be said to carry all his wealth about him; his horse, sword, and pistols, beautifully wrought and inlaid with silver, are worth very great sums, and constitute the chief part of his riches. . . . These Mamalukes were so richly dressed and accoutred, that the French soldiers actually fished up the bodies of those who were drowned in the Nile, by which they obtained very considerable booty.[51]

But the consequence of the French invasion influenced most directly the Mamluks. They were doomed. It took another ten years, but in the end, the age of the Mamluks was over in Egypt, to be replaced by the khedival age of Muhammad Ali (Mehmed Ali in Turkish) and his successors until 1952. The struggle for the control of Egypt split three ways after the departure of the British: the Mamluks described above, the Ottoman provincial governor supported by the remaining Janissaries, and the volunteer militia bands of Albanians, who coalesced around their young leader, Mehmed Ali. It was he who in the end defeated the last of the Mamluk beys and set Egypt on a rapid and astonishing course of modernization. He observed the discipline of the Nizam-ı Cedid under Grand Admiral Küçük Hüseyin and the Anglo-Ottoman cooperation as a young recruit, but his reform model was French and his foreign advisors very largely French.

Mehmed Ali reorganized the Egyptian economy, introducing plantation cotton, which thrust Egypt into international markets in the early decades of the nineteenth century. He completely rebuilt and reformed both the navy and army. Initially, he served as the right hand of Mahmud II in the southern tier of the Ottoman Empire, particularly in repressing the earliest Wahhabi revolts in Mecca and Medina, and in the early stages of the Greek revolt in 1821. Frenchmen, Albanians, Circassians, and Turks of Anatolia made up his officer class, but Sudanese black Africans and Egyptian peasants (*fellahin*) were his recruits. He first attempted to create an army made entirely of black slaves from Sudan, but they proved vulnerable and unsuitable as the new model army he envisioned. Perhaps he had been influenced by observing the use of the native sepoys from India during the Anglo-British campaign. In 1822, however, he introduced conscription of his peasants (fellahin) and embarked on a full-scale militarization of his territories, the Egyptian version of the levée en masse.[52]

By contrast, the Ottoman center took longer to rid itself of the Janissaries, who were after all the heart and lungs of traditional Ottoman society. More than anything else, they were able to contain the worst excesses of the Ottoman sultan by their threat to revolt. Most advisors around the new sultan Mahmud II saw that they were useless as a military force, but the sultan had serious financial problems, empire-wide revolts, and resistance, of which Mehmed Ali would grow to be the largest and most threatening.

Mahmud II could not turn to the problem of the Janissaries until 1826, when he eliminated the last of them in Istanbul. What seems clear is that Mahmud II's set of reforms, while influenced by the Egyptian experience, was a much more hybrid production. The pool of manpower represented by the demobilized post-Napoleonic officer class, ubiquitous in Egypt, was not to be found in the inner circle of Mahmud II's court. The great reforming sultan was notoriously stingy and very resistant to outside assistance, with the exception of the Prussians, such as Helmut von Moltke, the elder, who served as an advisor to the sultan in the 1830s and was careful to maintain his status as such.

In fact, the question of the military leadership of the reforms and of the reconstructed army of Mahmud II is still very much a puzzle of late Ottoman history. The main architect of the reforms, Husrev Pasha (d. 1855), who served in Egypt in 1801, returned to Istanbul as the chief advisor to Mahmud II, and is credited with strong-arming the implementation of the reforms, but there is no convincing evidence of a sustained reform strategy and agenda beyond a very small group of ideologues and advisors. Husrev managed, by the end of Mahmud II's reign, to combine in himself the functions of the office of commander in chief of the new army and all other aspects of the military: commandant of Istanbul, chief of the general staff, and minister of war. In fact, it would not be until the 1860s and after that a modern military command structure, which was based on merit, rather than cronyism and seniority, could be said to have taken root. On the battlefield, as we have seen, military command was uncoordinated and extremely ineffective, with individual valor and mercenary mentalities dictating the performance of the diverse corps. In contrast to Mehmed Ali of Egypt, who established an officers' training school with French assistance, Mahmud II did not see the need for a military academy and drew the first cadre of officers for his new regiments from his imperial household. The first officers' training school was finally established in 1834, with insufficient teachers and texts. The impact of the academy on the command structure of the Ottoman reformed army remained small until the end of the century, when the officer elite became an important force in the modernization of the late empire.[53]

The performance of the Ottoman army in Egypt in 1801 needs another look as it represents the midway point between the old and new military systems, one of the last campaigns of the ancien régime. The accounts talk about terrific disorder and filth, and complete disarray, all indisputable. Equally indisputable is the lack of a central command and fierce rivalries between the Janissaries and the cavalry regiments, whether sipahis or delis.

Still, the Wittman observations reveal the Ottoman ability to deliver money, ships, soldiers, and provisions to specific locales, and to stand fast in sieges. While the surgeon in Wittman was dismayed at the lack of attention to the dead or ill soldier, the need to take care of the fighting man is obvious in the question of biscuits and water. The disarray is more closely to be observed, and more significant, in the hierarchy of command and the lack of ideological unity. Warrior cultures persisted, and the kinds of terrain and nature of warfare encouraged mobility and flight of volunteer militias. The soldier for hire had come to be both a necessity and a menace to Ottoman survival as the British themselves learned in India.[54]

In the Bonaparte invasion, we see the genesis of the interventionist school of British imperialism, but also the birth of the romantic ethnography, which backed the Mamluks, then the Greeks, then the Arab Bedouins, and then the Saudis. Khedival rule in Egypt prepared the way for the British occupation in 1882, while sultanic resistance and adroit if desperate use of the Russian card sustained Ottoman autonomy at the center. Both have their genesis in 1798. After rocky beginnings, British politicians settled on political support for the court in Istanbul by midcentury, having acquired free trading rights across the empire in the Anglo-Ottoman Treaty of 1838. For those on the ground, imperial attitudes took a different turn. The military men of the new British imperialism deplored the barbarism of the Turk and wanted to intervene on behalf of the many subject peoples of the empire. Many of them moved back and forth between British India and the Ottoman Empire and confronted in the arrogance of Ottoman rule a reflection of their own imperial arrogance. Sidney Smith left Egypt in 1801. "When Sidney Smith told the Turkish authorities that he was to be superseded by [Lord] Elgin, the Grand Vizier [Yusuf Ziya], reported Smith, asked if it was necessary, as they 'went on well together.' Smith replied that Elgin was a great landed proprietor of influence in Scotland, such as the Government habitually conciliated by appointments to high stations. 'Ah,' commented the Vizier, 'then I understand your government has also got its mountain chiefs to conciliate.'"[55] The Lord Elgins and the Yusuf Ziyas would have understood one another; the

Sidney Smiths inhabited a new world. The mountain men of both countries would play out their imperial rivalries once again in the Crimea, and finally on the beaches of Gallipoli.

Notes

1. The Mamluks had essentially assumed control over Egypt by the mid-1750s and governed by a council of twenty-three beys, with Murad and Ibrahim Beys in charge. The Ottoman-appointed governor had long since become little more than a puppet, and tribute owed to the Istanbul government seldom arrived. Joseph Shosenberg, "The Battle of the Pyramids: Futile Victory," in *Napoleon and the French in Egypt and the Holy Land 1798–1801,* ed. Aryeh Shmuelevitz (Istanbul: Isis, 2002), 241–43. For a historical background, see M. W. Daly, ed. *Cambridge History of Egypt,* vol. 2, *Modern Egypt from 1517 to the End of the Twentieth Century* (Cambridge: Cambridge University Press, 1998), in which there are several articles on this period.

2. Juan Cole, *Napoleon's Egypt: Invading the Middle East* (New York: Palgrave McMillan, 2007), 198–207; Darrell Dykstra, "The French Occupation of Egypt, 1798–1801," in Daly, *Cambridge History of Egypt,* 2:113–38; Abd al-Rahman al-Jabarti, *Napoleon in Egypt: Al-Jabarti's Chronicle on the French Occupation of Egypt, 1798,* trans. Shmuel Moreh (Princeton, N.J.: Markus Weiner, 1993).

3. Cole, *Napoleon's Egypt,* 168. An amusing side note is that Bonaparte employed Arabic translators from Malta, whose renditions were declared illiterate if not execrable by al-Jabarti; Mary Kathryn Cooney, "Egypt Was Worth a Turban: Bonaparte's Flirtation with Islam," in Shmuelevitz, *Napoleon and the French,* 93–94.

4. Norman Daniel, *Islam, Europe and Empire* (Edinburgh: University of Edinburgh Press, 1968), 98.

5. Anthony Pagden, *Worlds at War: The 2,500-Year Struggle between East and West* (New York: Random House, 2008), 396, quoting a contemporary source, Niqula (Nicholas) al-Turk.

6. The contribution of the Ottoman navy in this period is not inconsiderable. See Kevin McCranie, "The Operations and Effectiveness of the Ottoman Navy During Napoleon's Invasion of Egypt, 1798–1801," in Shmuelevitz, *Napoleon and the French,* 156–64.

7. Kahraman Şakul, "Ottoman Attempts to Control the Adriatic Frontier in the Napoleonic Wars," in *The Frontiers of the Ottoman World,* ed. Andrew Peacock (Oxford: Published for the British Academy by Oxford University Press, 2009). Over 4,000 Greeks and Albanians served in Tepedelenli Ali Pasha's Ionian units between 1799 and 1807, and many fought against the Ottomans after 1806 at Ruschuk and Vidin.

8. J. M. Wagstaff, "Colonel Leake and the Classical Topography of Asia Minor," *Anatolian Studies* 37 (1987): 24.

9. The figure varies from 2,500 to 4,000, the higher one in the Muslim/Ottoman accounts. The original garrison at Jaffa probably consisted of 12,000 Albanian and North African (Maghrebians) with a few

artillerymen. See M. C. Şehabeddin Tekindağ, "Yeni kaynak and vesika ışığı altında Bonaparte'in Akkâ Muhâsarası," *Istanbul Üniversitesi Edebiyat Fakültesi Tarih Dergisi* 15, no. 20 (1965): 8.

10. A. L. MacFie, *The Eastern Question, 1774–1923*, rev. ed. (London: Longman, 1996), 11, and al-Jabarti, *Napoleon in Egypt*, 9; Pagden, *Worlds at War*, 375. At one point, Bonaparte dressed in mufti and styled himself the Mahdi.

11. Cole, *Napoleon's Egypt*, 247.

12. Extract and excerpt: Daniel, *Islam, Europe and Empire*, 91–92; Cole, *Napoleon's Egypt*, 56–58. Franco-Ottoman diplomacy dated from the 1530–40s, when French King Francis I (1514–47) and Süleyman I (1520–66) proved allies of convenience against the Habsburgs. They briefly combined against Habsburg ally the Duke of Savoy in 1543, and Francis I went so far as to allow the Ottoman fleet to winter in Toulon in 1543–44 (Suraiya Faroqhi, *The Ottoman Empire and the World around It* (London: I. B. Tauris, 2004), 33. See also Christine Isom-Verhaaren, *Allies with the Infidel: The Ottoman and French Alliance in the Sixteenth Century* (London: I. B. Tauris, 2011). In the eighteenth century, French ambassador Louis Saveur Villeneuve is usually credited with securing the very favorable treaty of Belgrade for the Ottomans after the Austro-Russo-Ottoman War of 1736–39, for which France was rewarded with the renewal of favored trading rights in 1740. See Virginia Aksan, *Ottoman Wars, 1700–1870: An Empire Besieged* (Harlow, UK: Pearson, Longman, 2007), 116.

13. Michael Hochedlinger, *Austria's Wars of Emergence 1683–1797* (Harlow, UK: Pearson Longman, 2003), 205.

14. Mehmet Genç is the acknowledged expert on the late eighteenth-century financial state of the empire: "L'économie ottomane et la guerre au XVIIIe siècle," *Turcica* 27 (1995), 177–96. Absolutely central to the discussion of Ottoman finances in the transition period are Yavuz Cezar's *Osmanlı Maliyesinde Bunalım ve Değişim Dönemi (XVIII.yy dan Tanzimat'a Mali Tarih)* (Istanbul: Alan, 1986), especially his description of novel tax instruments such as the *imdad-i seferiye* (special campaign tax) for the use of provincial governors, 53–70, and Ahmet Tabakoğlu's *Gerileme Dönemine Girerken Osmanlı Maliyesi* (Istanbul: Dergâh, 1985).

15. Virginia H. Aksan, *An Ottoman Statesman in War and Peace: Ahmed Resmi Efendi, 1700–1783* (Leiden, Neth.: Brill, 1995).

16. See Şevket Pamuk, *A Monetary History of the Ottoman Empire* (Cambridge: Cambridge University Press, 2000), 150–71, who views the 1787 war measures such as price ceilings, and coin debasement as "the most comprehensive and ambitious package of intervention in the money and commodity markets that occurred during the eighteenth century." His book includes valuable tables of exchange rates with foreign currencies.

17. See Aksan, *Ottoman Wars*, chaps. 5 and 6.

18. Halil İnalcik and Donald Quataert, eds., *An Economic and Social History of the Ottoman Empire* (Cambridge: Cambridge University

Press, 1994), 659. These officials are frequently referred to as *mutasarrıfs*, most often used to designate governors of *sancaks*, or local tax officials.

19. Genç, "L'économie ottomane," 185; Evgenii Radushev, "Les dépenses locales dans l'empire ottoman au xviiie siècle," *Études balkaniques* 3 (1980): 74–94, discusses the full range of such taxes.

20. Described in Aksan, *Ottoman Wars*, chap. 4.

21. Ahmed Cevdet, *Tarih*, 1st ed. (Istanbul, 1858) 4:265–66. The advisors, of course, were the chief beneficiaries of the corrupted muster rolls.

22. All numbers are speculative (and conservative) as registers for this period are very inconclusive or nonexistent. See Aksan, *Ottoman Wars*, chap. 2; see also Gábor Ágoston, "Military Transformation in the Ottoman Empire and Russia, 1500–1800," *Kritika: Explorations in Russian and Eurasian History* 12, no. 2 (Spring 2011): 281–319, for more recent estimates.

23. Aksan, *Ottoman Wars*, 192–97.

24. The Ottomans would not send a permanent ambassador to Saint Petersburg until 1857.

25. Allan Cunningham, "The Ochakov Debate," in *Anglo-Ottoman Encounters in the Age of Revolution*, vol. 1 of *Collected Essays*, ed. Edward Ingram (London: Frank Cass, 1993), 3 ("The French barrier around the Ottoman Empire fell.").

26. Cunningham, "Ochakov Debate," 5–6, 6n11, 20.

27. The first translations of *1,001 Arabian Nights* by Galland, which appeared in 1797; Baron de Tott's bestselling *Memoirs*; and Montesquieu's *Persian Letters*, to name just a few works, had fashioned an oriental mania in the reading public. Europeans were avid readers of *Arabian Nights* and *Letters Writ by the Turkish Spy*, and must have delighted in the virtualization of their fantasies in the new ambassador.

28. Wajda Sendesni, *Regard de l'historiographie ottomane sur la révolution française et l'expédition d'Égypte: Tarih-i Cevdet* (Istanbul: Isis, 2003).

29. Cole, *Napoleon's Egypt*, 154–56. Forty-two officials and 1,800 private individuals were arrested, and their goods confiscated. Ruffin remained in prison in Istanbul until August 1801, the very last foreign representative to be so treated, but his wife and family were allowed to join him in 1800 under house arrest. See Henri Dehérain, *La Vie de Pierre Ruffin: Orientaliste et diplomatie, 1742–1824*, 2 vols. (Paris: Paul Geuthner, 1930), 2:145–46. Ruffin was one of the great orientalists of his time; he knew Turkish, Arabic, and Persian and was one of the few of the French representatives who eschewed the use of the dreaded dragomans. For a fascinating look at the dragoman dynasties, see Alexander H. De Groot, "The Dragomans of the Embassies in Istanbul, 1785–1834," in *Eastward Bound: Dutch Venturs and Adventures in the Middle East*, ed. Geert Jan van Gelder and Ed de Moor (Amsterdam: Rodopi, 1994), 130–58.

30. Mamluks and Druze ended up fighting on both sides in this particular engagement at Acre, a further measure of the complications facing both armies on its way into Syria. Bedouin Arabs who supplied the camels

and pitched the Ottoman army tents (see below), could be counted on to loot the camps of either side.

31. Tekindağ, "Akkâ Muhâsarası," 2–3. Some 12,000 were in Jaffa (8). See also Amnon Cohen, "Napoleon and Jezzar: a Local Perspective," in Shmuelevitz, *Napoleon and the French*, 79–86. The regiments of soldiers sometimes were called *sekban*, or referred to as *Çiftlik*, after the place where their barracks was, Levend Çiftlik, on the outskirts of Istanbul.

32. Lord Russell, *Knight of the Sword: The Life and Letters of Admiral Sir William Sidney Smith* (London: Gollancz, 1864), 80. Smith takes credit in his dispatches for convincing the chiefs and shaykhs of Mount Lebanon to join Ahmed Cezzar, where other sources record the latter's judicious use of coins for the same purpose (82–83).

33. Hamdi Köseoğlu, *Osmanlı devri 1798–1802: Osmanlı Fransiz harbi (Napolyon'un Mısır seferi) Türk silahlı kuvvetleri tarihi 3.cilt, 5inci kısım eki* (Ankara: Gnkr. Basımevi, 1978) 79–92 passim.

34. Ibid., 79–92.

35. Ibid. The official orders resemble the standard call to mobilization across the empire of the traditional army, to include the Janissaries and auxiliaries such as the mortar and armory corps, the timariots, the local soldiers under "influential *ayans*" (*nüfuslu ayans*), wagons and animals for transport, and bivouacs (*menzils*). In early June, 12,885 Janissaries; 657 artillerymen, and 1,450 armory soldiers began the march. I thank colleague Mesut Uyar for securing this source for me.

36. The general sentiment on the Ottoman land forces was summed up by Walsh, who was with the British forces at Alexandria: "For what could be effected by a disorganized army, composed of an assemblage of countries and nations, without discipline, with little or no authority in its chief, without any magazine, and afflicted with the exterminating plague." Thomas Walsh, *Journal of the Late Campaign in Egypt, Including Descriptions of that Country, and of Gibraltar, Minorca, Malta, Marmorice, and Macri: With an Appendix Containing Official Papers and Documents* (London, 1803), 52–54.

37. Ottoman records show 3,000 Nizam-ı Cedid troops; 3,500 volunteer infantry; one artillery battalion with one-half of a battalion of wagoneers under the Kapudan Pasha. Separately, Tepedelenli Ali Pasha was ordered to send a force of 2,000 Albanians in February 1801 (Köseoğlu, *Osmanlı devri 1798–1802: Osmanlı Fransiz harbi*, 95).

38. Walsh, *Journal*, 187–88. A monsoon prevented them from going up through Suez. They had to march across dessert with bullocks from India drawing their artillery. Sepoys suffered terribly from the heat and ophthalmia (190–93). With great difficulty, they marched down the Nile, reaching Rosetta in time for the final French capitulation in September. While not significant to the military operations, the idea of bringing them to the Middle East marks an important juncture in the colonial use of native troops. The French troops remaining in Egypt numbered around 20,000 (app. 29).

39. Ibid., app. 31.
40. We know this by an order sent to the Cyprus governor stating that there were deserters in their territories, who should be well treated, given ten or fifteen kuruş and surrendered to the army (Köseoğlu, *Osmanlı devri 1798–1802: Osmanlı Fransiz harbi*, 98).
41. William Wittman, *Travels in Turkey, Asia Minor, Syria, and across the Desert into Egypt during the years 1799, 1800, and 1801, in Company with the Turkish Army, and the British Military Mission* (1803; repr., New York: Arno Press, 1971), 122–23. Wittman's first impressions demonstrate his primary concern, which was the physical care of the mission and the soldiers. He was also researching the source of fevers and the plague.
42. Ibid., 125–31.
43. Ibid., 139–40.
44. Ibid., 141–49.
45. Ibid., 188–209.
46. Ibid., 303.
47. Ibid., 273–74.
48. Ibid., 286–87. This is a very small selection of the observations drawn from Wittman. The pages concerning the final march across the desert are reproduced in Aksan, *Ottoman Wars*, 270–89.
49. Caroline Finkel, *Osman's Dream: The Story of the Ottoman Empire, 1300–1923* (New York: Basic Books, 2005), 426.
50. Walsh, *Journal*, app. 35. To my knowledge, this is the first time that such European-style medals were created and awarded to foreigners.
51. Ibid., 152–54. It should be noted that this group of Mamluks is joining the British, not the Ottomans.
52. The single best book on the social impact of this transformation is Khalid Fahmy's *All the Pasha's Men: Mehmed Ali, His Army, and the Making of Modern Egypt* (Cambridge: Cambridge University Press, 1997); See also Aksan, *Ottoman Wars*, chaps. 8 and 10.
53. The best discussion of the problem remains Avigdor Levy, "The Officer Corps in Sultan Mahmud II's New Ottoman Army, 1826–39," *International Journal of Middle East Studies* 2 (1971): 21–39.
54. There are comparisons to be made between the state of native armies in Mughal India and the Ottoman Empire at this juncture in world history, but they are just beginning. Kaushik Roy, "Military Synthesis in South Asia: Armies, Warfare and Indian Society, c. 1740–1849," *Journal of Military History* 69, no. 3 (2005): 651–90, has some interesting insights into this question.
55. Daniel, *Islam, Europe and Empire*, 141.

Contributors

Virginia H. Aksan, Professor of History at McMaster University, Ontario, specializes in Ottoman History.

Edward J. Coss, Associate Professor of Military History, U.S. Army Command and General Staff College, studies the British army in the eighteenth and early nineteenth centuries.

Charles Esdaile, Professor of History, University of Liverpool, is a world-renowned historian in Napoleonic studies with a particular focus on Spain.

Lee Eysturlid teaches history at the Illinois Mathematics and Science Academy. He received his doctorate at Purdue University, where he studied Habsburg military history under the direction of Gunther E. Rothenberg.

Janet M. Hartley, Professor of International History, London School of Economics and Political Science, is an expert on eighteenth- and nineteenth-century Russian history.

Ciro Paoletti is an independent scholar who has written more than twenty books on Italian military history.

Frederick C. Schneid, Professor of History, High Point University, North Carolina, specializes in French and Italian military history from the French Revolution to the Wars of Italian Unification.

Dennis Showalter, Professor of History at Colorado College, is a prolific historian specializing in German military history.

Peter H. Wilson is G. F. Grant Professor of History at the University of Hull, UK. He is a world-renowned scholar of early modern German history and the Holy Roman Empire.

Index